THE KEY HORSES

THE STATS

MICK APPLEBY

Old favourite Danzeno primed for final season

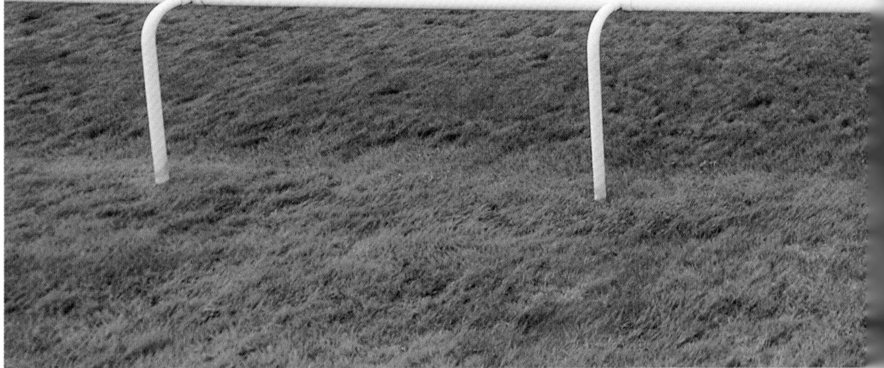

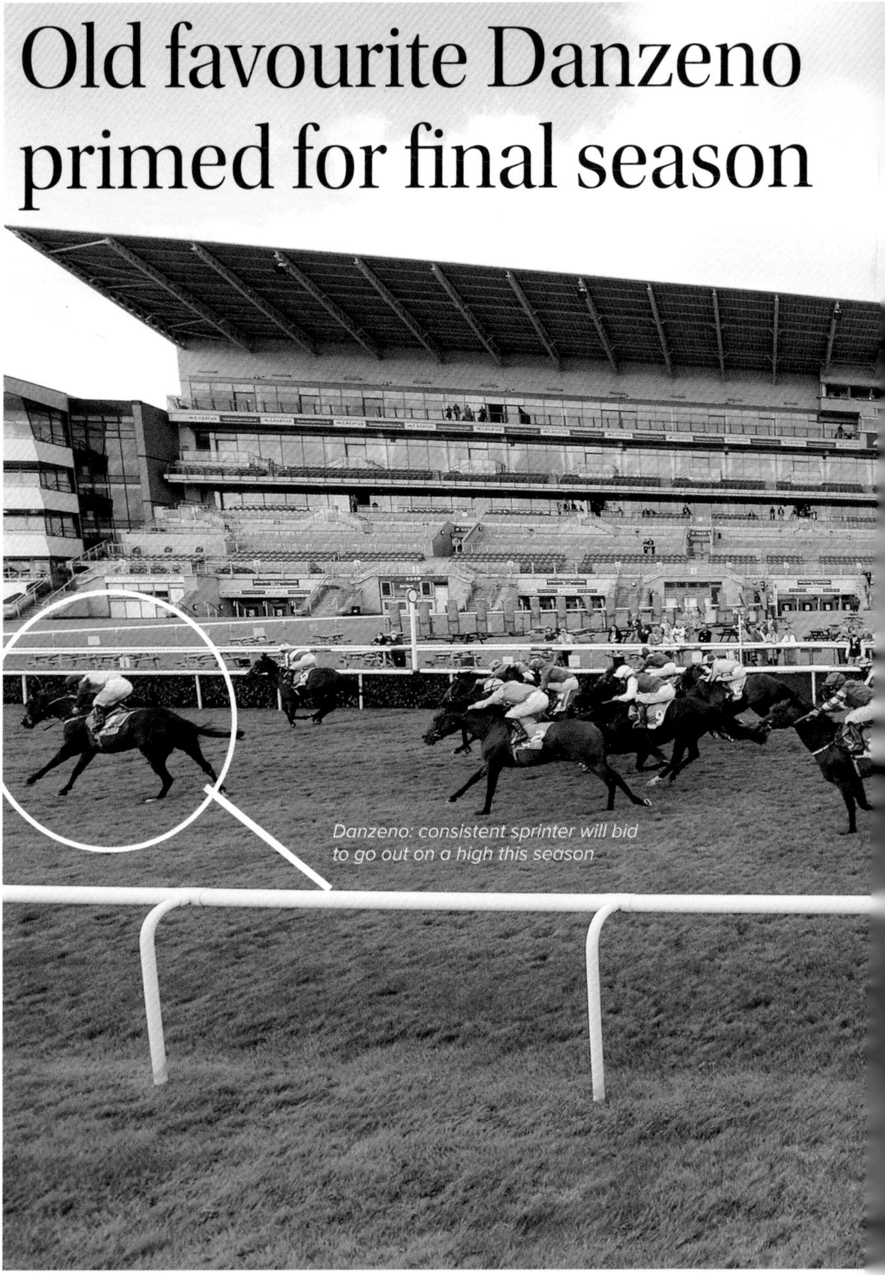

Danzeno: consistent sprinter will bid to go out on a high this season

WINNERS IN LAST FOUR YEARS 109, 99, 99, 94

DANZENO is one of those rare horses who receives fan mail. Not a lot – certainly not in Red Rum-Desert Orchid class – but it's a steady reminder to his trainer Mick Appleby that the old boy retains his enthusiasm for racing.

And old boy he definitely is. He's now in his 11th year – and still winning – but Appleby reveals this could be the stable favourite's last season before honourable retirement after a career that has brought ten victories and more than £431,000 prize-money.

"Yes, he's a popular horse and some people do write to him," says Appleby. "He had a good year last year. He's had the whole winter off and he's wintered well. He'll run in similar races to last year, those five- and six-furlong conditions races because he's a bit high in the handicap at 101. They tend to be small fields and he's better in those races rather than big fields.

"This will possibly be his last season, so it would be nice if he could win a few more races and go out on a high."

Last season Danzeno ran in the Wokingham and Stewards' Cup cavalry

charges and finished among the also-rans, but he won three conditions races, and those will be his targets this season.

His "farewell tour" will start at Musselburgh's Easter meeting where there is an ideal five-furlong conditions race for him.

Raasel has quickly become another favourite among Appleby's string of 90 at his stable in Langham, Rutland, where he moved from a rented yard at Danethorpe, near Newark, five years ago.

After landing his last five races he is almost certain to add to Appleby's score of 944 winners on the Flat since taking out a licence in 2009, a total which rises to 975 when jumps victories are added on.

"With a bit of luck we should get through the 1,000-winner mark this year, which will be quite good," says Appleby modestly, "and hopefully Raasel will help us there. He's still progressing. So, off a mark of 94, we'll be looking at some of the big handicaps at the festival meetings at Ascot, York and Goodwood.

"I'm sure he can win off his mark but he'll have to improve to a mark of around 100, so we could be looking at the Wokingham or Stewards' Cup. He'll be entered in all those big sprints. He's effective at five or six."

King Of Stars is another sprinter who has done well for Appleby, winning five times after being bought out of the Joseph O'Brien yard. He was sent to Dubai this winter, where he ran twice but wasn't suited by the watered track.

"Over here he wants quick ground. He was unplaced at Southwell and we might give him a break and wait for the turf; we'll play it by ear."

Raasel (left): a favourite at the Appleby yard in Rutland

United Front is an ex-Aidan O'Brien horse who won twice and finished second four times for Appleby on the all-weather early last year, and one of the horses who helped the Yorkshireman win his fifth All-Weather Championship.

United Front was gelded in the spring, given a long break and returned to win twice more and be placed four times to aid Appleby in his quest for a sixth all-weather title.

Appleby has him in the Lincoln but the five-year-old gelding is unlikely to make the cut with a turf mark of 92, which is 12lb lower than his all-weather rating.

"He's more likely to run in the Spring Mile where he'd probably have a better chance," says Appleby.

A planned warm-up on the all-weather came in a 1m2f handicap at Kempton in early March when a neck second to stablemate Baldomero did his Doncaster chances no harm at all.

"That should put him spot on," says Appleby.

Boundless Power won two small sprint handicaps at Nottingham early last year, as well as finishing a close second in two others, before finishing unplaced in the Stewards' Cup. He rounded off the year in great form with victories in big handicaps at Ascot and Doncaster.

"He's wintered really well. Hopefully, he'll progress again this year and if he does, the main aim will be the Abbaye.

"He's off 100 now but I don't think we've seen the best of him yet. I think we can get him up another 10lb yet."

Appleby's ambition is to win a Group 1. Could Boundless Power be the one?

DID YOU KNOW?
Mick Appleby has won five of the eight all-weather championships, including the last four, and was leading the latest trainer title race in mid-March.

"Yes, he could be. He loves the soft ground and it would suit him out there, which you normally get for the Abbaye."

Cairn Gorm won his first three races for Mick Channon, including a Group 3 at Deauville, and was thought good enough to run in the Prix Morny in 2020. But he went off the boil and never won again, although he was placed in a Listed race and several decent handicaps.

Appleby bought the 93-rated colt for 105,000gns at the Tattersalls horses-in-training sale last October.

"He's an exciting horse who I hope can progress even more at sprinting. I know Mick Channon thought highly of him."

An Appleby buy at the horses-in-training sale in August was **Night On Earth**, rated 80 at the time of purchase and now 84 after two wins and two seconds.

"I think there's more improvement left and I'd like to think we can get him into the mid-90s. He's a bit quirky but he's definitely going in the right direction."

Annaf is another ex-Shadwell colt bought at the October horses-in-training sale, this one for only 16,000gns, and is a purchase that has Appleby dreaming of far higher things for the well-bred son of Muhaarar than his current rating of 86.

"I think he's a Group horse," says Appleby. "He's had only two runs for us, a first and second. We might run him in a novice or a fast-track qualifier, but we're not going to over-run him on the all-weather. We'll wait for the turf and give him a light campaign this year and let him progress as a four-year-old."

Ayr Harbour won five races in 2020 and early 2021, then had a long break after a gelding operation before returning to be second at Wolverhampton over Christmas, failing by a neck, and finishing third at Lingfield and Southwell.

"He ran an absolute blinder at Southwell behind My Oberon, who was the highest rated horse to run at the track.

"It looked as though he was going to win at one point and it appears that he's improved this year and strengthened up even more.

"His main aim this season will be Sweden's Group 3 Pramms Memorial at Jagersro in May over 1m½f. Pearl Nation was sixth for us in 2015. It's a Fibresand surface and Ayr

MICK APPLEBY

OAKHAM, RUTLAND

RECORD AROUND THE COURSES

	W-R	Per cent	Non-hcp 2yo	Non-hcp 3yo	Non-hcp 4yo+	Hcp 2yo	Hcp 3yo	Hcp 4yo+	£1 level stake
Southwell (AW)	210-1401	15.0	0-38	8-74	20-112	8-34	36-212	138-931	-327.44
Wolverhampton (AW)	131-1218	10.8	2-13	6-87	17-126	2-22	21-185	83-785	-350.81
Chelmsford (AW)	91-818	11.1	0-25	6-27	2-55	0-17	14-129	69-565	-215.19
Nottingham	72-444	16.2	2-30	1-30	1-7	2-11	20-94	46-272	+148.19
Kempton (AW)	48-445	10.8	2-15	1-19	0-19	2-16	6-70	37-306	-82.00
Lingfield (AW)	33-323	10.2	1-5	0-8	3-36	0-5	10-59	19-210	-69.80
Newcastle (AW)	31-289	10.7	1-2	1-19	1-14	0-8	10-68	18-178	-30.65
Leicester	22-245	9.0	1-23	1-22	1-13	1-7	6-46	12-134	+40.83
Yarmouth	22-254	8.7	0-14	1-7	1-7	0-6	3-58	17-162	-71.11
Catterick	19-158	12.0	1-8	0-13	4-13	1-3	4-37	9-84	-0.05
Doncaster	19-235	8.1	0-13	0-14	1-22	0-2	3-21	15-163	-51.65
Pontefract	18-172	10.5	1-13	1-14	1-8	1-4	0-22	14-111	-73.10
Thirsk	12-121	9.9	1-4	0-9	0-7	0-2	7-28	4-71	+57.25
Beverley	11-112	9.8	0-14	0-11	2-13	0-0	5-26	4-48	-11.67
Brighton	10-75	13.3	0-2	0-2	0-1	1-1	2-19	7-50	-35.05
Haydock	10-119	8.4	0-9	0-8	2-10	1-2	1-23	6-67	-59.93
Musselburgh	9-44	20.5	0-2	0-0	1-7	0-0	1-6	7-29	+21.31
Newmarket (July)	9-66	13.6	1-3	0-1	1-4	0-0	2-12	5-46	+37.75
Chester	8-70	11.4	0-3	0-2	0-5	0-2	1-11	7-47	+13.50
Bath	8-79	10.1	0-0	0-2	1-6	0-0	4-26	3-45	-16.06
Newmarket	8-85	9.4	0-5	0-3	0-0	0-2	4-12	4-63	-18.25
Redcar	8-99	8.1	1-8	0-8	0-6	0-1	1-21	6-55	-43.75
Hamilton	7-35	20.0	0-1	2-3	0-1	0-0	0-8	5-22	+16.23
Ripon	7-61	11.5	0-3	0-6	1-2	0-1	1-10	5-39	-8.50
York	7-120	5.8	0-5	0-2	0-7	0-0	1-18	6-88	-57.25
Lingfield	5-24	20.8	0-0	1-1	1-1	0-1	2-9	1-12	+2.75
Windsor	5-66	7.6	0-1	0-9	1-4	0-0	1-13	3-39	-15.00
Ascot	5-86	5.8	0-2	0-1	0-11	0-0	0-9	5-63	-58.00
Goodwood	4-48	8.3	0-0	0-1	0-2	0-1	2-8	2-36	-20.17
Warwick	3-18	16.7	0-1	0-1	0-3	0-0	1-4	2-9	+24.00
Newcastle	3-33	9.1	0-3	1-4	0-2	0-1	0-0	2-23	-15.25
Epsom	2-13	15.4	0-0	0-0	0-0	0-0	1-2	1-11	+7.50
Salisbury	2-21	9.5	0-0	0-0	0-1	0-1	2-7	0-12	-15.38
Newbury	2-38	5.3	0-4	0-1	0-2	0-0	1-4	1-27	-20.50
Chepstow	2-49	4.1	0-2	0-0	0-1	0-1	0-16	2-29	-43.30
Sandown	2-54	3.7	0-7	0-3	0-3	0-0	0-11	2-30	-48.63
Carlisle	1-28	3.6	0-1	0-0	0-1	0-1	1-11	0-14	-22.00
Ayr	1-35	2.9	0-0	0-1	0-2	1-1	0-4	0-27	-30.00
Ffos Las	0-8	0.0	0-0	0-0	0-0	0-1	0-5	0-2	-8.00
Wetherby	0-13	0.0	0-0	0-1	0-1	0-0	0-3	0-8	-13.00

Number of horses racing for the stable **672**
Total winning prize-money **£4,484,617.96**

It's rare to find Jim Crowley in the saddle for the stable, but his 2-3 record in the last five years speaks volumes

Boundless Power (left): the Doncaster winner has wintered well, and Appleby feels he could be the horse to provide him with a top-level victory

Harbour goes well on the surface.

Fox Power, who won a Listed race at Newcastle when trained by Richard Hannon, was another purchase at the October horses-in-training sale and won first time out for Appleby in a mile handicap at Wolverhampton in early February.

He'll get a couple of outings on the all-weather before running on turf over a mile or 1m2f.

Khatwah has lots of ability but plenty of temperament too. "She's very well bred and we've had quite a few offers for her, so she may be sold to race abroad."

Mega Marvel is lightly raced and won over six furlongs at Newcastle on his third start.

"He's had a little break. He's a nice horse and could progress through the ranks. He'll prefer a bit of cut in the ground. He'll be ready for the start of the turf and looks to be on a workable mark of 70."

One horse off an even more "workable mark" is yet another Shadwell cast-off, **Mawkeb**.

"He was a short-head second first time out at Newcastle over seven and then a close third over a mile at Newcastle when he should have won, according to Appleby.

"He's had another couple of races but to be fair he's not had much luck and I think he could end up being better on the turf.

"He could be a very nice horse on the turf and off 71 he's on a very workable mark. He looks like a 90-plus horse to me and could be very well handicapped."

Edraak has done well for Appleby since being bought from Shadwell two years ago, winning five, being placed five times and running a stormer to finish fifth in last season's Ayr Gold Cup.

"He's off 105 now and he'll be entered for a lot of the big handicaps at the festivals, such as the Wokingham and Stewards' Cup.

Ayr Harbour (noseband): five times a winner and reportedly stronger this season

He does stay seven, although his optimum trip is six, but the thing with him is he needs quick ground. The ground beat us at Ayr last year but he ran an absolute blinder."

De Vega's Warrior was bought out of the Joseph O'Brien stable for 80,000gns after four starts, which brought a second at Limerick.

"I ran him at Southwell in February over a mile and he ran well enough to finish fourth because I think he's going to be a mile-and-a-half horse.

"Off 83, I think he's very well handicapped; there's a lot of improvement in him once we up him in trip.

"We gave him an outing at Wolverhampton, when he was second over a mile and a half, and we'll switch him to turf over a mile and a quarter. Once we know he stays we can map out a campaign for him," says Appleby.

The Shadwell dispersal was a lucrative hunting ground for Appleby, and **Saatty** has been another success story.

"He won easily first time out for us at Chelmsford over five, then finished third at Epsom before winning at Kempton over six.

"He's had a few little issues and has had a long break, but off 71 he should be coming back and winning. He's wintered very well and looks fully furnished now. He'll be back on the turf in April."

Zoom Zoom Babe, a winner in Ireland for Joseph O'Brien, broke her duck for Appleby in gutsy fashion over a mile on the all-weather at Kempton in mid-February, battling back to win by a short head.

"She likes soft ground on turf and over a mile and a half she'll progress even more. Off 63, she should be winning more races," is Appleby's confident prediction.

Reporting by LAWRIE KELSEY

GEORGE BOUGHEY

WINNERS IN FIRST THREE YEARS 85, 26, 2

Cachet leads the way for yard destined for the top

GEORGE BOUGHEY exploded on to the racing scene last year like a supernova as he piled up winners from Ayr to Ascot.

At the start of the year he was little known outside Newmarket after a second season that had yielded 26 winners, but by the end of 2021 the whole of racing had heard of the Dorset farmer's son as his total rocketed to 85.

Astronomically, supernovae are temporary bright new stars, but Boughey looks a permanent fixture in racing's firmament with the backing of some powerful owners, such as Nick Bradley.

Leading his charge for more success this year is stable star **Cachet**, who heads to the Nell Gwyn at Newmarket, one of the traditional trials for the 1,000 Guineas.

Although she won only once as a two-year-old, on her debut over six furlongs at Newmarket, she has some terrific form. She was fifth in the Albany at Royal Ascot,

Getting ready for a new day at Saffron House

second in the Group 2 Rockfel, third in the Group 1 Fillies' Mile and fourth in the Breeders' Cup Juvenile Fillies Turf at Del Mar, where she led until 75 yards from the line. She ended the season on a mark of 109.

"She's done very well over the winter and filled out, although she was a decent-sized filly at two," says her trainer. "She just about got the mile at two, but as a stronger filly I think she'll be better equipped to get the mile at three.

"She's in the English and French Guineas but it will depend on how she runs in the Nell Gwyn."

Bargain buy **Oscula**, who cost 4,000gns, was another filly from Saffron House to acquit herself well at two, earning almost £138,000 from victories in a Brighton maiden, a conditions race at Epsom and a Group 3 at Deauville, as well as being placed in the Group 3 Albany at Royal Ascot, the Group 2 Duchess of Cambridge, and Group 2 Rockfel.

Her final rating of 105 earned her a trip to Saudi Arabia for the $1.5 million Saudi Derby in February, and she could take in the UAE Derby on World Cup night on March 26.

"She's a filly who I think gets the mile well and will probably go the same route as Cachet after Saudi. She takes her racing well, but we'll give her a short break and she'll possibly be a Nell Gwyn-Guineas candidate.

"After that she'll tell us, but perhaps the Group 3 Princess Elizabeth at Epsom and later we might get her passport out for invitational races in America or Canada."

Like Oscula, **Corazon** is owned by a Nick Bradley syndicate, and another to bring a fair return on her £11,000 price tag.

After landing a modest all-weather novice race at Lingfield, three weeks later she won a Group 3 at Longchamp before finishing third in the Group 2 Flying Childers at Doncaster after picking up a slight injury.

Two weeks later she was unplaced in the Group 1 Cheveley Park over six furlongs, which probably stretched her stamina.

"She's fast and she almost won a Flying Childers. If she had been drawn on the stands' side and had a bit of company, I think she may have beaten the colts [Caturra and Armor]. So she's obviously a very high-class sprinter and one for the second half of the year.

"I said to Nick Bradley we should be working back from races such as the Flying Five [at the Curragh in September] and the Abbaye at the end of the year.

"I'm not going to rush her. Her dam was a five-furlong horse and she's by Markaz, who was a sprinter, so I'd be very surprised if we saw her starting over six. There are limited options over five, but very lucrative if you get it right."

Air To Air was unlucky last year, losing a shoe as he left the stalls when favourite for the Britannia [finished ninth of 29] and was caught in the final strides of a round of the Racing League at Windsor, after a previous round at Doncaster where he was repeatedly hampered when making a run, yet was beaten under two lengths.

"He's a horse I've always held in very high regard. He's a miler and from a family that doesn't get going until they're older. I'm not going to rush him back to the track. He's a horse rated 92 and 93 got in the Hunt Cup last year.

"The straight mile at Ascot I've always thought was his gig. He's a top mile handicapper and an exciting horse. I think we'll see him at all those top festivals."

Hellomydarlin won only once at two but was placed in Group and Listed races. She begins this season on a mark of 100 and could go down the All-Weather Championships route.

"She's a very well-balanced filly who took her racing well at two. She's done well from two to three and I'm looking forward to running her," says Boughey.

Last season Boughey landed Chester's Lily Agnes with **Navello**, who will be aimed at a repeat in early May. Before his Chester

victory he had picked up little sprints at Wolverhampton and Brighton.

He was then stepped up to the Group 2 Norfolk Stakes at Royal Ascot but found that level too high. After a gelding operation in July he won once and finished second twice.

"He's in very good shape and gasping for a run," says Boughey. "After Chester he could run in Royal Ascot's Palace of Holyroodhouse Stakes over five furlongs for three-year-olds. He'll get in off 90 and should be there or thereabouts.

Al Ameen is by the National Stud's Aclaim, who sired more two-year-old winners in 2021 than any other British-based, first-season sire.

He cost Shadwell Estates 140,000gns as a yearling and was snapped up for 20,000gns at the October horses-in-training sale.

He has begun to repay that outlay with a victory and two seconds on the all-weather this winter.

"He'll improve as he matures and could turn up at some of the fun meetings," says Boughey.

Cashew, a dual winner at two, has a

similar profile to Al Ameen and will be running in six- and seven-furlong handicaps.

"She had a busy two-year-old career and I slightly questioned whether she was going to go on, but her physical progression is pleasing.

"She was never really allowed a chance to develop and grow at two because she was so busy, but she's done well for having an extended break. She's rated 81 and will end up at some of the nice meetings."

Boughey has high hopes for **Fiorina**, a sister to Shadwell's sire Tasleet.

"She's rated 74 and I'd like to win a handicap or two, then take her to Royal Ascot for something like the Sandringham. She was weak at two and couldn't quite finish off her races, but she's probably done best of the fillies from two to three," he says.

"She was learning with each run and the mile there on a straight track is probably right up her street. She's got a great pedigree and the main aim is to get some black type."

Another ex-Shadwell horse is **Sip And Smile**, a winner of his first two starts over six furlongs this year.

Cashew scores at Windsor last season and remains open to plenty of improvement

GEORGE BOUGHEY

NEWMARKET, SUFFOLK

RECORD AROUND THE COURSES

	W-R	Per cent	Non-hcp 2yo	Non-hcp 3yo	Non-hcp 4yo+	Hcp 2yo	Hcp 3yo	Hcp 4yo+	£1 level stake
Wolverhampton (AW)	16-104	15.4	3-26	1-9	2-2	2-11	3-29	5-27	-25.21
Southwell (AW)	14-41	34.1	1-3	3-8	2-3	1-1	0-6	7-20	+9.11
Lingfield (AW)	13-85	15.3	4-18	5-21	1-3	0-2	0-12	3-29	+3.57
Newcastle (AW)	12-50	24.0	1-7	4-10	0-1	1-4	1-9	5-19	-1.43
Kempton (AW)	9-65	13.8	3-20	1-8	0-2	1-3	1-12	3-20	-40.17
Newmarket	7-41	17.1	2-17	2-3	0-0	1-6	0-3	2-12	+4.50
Brighton	6-13	46.2	3-4	0-0	0-0	1-1	1-5	1-3	+11.00
Yarmouth	6-24	25.0	0-7	0-2	0-0	2-5	2-4	2-6	+2.08
Windsor	5-20	25.0	2-4	1-6	0-0	0-1	1-3	1-6	+18.27
Bath	5-23	21.7	1-7	2-4	0-1	0-1	0-1	2-9	+7.00
Chelmsford (AW)	5-64	7.8	0-26	1-6	1-2	0-4	2-11	1-15	-38.27
Haydock	3-8	37.5	1-2	0-1	0-0	1-2	0-0	1-3	+4.33
Chepstow	2-6	33.3	1-2	0-0	0-0	0-1	0-1	1-2	-1.13
Salisbury	2-8	25.0	1-3	0-1	0-0	1-1	0-2	0-1	-2.50
Nottingham	2-9	22.2	0-3	0-0	0-1	2-2	0-1	0-2	+3.00
Leicester	2-10	20.0	0-2	0-0	0-2	0-2	1-2	1-2	-5.26
Newbury	2-11	18.2	1-4	0-1	0-0	0-1	0-1	1-4	-2.90
Newmarket (July)	2-15	13.3	0-4	0-0	0-0	0-2	0-2	2-7	+12.50
Goodwood	1-4	25.0	1-2	0-0	0-1	0-0	0-1	0-0	+4.00
Ayr	1-4	25.0	1-3	0-0	0-1	0-0	0-0	0-0	-1.90
Catterick	1-4	25.0	0-0	0-0	0-0	1-2	0-0	0-2	-2.33
Chester	1-5	20.0	1-2	0-0	0-0	0-1	0-0	0-2	-2.75
Beverley	1-6	16.7	1-4	0-0	0-0	0-0	0-0	0-2	+0.50
Redcar	1-6	16.7	1-3	0-0	0-0	0-2	0-1	0-0	-2.88
Sandown	1-7	14.3	1-5	0-1	0-0	0-0	0-0	0-1	-5.43
Thirsk	1-8	12.5	1-4	0-0	0-0	0-0	0-2	0-2	-6.09
Epsom	1-9	11.1	1-2	0-1	0-1	0-1	0-2	0-2	-0.50
Lingfield	1-10	10.0	0-3	0-1	0-0	0-1	0-1	1-4	-9.00
Doncaster	1-12	8.3	0-5	0-0	0-0	0-1	1-3	0-3	-9.50
Carlisle	0-1	0.0	0-1	0-0	0-0	0-0	0-0	0-0	-1.00
Ffos Las	0-1	0.0	0-1	0-0	0-0	0-0	0-0	0-0	-1.00
Musselburgh	0-1	0.0	0-0	0-1	0-0	0-0	0-0	0-0	-1.00
Pontefract	0-7	0.0	0-4	0-0	0-0	0-0	0-3	0-0	-7.00
Ripon	0-8	0.0	0-5	0-0	0-0	0-0	0-1	0-2	-8.00
York	0-9	0.0	0-3	0-1	0-0	0-2	0-0	0-3	-9.00
Ascot	0-17	0.0	0-10	0-1	0-0	0-0	0-2	0-4	-17.00

Number of horses racing for the stable **131**
Total winning prize-money **£588,976.19**

DID YOU KNOW?

George Boughey's racing interests came from his family's roots in jump racing on their Dorset farm, where his father owned the stallion Riverwise, sire of the 2003 Champion Hurdle winner Rooster Booster.

"He's rated 80 and has lots of options. It wouldn't surprise me if he got a mile – he looks like a miler – and a race like the Britannia at Royal Ascot could be a summer target for him.

"**Ochil House** is a new horse for us. He ran once last year when he finished mid-div at Kempton on the all-weather. He's a big strong horse by Gleneagles who I imagine would end up in some nice staying handicaps. The further he gets, possibly the better he'll be."

Look out for **Totally Charming**, who was bought at the horses-in-training sale in October and won impressively first time out for Boughey over a mile in January. He was a little unlucky in his next two starts when second and third.

"There'll be races for him in those ten-furlong handicaps at Ascot, Goodwood and York, all those sorts of meetings. He's rated 87 but it's worth stressing there's a bit of room left in there for improvement. Big-field handicaps with a strong pace is where he can be effective, where he can drop the bridle and hit the line running."

Inver Park is another horse who could have Royal Ascot on his agenda. Bought at the sales in December, he has been gelded and given a break before a likely return in a seven-furlong handicap at the Lincoln meeting at Doncaster.

Oscula: bargain buy has proved incredible money-spinner

Runners at Brighton are always worth a second look. A 46% strike-rate (6-13) has turned a profit of £11

Inver Park: likely to reappear at Doncaster and could have engagements at Royal Ascot during mid-season

"We nearly won the race last year with Dirty Rascal, who then won his next two races, and we'll try to do the same with Inver Park.

"We'll be working back from the Wokingham or Buckingham Palace at Royal Ascot. He's a winner at Ascot already in a handicap and he looks a nice recruit."

Arguably the most interesting addition to Boughey's string is an American three-year-old colt by Quality Road out of the Sea The Stars mare Beauly, named in the States Lahiq, but renamed **Missed The Cut** over here.

"He was an expensive yearling costing $400,000, and resold as an unraced three-year-old. We bought him at the Tattersalls February sales for 40,000gns.

"He's unraced and unproven but he's a horse with a good pedigree and as good a physical [specimen] as I have in the yard.

"He'll start in a mile maiden and he might end up getting a mile and a half. He's a dirt bred but I think he'll probably like fast ground."

Of his band of two-year-olds he picks out: **Mr Rascal**, by Showcasing out of A Huge Dream; the filly **Time In Motion** by Time Test out of Bridge Poseidon "who is doing everything right at the moment"; an unnamed filly by Profitable out of Roxelana; the "very precocious filly" **Pastiche** by Zoustar out of Crying Lightening; **Starshot**, a colt by Acclamation out of Sea Meets Sky; the colt **Apex** by Kessaar out of Bisous Y Besos, a half-brother to the stable's Oscular; and an unnamed colt by Lightning Spear out of Molly Mayhem.

Reporting by LAWRIE KELSEY

Burke's sprinting peerage

WINNERS IN LAST FOUR YEARS 99, 60, 68, 71

THERE will be few trainers with a sprinting team as strong as Karl Burke's this year judged on the early season confidence he has in his speedsters.

The Middleham trainer, whose Spigot Lodge yard overlooks the picturesque Yorkshire Dales National Park, is hoping last season's band of two-year-old 'swans' do not turn into this year's three-year-old 'geese'.

The early signs are promising, however, for what Burke describes as "the strongest team of three-year-olds we've ever had". In fact, so high is the confidence emanating from Spigot Lodge, that Royal Ascot has been pencilled in for several of his sprinting squad.

Whether the pencil marks are rubbed out as the season progresses will obviously depend on how they perform on the track.

"We're top-heavy with speed horses this season," he admits. "The only problem will be placing them to keep them apart, but that's a nice problem to have, although it's

DID YOU KNOW?
Karl Burke is on record as saying that if he hadn't become a trainer, he would have applied to be a deckchair attendant on a Caribbean beach.

going to be tough for them in the first half of the season."

Attagirl is one of those with Royal Ascot aspirations following a juvenile season packed with promise.

After finishing a close third in a Haydock fillies' novice stakes, then winning a fillies' maiden back at the same track, she stepped straight up to Group 3 level and finished a creditable seventh in the Princess Margaret Stakes at Ascot in July after being hampered in the last furlongs.

A month later she was caught in the final strides of a Listed race at Newbury before landing a York Listed race a week later.

A sixth in the Flying Childers, in which she was beaten only three lengths, meant she ended the season rated 97 and her connections brimful of hope.

"She's wintered well and looks a really powerful filly," says Burke. "She'll probably, but not definitely, go for a Listed race at Bath in April, although she could wait for a three-year-old Listed race at York. And, depending on whether she gets six furlongs or not – and I always thought she would last year – we'll think about the Commonwealth Cup at Ascot and other Group races in the second half of the season.

"She's very useful. Whether she's good enough for the Abbaye at the end of the season, we'll have to see."

Kaboo was thrown straight into the deep end last season with a racecourse debut in the Listed Windsor Castle at Royal Ascot. He might not have won but was far from disgraced in sixth.

It was a run which delighted Burke, who says: "If he'd been drawn on either wing I think he'd have finished second and maybe challenged the winner."

He finished 2021 rated 90 after winning a couple of all-weather sprints and is now on 95 after completing his hat-trick over six furlongs at Kempton in January.

"He's a big, powerful, high-class horse who is American-bred and so likes artificial

Attagirl (noseband): promising juvenile form and could find her way to Royal Ascot

surfaces," says Burke. "He'll go to the all-weather finals on Good Friday and we might see about sending him out to Dubai.

"He definitely gets six and wouldn't want anything but fast ground on turf. He has a dirt action with a high-cruising speed."

Last Crusader is another member of Burke's sprinting peerage. His last run was a neck second in the Listed Two-Year-Old Trophy at Redcar and is pleasing his trainer after doing really well through the winter.

"He's another very powerful horse. He's rated 98, so it will be difficult for him. There aren't many handicaps for him, so we're

going to have to throw him in at the deep end, possibly in a Listed or Group 3.

"We've got to make a decision – see how he works through March – and see whether we go six or seven with him. Depending on what trip we're looking at, it wouldn't be out of the question, if he goes seven, a Jersey, or six, the Commonwealth.

Korker was another precocious juvenile who performed well in his debut season. He finished ninth in the Norfolk at Royal Ascot and, although he was last in the Group 2 Flying Childers at Doncaster, he ended the year with three wins and two seconds from eight outings, and a rating of 95.

"He's a very quick horse, five furlongs is definitely his game," says Burke. "We tried him over six but he was a bit too keen and didn't quite see it out. He's been gelded and goes to Sandown in April for a handicap, then we'll take the rest of the season from there."

Lord Of The Lodge is described as "a revelation".

"He's been so consistent this winter. He was just collared by our other horse [Spycatcher] at Lingfield in early February.

"I was hoping he'd get an invite to Saudi

KARL BURKE

MIDDLEHAM, NORTH YORKSHIRE

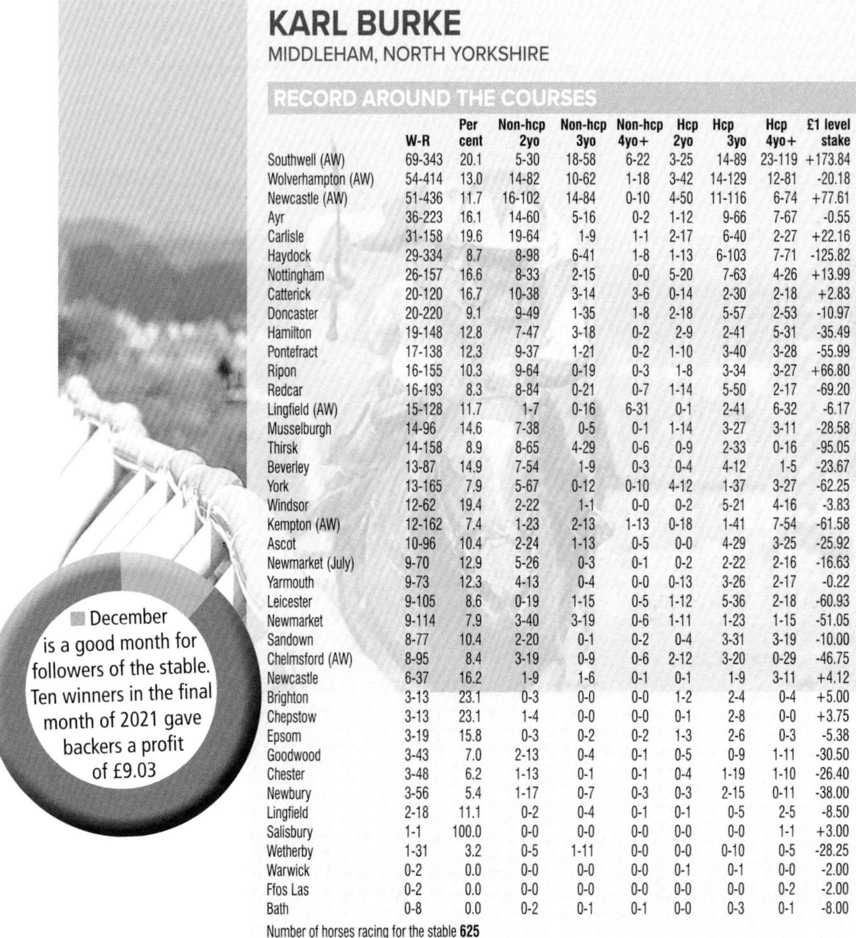

RECORD AROUND THE COURSES

	W-R	Per cent	Non-hcp 2yo	Non-hcp 3yo	Non-hcp 4yo+	Hcp 2yo	Hcp 3yo	Hcp 4yo+	£1 level stake
Southwell (AW)	69-343	20.1	5-30	18-58	6-22	3-25	14-89	23-119	+173.84
Wolverhampton (AW)	54-414	13.0	14-82	10-62	1-18	3-42	14-129	12-81	-20.18
Newcastle (AW)	51-436	11.7	16-102	14-84	0-10	4-50	11-116	6-74	+77.61
Ayr	36-223	16.1	14-60	5-16	0-2	1-12	9-66	7-67	-0.55
Carlisle	31-158	19.6	19-64	1-9	1-1	2-17	6-40	2-27	+22.16
Haydock	29-334	8.7	8-98	6-41	1-8	1-13	6-103	7-71	-125.82
Nottingham	26-157	16.6	8-33	2-15	0-0	5-20	7-63	4-26	+13.99
Catterick	20-120	16.7	10-38	3-14	3-6	0-14	2-30	2-18	+2.83
Doncaster	20-220	9.1	9-49	1-35	1-8	2-18	5-57	2-53	-10.97
Hamilton	19-148	12.8	7-47	3-18	0-2	2-9	2-41	5-31	-35.49
Pontefract	17-138	12.3	9-37	1-21	0-2	1-10	3-40	3-28	-55.99
Ripon	16-155	10.3	9-64	0-19	0-3	1-8	3-34	3-27	+66.80
Redcar	16-193	8.3	8-84	0-21	0-7	1-14	5-50	2-17	-69.20
Lingfield (AW)	15-128	11.7	1-7	0-16	6-31	0-1	2-41	6-32	-6.17
Musselburgh	14-96	14.6	7-38	0-5	0-1	1-14	3-27	3-11	-28.58
Thirsk	14-158	8.9	8-65	4-29	0-6	0-9	2-33	0-16	-95.05
Beverley	13-87	14.9	7-54	1-9	0-3	0-4	4-12	1-5	-23.67
York	13-165	7.9	5-67	0-12	0-10	4-12	1-37	3-27	-62.25
Windsor	12-62	19.4	2-22	1-1	0-0	0-2	5-21	4-16	-3.83
Kempton (AW)	12-162	7.4	1-23	2-13	1-13	0-18	1-41	7-54	-61.58
Ascot	10-96	10.4	2-24	1-13	0-5	0-0	4-29	3-25	-25.92
Newmarket (July)	9-70	12.9	5-26	0-3	0-1	0-2	2-22	2-16	-16.63
Yarmouth	9-73	12.3	4-13	0-4	0-0	0-13	3-26	2-17	-0.22
Leicester	9-105	8.6	0-19	1-15	0-5	1-12	5-36	2-18	-60.93
Newmarket	9-114	7.9	3-40	3-19	0-6	1-11	1-23	1-15	-51.05
Sandown	8-77	10.4	2-20	0-1	0-2	0-4	3-31	3-19	-10.00
Chelmsford (AW)	8-95	8.4	3-19	0-9	0-6	2-12	3-20	0-29	-46.75
Newcastle	6-37	16.2	1-9	1-6	0-1	0-1	1-9	3-11	+4.12
Brighton	3-13	23.1	0-3	0-0	0-0	1-2	2-4	0-4	+5.00
Chepstow	3-13	23.1	1-4	0-0	0-0	0-1	2-8	0-0	+3.75
Epsom	3-19	15.8	0-3	0-2	0-2	1-3	2-6	0-3	-5.38
Goodwood	3-43	7.0	2-13	0-4	0-1	0-5	0-9	1-11	-30.50
Chester	3-48	6.2	1-13	0-1	0-1	0-4	1-19	1-10	-26.40
Newbury	3-56	5.4	1-17	0-7	0-3	0-3	2-15	0-11	-38.00
Lingfield	2-18	11.1	0-2	0-4	0-1	0-1	0-5	2-5	-8.50
Salisbury	1-1	100.0	0-0	0-0	0-0	0-0	0-0	1-1	+3.00
Wetherby	1-31	3.2	0-5	1-11	0-0	0-0	0-10	0-5	-28.25
Warwick	0-2	0.0	0-0	0-0	0-0	0-1	0-1	0-0	-2.00
Ffos Las	0-2	0.0	0-0	0-0	0-0	0-0	0-0	0-2	-2.00
Bath	0-8	0.0	0-2	0-1	0-1	0-0	0-3	0-1	-8.00

Number of horses racing for the stable **625**

Total winning prize-money **£4,879,554.22**

but he didn't quite get high enough in the handicap for there.

"He's a strong possibility for Meydan Super Saturday for the six-furlong sprint there, and if he performs well we're hoping he'll get an invite to World Cup night at the end of March.

"He'll definitely come back for the Good Friday meeting at Newcastle and then he'll have a break."

Spycatcher, who was eighth in the Jersey Stakes last season after being placed in Listed and Group 3 races, ended the year on 101.

He rose to a rating of 109 after beating stablemate Lord Of The Lodge by a neck in the Listed Kachy Stakes at Lingfield, earning a place in the All-Weather Championships Finals Day at Newcastle on Good Friday, and will probably go straight to Royal Ascot after that.

"He'll have a target at Royal Ascot but I don't know what at the moment. We'll have a word with the owner," says Burke.

"He'll get seven but is better at a stiff six or a fast-run six. His best runs have been when he's flying at the end. He could be one for

El Caballo: "a lovely horse" who could have big races on his agenda

something like the Wokingham."

El Caballo is yet another inmate to have delighted Burke, especially after finishing a length behind Richard Hannon's well-regarded Armor at Doncaster on debut last April. That horse went on to have a rating of 111 after landing the Molecomb Stakes and finishing third in the Cheveley Park.

El Caballo cruised home in a Carlisle maiden the following month, but was then sidelined with an injury until December when he won a six-furlong all-weather qualifier at Wolverhampton.

"He'll go to the finals at Newcastle and then we'll see about the Jersey or the Commonwealth at Ascot. He's a lovely horse and deserves to run in those types of races. I'm sure he'll get seven," says Burke.

Joining Burke's Royal Ascot team will be the 104-rated **Significantly**, winner of the Palace of Holyroodhouse Handicap for three-year-olds over five furlongs at the royal meeting last year.

He returned to Ascot a month later to win another five-furlong handicap, but he began to develop a problem at the start of his races, so Burke decided to have him gelded.

"When he's started he's always performed very well and I'm hoping he can step forward now he's been gelded," says his trainer. "We took him to Ireland for a Group 1 and he lost a couple of lengths at the start but was still in with a chance at the furlong pole.

"So he's been knocking on the door of being a high-class sprinter. He's an exciting horse."

White Lavender is a four-year-old filly who has been sent over from Joe Murphy in Ireland where she won once and was placed twice.

"We'll probably start her off in a fillies' Listed race at Bath in April and I'm hoping we can pick up some black type.

Almohandesah, fourth in a back-end mile Newmarket Listed race, is the first horse Burke has trained for Sheikh Mohammed

Obaid Al Maktoum.

"She's wintered well. We could start her off in one of the Guineas trials, maybe something like the Nell Gwyn," says Burke. "She's bred to want more than a mile but I'm not sure she does. She's been knocking on the door of getting black type and with a bit of luck this year she can."

French Listed winner **Honey Sweet**, on 103, is the highest-rated filly at Spigot Lodge but Burke says she's "still a work in progress".

"She's still getting stronger; she's done well through the winter but there's still a bit more to come from her.

"She's a filly I like a lot and hopefully we can get some Group black type with her this year. She could start her season in either the Free Handicap or the Fred Darling."

Is she a Guineas filly? "It's possible; it'll be interesting to see. She definitely stays seven but to be honest I don't think she wants further than seven because she's from a very fast family."

Yet another member of the Spigot Lodge sprinting squad is the "very high-class" filly **Illustrating**.

"She was very unlucky not to win a Group 3 race in France last September [hung left, finished third beaten a neck and short neck]. She had no run whatsoever. It was very frustrating, to say the least. I would expect her to definitely get some more black type this year.

"She could be out in April at Bath, but we have three or four fillies going there – we'll see how they're all working before deciding – or she could go to France for the Group 3 Prix Sigy, which we won with Quiet

White Lavender (left): new recruit from Ireland

Reflection in 2016. Then, if she performs well, she could go for one of the Commonwealth Cup trials over here."

Among the colts singled out by Burke to follow is **Al Qareem**, an ex-Shadwell colt bought at the October sales.

He was second first time out at Kempton and won at Newcastle, both over seven furlongs.

"We gelded him and I think he's well handicapped," says Burke. "We'll probably run him over a mile and a quarter at the Lincoln meeting."

Taj Alola won twice and was second twice from five outings and is "a very nice horse who needs a mile or mile and a quarter and can progress".

Tothenines is a definite winner-in-waiting. He had only one outing last year when splitting Gubbass, who developed into a Group horse for Richard Hannon (second in the Richmond at Goodwood) and Ralph Beckett's Angel Bleu (won the Group 2 Vintage Stakes at Goodwood and two Group 1s in France in October).

"He'll go for a little novice in April and we'll see where we progress from there; but his form looks ridiculously strong," says Burke.

It's early days to differentiate between two-year-olds but the master of Spigot Lodge says he has "a lovely team" of juveniles from which he has pinpointed fillies to follow by Dark Angel, first-season sire Jungle Cat, Shalaa and Unfortunately, as well as colts by Saxon Warrior and Ulysses.

Reporting by LAWRIE KELSEY

Caturra tops quality bunch for stable on the march

CLIVE COX has become synonymous with top-grade sprinters and he's hoping this year will enhance a reputation burnished by the exploits of horses such as Harry Angel, Golden Horde, Profitable and Supremacy.

He's already pencilled in all the top sprint races as he aims to break through the £1 million prize-money target for the first time since 2019, which had marked the fourth year in succession he had earned seven figures.

Last year was Cox's best numerically with 79 winners, but prize-money was tantalisingly £10,000 short of the million mark.

So, does Cox's string of around 120, divided between Beechdown Stables in Lambourn and an overspill yard at nearby East Garston which houses another 20 boxes, have either the quality or quantity to make the goal of improving last year's figures feasible?

Cox answers with an emphatic yes. "I was very pleased with

WINNERS IN LAST FOUR YEARS 79, 47, 71, 68

Stable star: Flying Childers winner Caturra with Clive Cox

last year and I'm delighted with the quality we have this year, which is a dream.

"I'm proud to have the strength in depth and I'm as excited as I have been for many years. I certainly don't need an alarm clock! It's great to come out to the bunch of horses I have waiting for me."

Leading the Beechdown brigade this year is **Caturra**, winner of Doncaster's Group 2 five-furlong Flying Childers sprint, as well as a Newbury Listed race.

The colt ran some equally big races in defeat over six furlongs, including seventh in the Coventry at Royal Ascot and fifth in the Group 1 Middle Park at Newmarket where the first seven home could have been covered by a king-sized duvet with the rest of the bedding only a few feet away in eighth and ninth.

Cox feels with a winter on Caturra's back his stable star could get six furlongs well this year, in which case the Commonwealth Cup comes into careful consideration.

"He was a very pleasing two-year-old last year who ran very well in the Coventry and won the Flying Childers.

"He's matured very well, he's certainly not small and is undoubtedly a stronger individual – he's 520 kilos and a bull of a horse. With the physical progression that is evident from two to three, I'd be very hopeful he can be an exciting sprinting prospect this year.

"To be beaten only a length in the Middle Park means he clearly gets six, but he's also quick enough for five, so we won't be stretching him out further."

His starting point will be the Pavilion Stakes at Ascot, a trial for the Commonwealth Cup, which is his main target.

"He's won on an easy surface and clearly doesn't mind quicker ground, which is a pleasing quality," says Cox. "Depending on how those early targets go, we'll decide later on where he'll race. With the right sort of progress I'd be looking at taking on the older horses in the second half of the season."

Can he compare Caturra with his previous top-level sprinters, such as Profitable, Harry Angel and Supremacy?

"From a physical sense, he fits that mould – wonderfully strong and a great strong hip on him. At this stage I would be very impressed with his whole approach and development. He has a wonderful mind at the races. We actually had to wake him at Doncaster before the Flying Childers; he was flat out lying down."

The Commonwealth Cup could also be on the agenda for **Wings Of War**, who ended the season on a rating of 109, 2lb behind Caturra, after winning the Group 2 Mill Reef at Newbury "in very pleasing style" following a second in Kempton's Group 3 Sirenia Stakes and third in a big sales race at York.

"He's another son of Dark Angel. We did well with Harry and Lethal Force, who were also by Dark Angel. He was a strong two-year-old but the progression over the winter is obvious to see; he's much stronger through his back and quarters and as we continue to step the workload up he's pleasing us very much.

"With a Group 2 penalty he's going to be going in the same direction as Caturra, which is a shame, but very satisfying to have two horses of that calibre.

"This fella is a little bit more ground dependent, not wanting it too soft, which would be the only limiting aspect of his programme. Comparing him with Caturra, he has more of a sprinting mentality, whereas the other one is so laid-back."

Joining those two in Cox's squad for top sprinting honours is a phenomenon called

DID YOU KNOW?

Clive Cox made Royal Ascot history in 2020 when Nando Parrado won the Coventry Stakes at 150-1, the longest winning starting price at the royal meeting.

Wings Of War: the Group 2 Mill Reef Stakes winner could take in Royal Ascot's Commonwealth Cup

Tis Marvellous, an eight-year-old gelding whom the official handicapper decided was still improving at the age of seven by raising his rating from 101 to a career high of 113.

The handicapper was clearly impressed with the gelding's last three runs: a win in the Listed Beverley Bullet and Ascot's Listed Rous Stakes, either side of third place in a Newbury Group 3.

"He's absolutely amazing and such a gentleman to deal with," says Cox. "It gives me huge satisfaction to have a horse with an appetite to race at that level.

"He still holds the record at Maisons-Laffitte, which he set in 2016 in the Robert Papin, and broke the record at Beverley last season, which was all the more satisfying with the additional Covid weight he had to carry."

Four of Tis Marvellous's eight victories have come at Ascot and he'll be gracing the place again this year.

"He loves Ascot and we'll definitely be targeting the King's Stand," says Cox. "He's a five-furlong specialist now and we'll work back from Royal Ascot to see where he'll go."

Diligent Harry won the all-weather final at Lingfield and is the fourth member of Cox's sprint relay team aiming for gold.

"We gave him a winter break and I'm pleased we did because he came a long way in a short time last spring. His only disappointing run came at Ascot on testing ground [in the Group 3 Bengough Stakes] and on a higher level on turf we didn't quite see what I think is the real Harry. He's rated 109 and I genuinely feel he's another sprinter in the older brigade.

"He's benefited from not having a winter campaign and he's done very well. The ground will decide where he goes. If it's dry, the Listed Cammidge Trophy at Doncaster could be a start."

Cox's enviable dilemma is keeping his flyers out of the same airspace.

"We'll feel our way according to the ground with him, likewise with the others. Our first steps will determine where we go, but potentially he could be a horse who'll be heading to Ascot in June."

Aratus won his last four races, all over seven furlongs, including a decent handicap at Goodwood on his last start, and opens this season on a rating of 102.

"I think he'll get a little further. He's training nicely and seems a little more relaxed now he's been gelded," reveals Cox. "We'll feel our way with him in the hope that he'll make the step up to a mile. He has a tentative entry in the Lincoln but I wouldn't want to be running him on soft or good to soft ground."

CLIVE COX
LAMBOURN, BERKSHIRE

RECORD AROUND THE COURSES

	W-R	Per cent	Non-hcp 2yo	Non-hcp 3yo	Non-hcp 4yo+	Hcp 2yo	Hcp 3yo	Hcp 4yo+	£1 level stake
Kempton (AW)	76-572	13.3	14-128	16-91	1-16	5-32	25-143	15-162	-28.80
Windsor	55-337	16.3	17-81	8-52	1-6	0-4	18-113	11-81	-57.37
Bath	53-235	22.6	16-46	7-30	2-9	2-8	23-103	3-39	+40.93
Wolverhampton (AW)	47-312	15.1	7-57	11-62	2-9	5-23	12-89	10-72	-21.23
Salisbury	34-224	15.2	11-80	6-38	1-4	4-12	9-64	3-26	-52.32
Sandown	29-217	13.4	7-49	2-23	1-9	1-7	14-99	4-30	-44.67
Ascot	28-257	10.9	9-59	1-29	4-29	1-2	6-65	7-73	+96.93
Nottingham	27-150	18.0	7-32	6-27	1-6	1-9	9-60	3-16	-3.55
Lingfield (AW)	26-229	11.4	2-36	6-43	0-7	2-12	15-88	1-43	-74.23
Leicester	25-196	12.8	7-57	4-19	3-6	1-11	7-76	3-27	-59.10
Newbury	25-311	8.0	10-126	3-45	2-18	1-10	5-56	4-56	-148.33
Haydock	22-131	16.8	9-31	3-19	2-17	0-7	6-40	2-17	+12.90
Goodwood	21-194	10.8	7-47	1-22	1-13	0-6	7-53	5-53	-30.45
Chepstow	16-97	16.5	5-17	2-14	0-1	0-3	6-45	3-17	-29.55
Doncaster	16-141	11.3	6-32	4-22	0-9	0-6	4-33	2-39	-24.47
Newmarket	12-129	9.3	6-48	1-11	1-13	2-14	2-26	0-17	-19.05
Brighton	11-39	28.2	3-6	0-0	0-0	0-1	5-23	3-9	+8.98
Lingfield	9-72	12.5	4-16	3-18	0-1	0-1	1-25	1-11	-2.90
Chelmsford (AW)	8-60	13.3	1-13	2-12	0-1	2-5	2-15	1-14	-29.12
Newmarket (July)	7-75	9.3	1-14	1-7	1-2	0-0	3-35	1-17	-43.76
York	6-71	8.5	2-19	1-9	1-10	0-5	2-12	0-16	-9.06
Epsom	5-36	13.9	1-2	1-4	0-0	0-4	3-14	0-12	+9.50
Ffos Las	4-32	12.5	1-10	1-3	0-0	0-2	2-13	0-4	-12.39
Southwell (AW)	3-23	13.0	0-3	0-4	0-1	0-0	2-8	1-7	-7.25
Ripon	2-12	16.7	1-2	0-0	0-1	1-1	0-2	0-6	-5.88
Ayr	2-15	13.3	0-1	0-3	0-0	0-0	2-4	0-7	+5.00
Wetherby	1-3	33.3	0-0	0-1	0-0	0-0	1-2	0-0	+3.50
Beverley	1-4	25.0	0-0	0-0	1-3	0-0	0-1	0-0	+4.00
Newcastle (AW)	1-6	16.7	0-0	0-1	0-1	0-0	1-3	0-1	+9.00
Pontefract	1-15	6.7	1-2	0-4	0-3	0-1	0-4	0-1	-5.00
Musselburgh	0-1	0.0	0-0	0-0	0-0	0-0	0-1	0-0	-1.00
Redcar	0-2	0.0	0-1	0-0	0-0	0-0	0-0	0-1	-2.00
Thirsk	0-2	0.0	0-0	0-0	0-0	0-0	0-1	0-1	-2.00
Carlisle	0-3	0.0	0-0	0-1	0-0	0-0	0-2	0-0	-3.00
Warwick	0-7	0.0	0-1	0-3	0-1	0-0	0-1	0-1	-7.00
Yarmouth	0-12	0.0	0-1	0-1	0-0	0-0	0-7	0-3	-12.00
Chester	0-13	0.0	0-2	0-1	0-0	0-1	0-4	0-5	-13.00

Number of horses racing for the stable **590**
Total winning prize-money **£6,680,572.70**

Backing September runners for the last four years has turned profits of £50.52, £5.28, £19.67 and £12.04

Tis Marvellous, winning at Beverley, continued to improve last season at seven

Get Ahead produced an impressive victory at Ascot on her racecourse debut but suffered a hairline fracture in running sixth in the Queen Mary on her return to the Berkshire track and had the rest of the year off.

"She has thrived since her two-year-old campaign. She's wintered well and is back in and training really nicely. She's another filly who looks exciting in the sprinting department.

"She has a rating of 89 and could run in a handicap or even a novice if need be, but she's most definitely a stakes filly with undoubted class and ability. She's just a ball of muscle to look at and pure speed. We'll be looking at the Lansdown Stakes at Bath to get the show on the road."

That's a five-furlong fillies' Listed race on April 17 which Cox has won with Priceless (2017), Place In My Heart (2013) and Gilt Edge Girl (2010).

"She's coming back off an injury, so I just want to take a couple of positive steps before getting too entrenched in a long-term plan for her, but at the moment I couldn't be more pleased."

Bermuda looks a very promising filly owned and bred by Cheveley Park who won her only start at two over seven furlongs at Newmarket in late October.

"She was very professional that day. She's a very strong, good-looking filly. I'm not sure she'll get a mile but with most of ours, if they win like that first time out, normally they show further progress.

"She's wintered well but we won't be hurrying her. I'm very pleased with her; she's looking the part and doing everything we want at the moment."

Mine's A Double didn't race as a two-year-old but was unbeaten in three outings at three, all over five and six furlongs on good to firm ground.

"He's very interesting, another exciting horse who's very quick. He won over six at Leicester first time out, then dropped back to five for his next two races and was very pleasing.

Mine's A Double: three wins out of three starts last season

"He's without doubt by far the heaviest horse I've trained at 560 kilos, which is huge. He's quite a force to be reckoned with and at 16.2hh he's a monster; hopefully he can keep his unblemished record intact.

"He would have another step to take in handicap company and progress from that."

Cheveley Park's well-bred filly **Benefit**, by Acclamation out of a Pivotal mare, won her first two starts, the second "very pleasingly" at Leicester, before finishing 11th of 13 at Newmarket, where she didn't handle the undulations, particularly the Dip.

"I'm hoping she can progress into Listed or Group 3 class this year. She was a big filly at two and she's grown into that frame over the winter. I'm very happy with the way she's progressing. She could have a start in a trial, probably Newbury for the Fred Darling, because she doesn't mind ease in the ground.

"She's from a quick family. She'll definitely get seven but I don't know whether we could stretch it out to a mile. I'm not ruling it out but we'll cross a few bridges first."

River Nymph is a 103-rated five-year-old gelding who has managed to win in each season so far, including the Victoria Cup last year.

"He's a very solid performer whose form tailed off after Ascot. I'm hoping he's a horse who can take a step forward and make his presence felt in Listed company when conditions are right. Seven furlongs seem ideal for him.

"We'll feel our way but the ground is a factor with him – the more ease the better – and we might have another crack at the Victoria Cup."

Mohi finished off well last year. After winning twice on the all-weather at Wolverhampton he was just beaten in Listed company at Doncaster.

"He's by Acclamation but from a family that generally shows good progress from two to three. That performance in the autumn was clearly very progressive and hopefully can pick up in the spring," says Cox.

"He'll definitely get seven but whether he'll get a mile I'm not sure. We'll see how his work is."

Tregony won five times last year to earn a rating of 81 but Cox feels she could be well treated for the new season.

"Hopefully, we've still got plenty of manoeuvres to make with her but she wouldn't want conditions too slow. She's from a family that generally improves with age and is one to keep an eye on."

Harry Three, Diligent Harry's half-brother, won his first two starts on the all-weather. "We gave him a break and ran him at Southwell in January and I was disappointed things didn't go well, but he's not too badly handicapped on 89."

After winning three times last year and being placed four times **Fernando Rah** earned a rating of 97 and Cox hopes he can transfer his all-weather form to the turf. "We've given him a break after a winter campaign, so he'll be a fresh horse for the summer."

Whoputfiftyinyou won both his starts at two, both over six furlongs, and hit the line well at Kempton, suggesting an extra furlong would be no problem.

"He's had a long welcome break and done very well over the winter and I hope he can continue to progress. We'll just feel our way with him."

Cox has around 50 well-bred two-year-olds, the same as the last few seasons and, as he has done in previous years, he is almost certain to produce some exciting talent.

He has half a dozen sired by his dual Group 1-winning sprinter Harry Angel, four colts and two fillies, and has picked out **Redemption Time**, a colt out of Red Box. He has also selected **Heroism**, a colt by Invincible Spirit out of Liberating.

Two fillies chosen are both unnamed, one by Kingman out of Place In My Heart and the other is by Havana Grey out of Showstoppa.

Reporting by LAWRIE KELSEY

KEITH DALGLEISH

Royal Ascot aim

WITH a name like K Dalgleish, scoring should be second nature – and so it has proved, both as a jockey and as a trainer.

Like his Scottish namesake (whose surname omits the letter e), legendary goal machine Sir Kenny Dalglish, who played 338 times for Celtic and made 515 appearances for Liverpool on his way to 102 caps for his country, and scoring 375 goals throughout his career, Keith Dalgleish is carving out his own impressive statistics.

As an apprentice jockey with Mark Johnston he rode just short of 300 winners at home and abroad, including two at Royal Ascot and a German Group 1, and since he switched to training in 2011 has saddled 750 winners on the Flat and 151 over jumps up to the middle of February.

Dalgleish holds the record for the most wins by a trainer based in Scotland in a calendar year – 118 in 2019 (80 Flat, 38 jumps). He also holds the Flat-only record with 93 last year.

If he maintains his impressive strike rate, towards the end of 2022 Dalgleish ought to have reached a landmark four figures between both codes.

As an apprentice, Dalgleish rode two Royal Ascot winners, Helm Bank in the 2002 Chesham and Fantastic Love in the 2003 King George V Stakes, but has yet to saddle a winner at the royal meeting, although he's hit the post and crossbar with Stonefield Flyer's second in the 2011 Windsor Castle, Tommy Docc's second in the 2015 Queen's Vase and Glasvegas's third in the 2019 Windsor Castle.

Could this season be the one Dalgleish finally smashes one into the net? Well, stable favourite **What's The Story** will give it his customary go with a fifth successive appearance in the Hunt Cup since finishing fourth in 2018.

WINNERS IN LAST FOUR YEARS 93, 43, 80, 73

"He's been around a while and is a stable favourite, and a very good horse on his day," says Dalgleish. "He was injured on his last run in August [John Smith's Cup at York], that's why he hasn't run since then, but he's fully recovered and is in full work. He should be ready to run around the end of March or beginning of April.

"He'll probably have a run on the all-weather and then go for a mile handicap at the York May meeting.

"Then he'll probably compete in all the same races as last year, the John Smith's Cup and Royal Hunt Cup, and those premier mile or mile and a quarter handicaps."

Another couple of Royal Ascot runners could be **Gioia Cieca**, who was unplaced in last year's Britannia, and **Summa Peto**, who was last in the same race.

"Gioia Cieca wasn't quite there physically last year, so we weren't too hard on him, but he's a horse who hasn't shown his true potential yet and there's more to come," says Dalgleish.

"I can see him ending up similar to What's The Story, a good mile handicapper. He's level-headed and has done really well over the winter; hopefully we can reap the reward of being patient with him."

Summa Peto has had a little break. He'll run from May onwards and we may try him a little bit up in trip because he was just being caught when the pressure was being put on two out.

"If he stays a mile and a half it opens more doors. He's a dead-honest horse and he's another who could end up on a higher mark than he is presently, and could go to Royal Ascot."

Red Bond has been "a little bit frustrating" over the last year and a half or so, but is clearly a horse with talent after winning three times and being placed three times before running a cracker to finish fifth in the Silver Hunt Cup at Royal Ascot in 2020.

"He was a really nice horse early on and then he just got a few problems, but he's back now. He ran in February and was just beaten half a length at Wolverhampton.

"He looks as though he's ready to win, but he should do because he's off a considerably lower mark than in the past [from 92 to 67]. Let's hope he can rise in the weights and give us some fun again."

As a two-year-old **Volatile Analyst** had the class to finish fourth in the Richmond Stakes at Glorious Goodwood and last year landed the Coral Sprint Trophy over six furlongs at York.

He has maintained his form and won over a furlong further at Wolverhampton in January.

"He's had a lot of issues but on his day is very talented. I'm really looking forward to this year with him but I think seven will stretch him running at the level we'll be targeting, so we'll keep him to six on turf.

"I think he's good enough to compete at Group 3 level, so we'll target races at that level, the likes of the Wokingham, the Coral Sprint Trophy he won last year, and the Ayr Gold Cup.

Alright Sunshine did very well in his first two seasons, winning seven times in 11 outings and being placed in the other four.

He had a long break and was not disgraced in finishing fifth in the Group 3 Sagaro Stakes at Newcastle but ran down the field in the Cesarewitch.

Dalgleish gave him a few spins over hurdles mixed with outings on the Flat and felt he was returning to his earlier form.

"I think we know how to ride him now – give him plenty of cover and don't show him much daylight. He'll probably run at the Musselburgh spring meeting in the Queen's Cup, a £75,000 handicap at Musselburgh in

DID YOU KNOW?

Keith Dalgleish retired from the saddle in 2004 after a battle with his weight, announcing quite suddenly that he was quitting – despite having four booked rides at Hamilton.

Horses in Training 2022
Edited by Graham Dench

PB £24.99

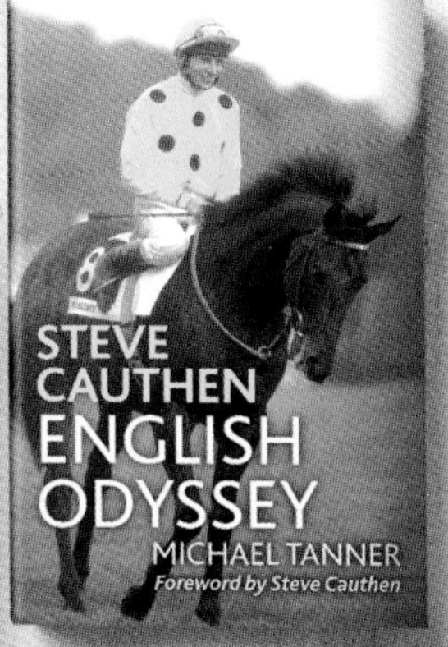

Steve Cauthen
English Odyssey
Michael Tanner

HB £19.99

Guide to the Flat 2022
PB £12.99

100 Winners
Jumpers to Follow 2021-2022
Rodney Pettinga
PB £5.99

New for 2022

www.racingpost.com/shop
01933 304858

The History of Horse Racing in 100 Objects
Steve Dennis
HB £19.99

Puzzle Book
240 Puzzles
Alan Mortiboys
PB £9.99

A4 Notebook
£16.99

A5 Notebook
£14.99

Mug
£11.99

Drinks Bottle
£21.99

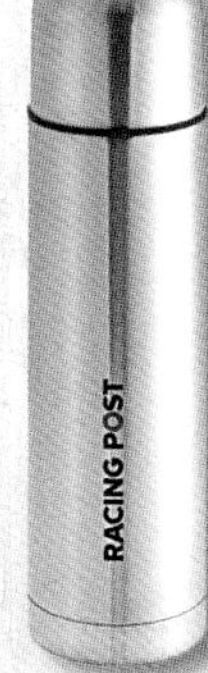

Travel Flask
£20.00

Parker Jotter Pen
£24.99

Stylus Pen
£7.99

Bottle Opener Key Fob
£7.99

Haizoom: Musselburgh Gold Cup winner has his trainer excited about this season

the spring. Then he'll run in some of the staying heritage handicaps throughout the year, including those at Royal Ascot.

The ex-Sir Michael Stoute gelding **Chichester** did Dalgleish proud after being bought in April and six days later he won at Newcastle. In June he landed the Carlisle Bell, sluiced home in a handicap at the Ayr Western Meeting and ended the year unplaced in the Cambridgeshire.

"That came too soon after Ayr really, but he had a fantastic year. I think we'll probably step him up to a mile and a quarter. Long term the Cambridgeshire could be a target,

but the John Smith's Cup would be the main aim."

The former Marcus Tregoning-trained filly **Haizoom** was rated a mere 55 when winning a 1m6f Sandown handicap. Since her move north she's won twice and been runner-up three times in five outings.

"We stepped her up in trip and she ended up winning the Musselburgh Gold Cup over two miles. I think she was very well rated when we bought her and I think she can do well this year. I'm really looking forward to her.

"She's rated 76 now and I genuinely think

Bringitonboris: thought capable of landing a decent Saturday prize

she's still well handicapped and can have a fantastic year. I really like her."

Misty Ayr was so well regarded as a two-year-old last year that she ran in the Queen Mary at Royal Ascot and the Lowther at York, then finished the year running in Group 3s at Salisbury, Ayr and Newmarket giving her a rating of 94.

"She looked as though she needed to fill out a bit and she's done that," says Dalgleish. "She's wintered well and we're looking forward to her, but we'll wait to see how her fast work is before making any plans."

Bringitonboris ended last season with a run of three seconds and two wins. "He's one who, if we could get him up in the weights, we could send south to Ascot or York and he could spring up at a nice price at one of the Saturday meetings."

Evaluation is an ex-Sir Michael Stoute-trained gelding bought at the horses-in-training sale for 30,000gns last October.

Gometra Ginty: five-time winner at Musselburgh

"He's settled in really well and is enjoying his work. He stays two miles and is well rated off 68. We'll run him in two-mile races in Scotland. They never have huge fields and are never over-competitive. He's a horse I'm really looking forward to racing."

Dual-purpose horse **Raymond** had a good year in 2021, winning at York over two miles and going up in the ratings.

"We gave him a break at the back end because he'd been raced pretty heavily. He'll be ready to race in May when the ground dries out.

"He'll be capable at two miles off his mark of 86 but whether he can progress, I don't know. He's honest, always gives his best and is a good yardstick."

Gometra Ginty has a liking for

KEITH DALGLEISH

CARLUKE, SOUTH LANARKSHIRE

RECORD AROUND THE COURSES

	W-R	Per cent	Non-hcp 2yo	Non-hcp 3yo	Non-hcp 4yo+	Hcp 2yo	Hcp 3yo	Hcp 4yo+	£1 level stake
Hamilton	110-812	13.5	18-112	6-51	6-26	2-31	34-213	44-379	-54.65
Ayr	101-912	11.1	17-116	4-24	3-12	4-46	26-234	47-480	-133.07
Musselburgh	96-774	12.4	17-106	2-14	1-11	7-45	25-210	44-388	-124.44
Wolverhampton (AW)	76-564	13.5	2-39	4-38	13-38	6-41	11-122	40-286	-91.85
Carlisle	58-423	13.7	5-70	4-13	0-6	2-17	27-118	20-199	-32.10
Newcastle (AW)	48-489	9.8	4-48	3-36	1-12	5-40	13-140	22-213	-133.76
Southwell (AW)	37-241	15.4	3-17	2-15	2-13	2-10	10-57	18-129	-11.84
Catterick	34-206	16.5	8-52	2-6	1-9	1-16	9-55	13-68	+39.89
Kempton (AW)	18-108	16.7	1-7	0-2	3-13	1-4	2-17	11-65	+22.19
Thirsk	17-112	15.2	5-28	0-7	0-5	1-7	6-31	5-34	+24.45
Ripon	17-121	14.0	1-30	0-3	1-6	0-7	8-26	7-49	-38.40
Redcar	14-158	8.9	5-44	1-9	1-9	1-11	3-48	3-37	-41.75
Lingfield (AW)	13-102	12.7	0-5	0-4	4-26	1-3	1-6	7-58	-35.55
Beverley	12-93	12.9	2-21	0-3	0-3	0-3	6-30	4-33	-9.42
York	12-114	10.5	2-16	0-2	0-2	1-12	2-15	7-67	+9.75
Newcastle	10-95	10.5	2-17	0-3	0-0	1-5	2-22	5-48	-9.25
Doncaster	9-120	7.5	0-11	0-6	0-6	1-10	3-29	5-58	-27.84
Chelmsford (AW)	8-52	15.4	0-0	1-1	0-1	0-2	3-9	4-39	-12.95
Haydock	7-92	7.6	0-10	0-3	0-4	1-4	3-27	3-44	-48.00
Chester	5-74	6.8	0-5	0-1	0-3	0-3	1-15	4-47	-37.00
Pontefract	4-58	6.9	0-8	0-6	0-5	0-5	0-7	4-27	-46.88
Leicester	2-13	15.4	0-0	1-3	1-5	0-1	0-1	0-3	-7.13
Sandown	1-10	10.0	0-0	0-0	0-1	0-0	0-2	1-7	-5.00
Nottingham	1-13	7.7	0-1	0-0	0-0	0-3	0-7	1-2	-1.00
Wetherby	1-21	4.8	0-1	0-4	0-0	0-0	0-7	1-9	-12.00
Newmarket	1-32	3.1	0-5	0-1	0-2	1-2	0-5	0-17	-27.00
Ascot	1-56	1.8	0-13	0-3	0-4	0-0	0-5	1-31	-52.00
Salisbury	0-1	0.0	0-1	0-0	0-0	0-0	0-0	0-0	-1.00
Ffos Las	0-1	0.0	0-0	0-0	0-1	0-0	0-0	0-0	-1.00
Warwick	0-1	0.0	0-0	0-0	0-0	0-0	0-1	0-0	-1.00
Brighton	0-1	0.0	0-0	0-0	0-0	0-0	0-1	0-0	-1.00
Bath	0-2	0.0	0-0	0-0	0-1	0-0	0-0	0-1	-2.00
Epsom	0-2	0.0	0-0	0-0	0-0	0-0	0-0	0-2	-2.00
Windsor	0-3	0.0	0-0	0-0	0-1	0-0	0-1	0-1	-3.00
Yarmouth	0-5	0.0	0-0	0-0	0-0	0-0	0-1	0-4	-5.00
Newmarket (July)	0-11	0.0	0-2	0-1	0-0	0-1	0-2	0-5	-11.00
Newbury	0-15	0.0	0-10	0-0	0-0	0-0	0-0	0-5	-15.00
Goodwood	0-19	0.0	0-3	0-1	0-1	0-0	0-1	0-13	-19.00

Number of horses racing for the stable **481**
Total winning prize-money **£3,800,787.30**

The stable's five-year record with older horses in maidens is 7-36 (19%) for a profit of £86.37

Musselburgh, where she's run 15 times and won five. She's a tough mare and one to follow at the Scottish track.

From his string of 75, which is down slightly on last year, ten are two-year-olds and Dalgleish has picked out a colt by Bungle Inthejungle and a filly by Camacho out of Avomcic as types with "good attitude".

"I train the filly's half sister, Friendly Vegan, who ran only twice last year because she was big and I wanted to give her time. But I quite like her and that's why I bought this filly.

"This one is bigger, stronger and sharper. I guesstimate she'll be out in April/May and she's showing enough to say she could win."

Reporting by LAWRIE KELSEY

TIM EASTERBY

Tim Easterby with his stable star Winter Power

WINNERS IN LAST FOUR YEARS 136, 94, 126, 118

Looking for Power and glory

FLYING filly **Winter Power**, who helped Tim Easterby to a record season last year, is back this year for another tilt at the top five-furlong sprints.

"She's wintered well," reports the North Yorkshire trainer, whose stables at Great Habton house around 130 horses.

"She's filled out and looks tremendous, so we're really looking forward to her. We'll target all the top five-furlong sprints when she's ready."

That's likely to be in May, although no target has yet been decided. That will be selected later but one decision has definitely

GALLOP WITH CONFIDENCE

Art Power: top sprints await this talented performer

been made – a return trip to Royal Ascot in June.

Last year she ran away with a Listed race at York in May before going to Royal Ascot for a showdown with the country's speedballs in the King's Stand. She showed blistering speed early on until weakening to finish ninth.

"We haven't decided what her May target will be yet. We'll take it as it comes," he says. "We'll get her ready, then decide, because you don't know what's round the corner. We'll just keep training away and once she looks right, then we'll fire."

After Ascot last year Winter Power landed a Listed race at York before returning to her local track for the Nunthorpe – and blasted her rivals away for a brilliant victory.

Trips to Ireland for the Flying Five at the Curragh and France for the Abbaye at Longchamp were disappointing after Winter Power led in both before fading. Those races could be on the Winter Power agenda again.

Fellow sprinter **Art Power** is also likely to follow a similar route to last year's which took in the major six-furlong races, starting with the Group 2 at York's Dante meeting in May, which is likely to be rebranded to reflect the person in whose honour it was first named in 1895, Prince George, Duke of York, who became King George V.

After York, Art Power will go to Royal Ascot, probably for the Group 1 Diamond

TIM EASTERBY

GREAT HABTON, NORTH YORKSHIRE

RECORD AROUND THE COURSES

	W-R	Per cent	Non-hcp 2yo	Non-hcp 3yo	Non-hcp 4yo+	Hcp 2yo	Hcp 3yo	Hcp 4yo+	£1 level stake
Ripon	101-900	11.2	15-192	4-60	2-5	1-28	25-203	54-412	-186.27
Beverley	80-800	10.0	11-210	2-48	0-8	1-18	30-251	36-265	-278.20
Redcar	71-914	7.8	9-206	6-82	0-10	5-52	28-264	23-300	-299.01
Thirsk	65-784	8.3	8-177	4-71	0-11	3-39	16-170	34-316	-224.51
Catterick	63-559	11.3	5-78	4-51	1-5	4-51	19-139	30-235	-103.63
York	57-796	7.2	9-124	3-17	2-15	2-27	9-129	32-484	-86.63
Pontefract	53-465	11.4	5-76	3-31	0-3	0-26	9-117	36-212	-119.32
Carlisle	52-469	11.1	8-93	2-11	1-2	0-31	15-109	26-223	-82.09
Hamilton	41-266	15.4	3-14	0-6	0-0	3-12	11-83	24-151	+14.47
Ayr	40-335	11.9	3-17	0-1	1-3	2-20	12-77	22-217	+2.49
Musselburgh	39-373	10.5	4-24	1-7	1-7	2-31	13-104	18-200	-94.35
Haydock	37-493	7.5	3-63	0-17	0-11	1-28	10-112	23-262	-154.85
Southwell (AW)	36-220	16.4	2-16	5-13	0-7	1-14	9-63	19-107	+70.02
Wolverhampton (AW)	36-328	11.0	1-27	0-23	1-6	1-27	19-104	14-141	-67.97
Chester	33-273	12.1	2-28	0-8	0-9	0-12	8-45	23-171	-53.26
Doncaster	25-539	4.6	1-71	0-36	1-17	3-32	6-89	14-294	-315.75
Newcastle (AW)	24-398	6.0	1-48	2-20	1-7	1-37	6-98	13-188	-161.88
Nottingham	15-213	7.0	2-23	0-3	0-1	1-26	6-50	6-110	-115.47
Newcastle	13-151	8.6	2-24	3-15	0-2	0-8	1-40	7-62	-58.05
Leicester	8-79	10.1	0-6	0-3	0-1	1-10	5-28	2-31	-11.50
Wetherby	6-61	9.8	0-7	2-9	0-1	0-0	1-24	3-20	-11.70
Newmarket (July)	5-45	11.1	0-2	1-1	1-3	0-5	2-21	1-13	-16.00
Newbury	4-30	13.3	1-9	0-1	0-2	0-2	1-2	2-14	-1.50
Ascot	4-57	7.0	0-2	0-5	0-9	0-0	3-9	1-32	-17.00
Salisbury	1-1	100.0	0-0	0-0	0-0	0-0	0-0	1-1	+5.50
Sandown	1-9	11.1	1-1	0-1	0-3	0-1	0-1	0-2	-4.50
Warwick	1-9	11.1	0-0	0-3	0-0	0-0	1-1	0-5	-4.50
Yarmouth	1-14	7.1	0-0	0-0	0-0	0-2	1-7	0-5	-6.50
Epsom	1-22	4.5	0-0	0-1	0-0	0-0	0-1	1-20	-17.50
Chelmsford (AW)	1-30	3.3	0-1	0-0	0-2	0-1	1-7	0-19	-27.00
Goodwood	1-35	2.9	0-1	0-0	0-7	0-3	0-1	1-23	-30.00
Newmarket	1-36	2.8	1-3	0-1	0-2	0-2	0-8	0-20	-25.00
Brighton	0-1	0.0	0-0	0-0	0-0	0-0	0-0	0-1	-1.00
Lingfield	0-2	0.0	0-0	0-0	0-0	0-0	0-0	0-2	-2.00
Kempton (AW)	0-4	0.0	0-0	0-0	0-1	0-1	0-0	0-2	-4.00
Lingfield (AW)	0-8	0.0	0-0	0-1	0-2	0-0	0-0	0-5	-8.00
Windsor	0-10	0.0	0-1	0-1	0-0	0-0	0-1	0-7	-10.00

Number of horses racing for the stable **780**
Total winning prize-money **£6,460,292.89**

Keep an eye out for when Tony Hamilton rides for the stable. His five winners in five years yielded a profit of £17.38

Jubilee Stakes in which he was third last year, then the Group 1 July Cup in which he looked like winning last season until collared in the last 100 yards.

He could take in Goodwood before Haydock's Sprint Cup and the British Champions Sprint Stakes at Ascot in October.

The five-year-old entire looks a picture of health after the winter and is pleasing everyone at Great Habton.

"He looks tremendous, in really good form; we're very happy with him," says Easterby. "He'll race over six or seven furlongs. He'll start at York and will then go to Royal Ascot. We might target a couple of the good six-furlong Irish sprints this year too, although we're not sure yet."

In the same King Power ownership as Art Power is **Roach Power**, a three-year-old half-brother by Ribchester for whom high hopes are being held by the Great Habton team.

That is despite Roach Power's moderate beginning as a two-year-old, which brought two seconds and a fourth from his three outings.

"He was a neck second at York and was a

bit unlucky, but he's done tremendously well through the winter and looks a really nice horse. He'll be out early and if he gets seven furlongs he'll be aimed at a big handicap at York in June."

Copper Knight is a horse who takes his racing well and was kept busy last season, winning three of his 14 races and being placed four times.

"He's done tremendously well and is in really good health. He's a super little horse and in good form. He loves Chester and York. He started the year on 85 and he's on 105 now; that's all right. We'll target some Listed handicaps and big handicaps with him."

Boardman ran up a hat-trick of wins early last season, rising from a rating of 75 to 96, and ended up competing in some of the big heritage handicaps, including the Buckingham Palace Stakes, Bunbury Cup at Newmarket, Ripon's Great St Wilfrid and the Ayr Silver Cup.

The handicapper has dropped him to 90, the mark of his last victory, and Boardman is pleasing his trainer.

"He's made into a nice horse and has done great over the winter. He'll be out fairly early and go to Chester – and the softer the ground the better," stresses Easterby.

Cruyff Turn won four of his nine starts last year over seven furlongs and a mile, including the 18-runner heritage Clipper Logistics handicap at York, rising from a rating of 77 to 98 by year's end.

"He likes good ground and we'll be targeting the good mile handicaps with him this year," says Easterby. "He looks well and is in good form."

Copper Knight leads before scoring at York last summer

Delgrey Boy was another who was kept busy last season earning his keep, winning three times over a mile and being placed nine times in 14 outings. Apart from his opening race, the ultra-consistent gelding finished out of the first four once – when he was fifth.

"He did really well for us last year; he won some nice handicaps and plenty of good prize-money. He started off on 62 and ended on 84. He's done really well over the winter and he'll start off over a mile. He likes good ground."

Last year **Showalong** won at Chester and then ran in a big handicap at York after which he lost his form.

"He went completely off the boil," says Easterby. "We ran him in a big apprentice handicap at York in August and he slipped coming out of the stalls. We never got him right again after that, but he's okay now and in good form. Five furlong's his trip."

He's now rated 84, 1lb lower than when he won at Chester in May and should be running in April "all being well".

Staxton is another six-furlong Easterby sprinter expected to pay his way after a decent season in 2021.

He ran in some of the big handicaps last year: the Scottish Stewards' Cup, the consolation Stewards' Cup at Goodwood and the Great St Wilfrid Handicap (a race he won in 2020) before landing the Ayr Silver Cup, rewarding his backers at 25-1.

He'll be back on the heritage trail again this season with Easterby predicting big things.

"He'll win a big one this year – I'm not sure which one just yet. I'd love to get him in the Ayr Gold Cup – he'd have a great

shout – but he'll probably not rise high enough to get in.

"He's seven and just the sort of horse we like, stands his racing well. Loves Ripon."

Hard To Fault won a novice race over 1m3f at Carlisle in July but was then "overfaced a little", according to his trainer.

"He's a big horse and was a little bit weak. He's improved this year with age and has made a really nice horse. He'll be out in April or May over a mile and a half."

Count D'Orsay ran 15 times last season in some tough handicaps without winning, although he was placed four times, including third in a Listed race at Haydock and third in the Portland Handicap at Doncaster. He was just out of the money in the Ayr Gold Cup too.

He's been dropped from a mark of 100 to 95, which ought to give him a chance in similar handicaps this season.

"He was a bit unlucky last year in some of those good handicaps," says Easterby. "He's done great over the winter and with him, the softer the ground is the better. He looks ready to run."

Atomic Lady won twice and was placed four times from seven outings at two, including runner-up in a big sales race at York before finishing third in a Listed race at Ripon.

"She did really well for us last year. We were going to take her to the Ayr Western Meeting for a Group 3, but she got a little problem, so we put her away. She's got lots

DID YOU KNOW?

Tim Easterby's Bollin Eric in 2002 was the only northern-trained winner of the St Leger in almost half a century since Bill Elsey's Peleid in 1973.

Horses to watch out for: Atomic Lady (centre) and (from top) Hard To Fault and Count D'Orsay

of ability. She won't be out until May."

Mattice ran only three times as a juvenile before developing sore shins, but one of those runs was a three-quarter-length second at York to Lusail, subsequent winner of the Gimcrack.

He's by Mattmu, winner of a Group 2 and Group 3, as well as the Great St Wilfrid, when trained by Easterby.

"He's had some nice horses and Mattice looks like a decent horse to me," says Easterby. "He looks fantastic and will be out early, possibly at Thirsk in April or Chester."

Sixstar was another to run only three times as a juvenile and was an eyecatching third at Pontefract on debut. He ran two more moderate races, leaving him on a mark of 67, a rating Easterby feels can be exploited this season.

"He's by Pivotal and is a nice horse but was just a bit weak as a two-year-old. He's strengthened up well and I think he'll improve for age. We're very happy with him and I think he could be well handicapped."

Easterby has around 50 two-year-olds and has singled out five who he thinks could be worth following: a colt by Washington DC out of Rose Eclair; a Churchill colt out of Evangelical; a colt by Expert Eye out of Ventura Mist, whom Easterby trained to win the Two-Year-Old Trophy at Redcar in 2013; a colt by Bungle Inthejungle out of Pearl Power; and **Northcliff** by Dandy Man out of Colgin.

Reporting by LAWRIE KELSEY

It's all systems go for a brand new chapter

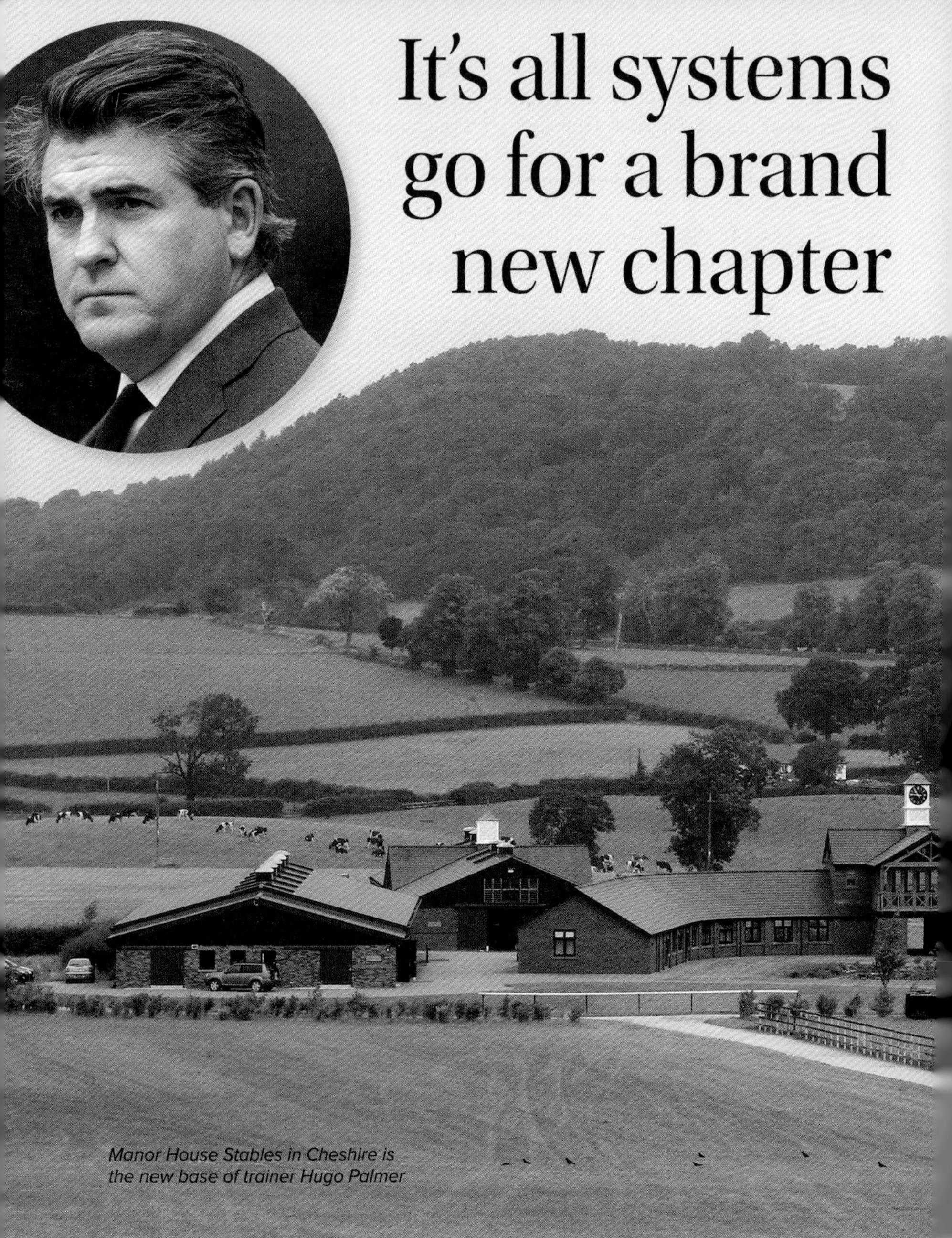

Manor House Stables in Cheshire is the new base of trainer Hugo Palmer

WINNERS IN LAST FOUR YEARS 54, 53, 87, 77

HUGO PALMER will be a force to be reckoned with at all major meetings this year as he begins a new phase of his career as salaried trainer for ex-England footballer Michael Owen.

His string of 60, being transferred from the Kremlin Cottage base he has occupied in Newmarket for the last ten years, joins Owen's 80-horsepower Manor House Stables 15 miles south of Chester racecourse in the Cheshire countryside to form a powerhouse of talent.

"There are another ten that haven't arrived yet and hopefully we'll be able to keep all the boxes full for the majority of the year," says Palmer, super keen to begin the next chapter of his already successful story.

"I'm enormously excited by it. I can't wait to get going. We'll have about 150 horses but there'll always be the sick, lame and lazy that

can do with a break somewhere else."

Owen, the former Liverpool and England international, was "absolutely thrilled" by the arrangement and described Palmer's move as "a huge coup for the area to welcome one of the country's leading trainers".

With such firepower, the Owen-Palmer alliance will hope to improve on their Classic score, which is 4-1 in Palmer's favour.

He saddled Covert Love to win the 2015 Irish Oaks, Galileo Gold in the 2,000 Guineas, and won the German 1,000 Guineas with Hawksmoor (2016) and Unfortgetable Filly the following year, while Owen landed the Irish St Leger with Brown Panther in 2014.

The star of Palmer's combined string is **Dubawi Legend**, who is in the 2,000 Guineas, for which he is as low as 20-1, and the Irish and French equivalents.

Last season Palmer's flag carrier was third in the Acomb at York before finishing second in the Dewhurst at Newmarket, then ending his season unplaced in the Breeders' Cup Juvenile Turf.

"He's done very well indeed during the winter, I'm very happy with him. Michael Hills rode him in his first bit of work and said he felt stronger and broader," says Palmer.

"Plan A is to go straight to the English Guineas. I always remember Henry Cecil being quoted over Frankel, saying he didn't feel clever enough to take a horse to the Guineas without a trial.

"I have to say I feel completely the opposite. I don't feel clever enough to take one there with a trial. The idea of asking a young horse to peak twice in a fortnight so early in the season scares me.

"I hate the thought of running horses that aren't fully ready. I think you run the risk of injury. I like to send my horses to races 100 per cent fit and fully prepared, although that doesn't mean they can't still improve for it.

"With a young horse like Dubawi Legend, who has raced only four times in his life, he will improve and has still got lots to learn. I hope he'll keep on improving all year – Dubawis have a habit of doing so."

Palmer isn't ruling out running in one of the other Guineas as well. "If Dubawi Legend were to win or nearly win, he could very easily go to one of the others subsequently."

Another Classic hopeful is **Flaming Rib**, winner of five races for Owen's previous trainer Tom Dascombe, including his last four outings. The final event was a Doncaster Listed race, which earned the Ribchester colt a rating of 108.

"He's bred to stay a mile. We've put him in the French Guineas but not the English Guineas. Talking to Michael, the feeling is he's more likely to get the downhill-turning mile at Longchamp rather than the uphill stiff mile at Newmarket or the Curragh.

"The plan with him is to go for a trial – probably the Greenham at Newbury – and then we can explore the seventh furlong and see from there. His rating would have him running well in a lot of Greenhams."

Manor House also has **Mr McCann**, who became a Classic hopeful when winning a 1m½f conditions race in September at Epsom, [the Cazoo Derby 'Wild Card'], which was a 'win and you're in' race, which meant the Derby first entry stage was free.

"He's by Kodiac, and there aren't many Kodiacs who stay a mile and a half, so he's also in the French Derby, which is 1m2½f," says Palmer. "They tend to go steady and then sprint in that, which may suit him. The plan is to run him in the Dee Stakes [over 1m2½f] at Chester first."

Ever Given and **Amor Vincit Omnia** are two sprinters Palmer will be inheriting at Manor House Stables, and both are expected to be fine prospects.

Ever Given won four times last year and was pipped in a valuable sale race at Doncaster, ending the year on a rating of 97.

Amor Vincit Omnia, a well-bred Caravaggio colt out of a Galileo mare, was an impressive winner of a Haydock nursery on the last of his four runs last year and begins this season on a mark of 90.

The duo will join a strong group of sprinters arriving from Kremlin Cottage, including **Hierarchy**, a three-year-old colt who won his first two races before finishing third in Kempton's Group 3 Sirenia Stakes, second in the Mill Reef and sixth in the Breeders' Cup Juvenile Turf Sprint.

"He was favourite for the Cornwallis [a 5f Group 3 at Newmarket] but I didn't like the look of him at evening stables on the day I declared him, so we took some blood, which wasn't right.

"I spoke to Sheikh Fahad [Qatar Racing owner], who said let's not risk him for £40,000 when we'll be running for a million in four weeks' time. So we turned him out in the field and the little brute lacerated his legs and ended up having to miss six days' exercise, which, in my view, certainly cost him second in the Breeders' Cup.

"He came to win his race but just ran out of puff and was beaten a length and a quarter. That week we missed meant we were always behind the eight ball in getting him back to where we were, but he ran a magnificent race.

"He's versatile as to ground and trip and he's so relaxed in his races, it wouldn't surprise us if he got seven at some stage, but not a mile. I think that would be stretching him."

The Commonwealth Cup for three-year-olds over six furlongs at Royal Ascot will be Hierarchy's first major target.

"The Commonwealth Cup programme has been written for horses like this. He's all muscle and looks like a sprinter. He's done well during the winter. He isn't a tall horse but he's a lot heavier and stronger and broader than he was, and he's a good deal bigger than an awful lot of champion sprinters."

His options before Royal Ascot will include the Group 3 Pavilion Stakes at Ascot in April, a Commonwealth Cup trial, and the Sandy Lane Stakes at Haydock the following month.

Another member of the Manor House sprint quartet is **Ebro River**, and Palmer will be juggling entries, which will also include the Duke of York Stakes and a Group 3 at Chantilly in May.

HUGO PALMER

MALPAS, CHESHIRE

RECORD AROUND THE COURSES

	W-R	Per cent	Non-hcp 2yo	Non-hcp 3yo	Non-hcp 4yo+	Hcp 2yo	Hcp 3yo	Hcp 4yo+	£1 level stake
Kempton (AW)	58-330	17.6	23-117	8-64	1-12	3-21	16-83	7-33	-7.90
Wolverhampton (AW)	48-191	25.1	13-40	10-47	3-11	5-18	10-54	7-21	+50.05
Chelmsford (AW)	38-209	18.2	13-52	7-49	1-8	1-12	8-56	8-32	-48.18
Newcastle (AW)	31-151	20.5	10-36	9-40	1-2	0-13	7-34	4-26	+2.46
Lingfield (AW)	30-196	15.3	4-44	7-53	2-14	0-7	9-49	8-29	-36.33
Haydock	21-83	25.3	7-18	4-18	2-8	0-2	7-27	1-10	+67.94
Newmarket (July)	21-162	13.0	6-55	1-16	3-6	3-8	8-65	0-12	-45.79
Doncaster	20-107	18.7	7-25	3-22	1-6	2-9	5-31	2-14	-4.09
Windsor	18-116	15.5	3-29	6-30	0-5	2-6	3-39	4-7	-21.28
Yarmouth	17-106	16.0	5-36	4-15	0-1	0-6	8-38	0-10	-8.37
Newmarket	13-180	7.2	6-69	3-41	0-8	1-11	2-38	1-13	-86.93
Newbury	11-108	10.2	6-37	2-18	0-12	0-0	3-27	0-14	-15.48
Lingfield	10-36	27.8	3-10	3-14	0-0	2-3	1-5	1-4	+10.64
Goodwood	10-83	12.0	3-18	1-15	0-7	0-7	4-22	2-14	-8.67
Thirsk	9-46	19.6	2-11	2-13	0-0	0-1	3-15	2-6	-12.87
Leicester	9-46	19.6	3-10	0-5	3-6	0-4	2-17	1-4	-18.54
Sandown	9-64	14.1	4-21	0-8	0-4	0-1	5-24	0-6	-17.00
Nottingham	9-67	13.4	5-22	0-16	0-1	0-5	4-20	0-3	-15.08
Ascot	9-113	8.0	3-17	3-22	0-3	0-1	2-38	1-32	-72.30
Salisbury	8-44	18.2	5-18	2-12	0-1	0-2	1-9	0-2	-3.01
Bath	7-25	28.0	2-4	0-5	1-2	0-2	4-12	0-0	+21.79
Redcar	7-50	14.0	4-17	1-9	0-0	0-1	2-20	0-3	+2.48
York	7-85	8.2	1-24	1-11	0-6	0-4	4-22	1-18	-5.00
Hamilton	6-10	60.0	1-2	4-4	0-0	0-0	1-3	0-1	+4.28
Carlisle	6-13	46.2	1-2	4-6	0-0	0-2	1-1	0-2	+3.43
Brighton	6-28	21.4	4-14	1-3	0-0	0-2	1-9	0-0	-11.04
Beverley	6-29	20.7	2-13	4-7	0-0	0-0	0-8	0-1	-5.78
Newcastle	5-13	38.5	2-7	2-3	1-1	0-0	0-2	0-0	+10.18
Ffos Las	5-16	31.2	1-4	2-3	1-1	0-0	1-5	0-3	-3.33
Catterick	4-13	30.8	1-3	1-1	0-0	1-4	1-5	0-0	+18.91
Ayr	4-19	21.1	0-2	3-4	0-1	0-1	1-8	0-3	-10.03
Southwell (AW)	4-33	12.1	0-1	2-11	0-2	1-8	0-6	1-5	-9.00
Pontefract	3-28	10.7	0-6	1-7	1-4	0-3	1-6	0-2	-6.39
Chester	3-31	9.7	1-5	0-1	0-2	1-4	1-10	0-9	-13.00
Chepstow	2-10	20.0	0-0	1-2	0-0	0-0	0-5	1-3	+19.00
Ripon	2-12	16.7	0-2	0-4	0-0	0-3	2-3	0-0	-6.93
Epsom	2-19	10.5	1-3	0-4	0-3	1-2	0-6	0-1	-9.75
Musselburgh	1-8	12.5	0-0	1-3	0-1	0-0	0-4	0-0	-4.50
Folkestone	0-3	0.0	0-2	0-0	0-0	0-1	0-0	0-0	-3.00
Warwick	0-3	0.0	0-1	0-0	0-0	0-0	0-2	0-0	-3.00
Wetherby	0-6	0.0	0-0	0-2	0-0	0-0	0-2	0-2	-6.00

Number of horses racing for the stable **452**
Total winning prize-money **£4,790,154.94**

Jason Hart has ridden nine times for the yard in the last five years. He won three times for a profit of £21.61

Ebro River: reported to have made great strides over the winter

"If we're clever, we can avoid running all four in the same race and bursting at least three bubbles before we start!" laughs Palmer, "but it's a nice problem to have."

Ebro River, winner of the Group 1 Phoenix Stakes and third in the Group 1 National Stakes, has changed hugely over the winter, according to Palmer.

"He's really matured, developed and grown. He's considerably over 500 kilograms, compared with his father [Galileo Gold], who weighed 481 kilograms the day he won the Guineas – and it's all muscle strength.

"He could go to the Pavilion Stakes as an unpenalised Group 1 winner, so that's a strong possibility. I think of him as a Commonwealth Cup horse, but if he were to be beaten over the stiff Ascot six in the Pavilion, then head to the Sandy Lane, which is a much sharper six, and win that, I would be strongly considering dropping back to five furlongs for the King's Stand."

DID YOU KNOW?

The Honourable Hugo Palmer is the eldest son of the 4th Baron Palmer, whose ancestral seat, Manderston, is in Berwickshire, and whose family were part of Huntley & Palmers, once the largest biscuit manufacturer in the world.

Dig Two won a couple of small races before finishing second in the Listed Windsor Castle at Royal Ascot last year and is likely to turn into a sprint handicapper rather than a Group horse, thinks Palmer.

"I think he's a notch below Ebro and Hierarchy, although he could reach Listed class," says Palmer. "He could run in a race at Newmarket on Guineas weekend or a handicap at York.

"He's done really well during the winter. He was a sharp two-year-old and looked physically as though there was more to come. I'm pleased to say he really has developed."

One of the best-bred members of Palmer's string is **Arion**, who is by Dubawi out of Filia Regina, a winning sister to Australia. She ran only twice last year, second in a good seven-furlong maiden at Newmarket, then won at Chelmsford over the same distance.

"She has bags of speed and we're hoping she stays a mile," says Palmer. "I don't think she's a Guineas filly, I think that will come too soon for her.

"She'll start in an Oaks trial, something like the Musidora at York. I think she's definitely up for getting black type and there's an awful lot of black type for three-year-old fillies in the month of May.

"She's a granddaughter of Ouija Board, who has been a difficult mare to breed from,

and she only has one filly, this filly's mother. This could be the end of the line."

Chocoya had a long year as Palmer tried to get winning black type for the filly. She was placed in a French Listed race in March, finished fourth in the Group 3 Nell Gwyn and was second in a Chelmsford Listed race, but despite running creditably in five more Listed races, the only victories came in two small handicaps.

"She's a tough filly whom we kept busy last year. She did really well for us but not as well as we wanted her to.

"One of her main targets will be a Chelmsford Listed race in July. There are other Listed targets but she needs to hear her feet rattle, so soft ground is out."

Scot's Grace will go the same route taken by Chocoya last year – a first outing in the Listed Prix Montenica over six and a half furlongs at Chantilly, the race in which Chocoya finished a close second last year. She has a 1,000 Guineas entry and will go for a trial, probably the Nell Gwyn at Newmarket.

Brunnera, a well-bred four-year-old filly by Dubawi out of a Galileo mare, was unlucky not to win a staying fillies' stakes race at Bath in October, when she got to the front easily but was "chinned on the line".

"She stays well. She's a fast-ground horse and I would love to think she could run in races such as the Group 2 Lillie Langtry at Goodwood and Doncaster's Group 2 Park Hill," says Palmer.

The four-year-old filly **Quenelle D'Or** had a busy year and ended up winning a moderate Listed race in France by a neck after running well in several handicaps in this country without winning,

"I was furious because they whacked her up from 86 to 100 after the French race. I couldn't see any justification. We got black type but I was planning to run her in the valuable Old Rowley Cup handicap at Newmarket but with an extra stone I couldn't."

This year the filly will take a similar route to last season with Palmer attempting to find a suitable programme in search of more black type on quick ground.

Of the two-year-olds moving from Newmarket, Palmer selects a quartet to follow: an unnamed Zoustar filly who looks "sharp, very forward and smart"; **Debater**, a 150,000gns filly by No Nay Never out of Now You're Talking who looks "strong and forward"; a Lope De Vega colt out of Maureen, "not very big but strong, athletic and forward who could be a Chesham type"; and a Havana Grey colt out of Chandresh, who is "strong, impressive-looking and peculiarly precocious".

Reporting by LAWRIE KELSEY

Michael Owen at Manor House Stables, where Hugo Palmer will now be based

JOHN QUINN

Safe Voyage will be bidding to find the winner's enclosure again this season

WINNERS IN LAST FOUR YEARS 52, 44, 36, 45

Safe Voyage could have Lincoln as an early target

THE first big race of the season, the Lincoln Handicap, is a race John Quinn knows how to win having landed it twice with Blythe Knight (2006) and Levitate (2013).

Quinn's entry this year is **Safe Voyage**, a nine-year-old winner of 13 races, including two Group 2s and a Group 3, and almost £570,000 prize-money.

The trouble is no horse of that age has won the Lincoln since it moved 44 miles to Doncaster when the Carholme racecourse closed in Lincoln in 1964.

But isn't age just a number? Safe Voyage doesn't know how old he is and, according to his trainer, he's performing admirably.

"He seems to have retained plenty of ability and we're happy with him. His work's good and he's training well," says Quinn.

The genial Irishman, who rode the best part of 200 winners as a journeyman jumps jockey before turning to training in the mid-1990s, isn't ruling out the Lincoln, but he is contemplating a Listed race in France on March 15 as an alternative, 11 days before the Lincoln.

"I think he's better round a bend, but he has won in a straight line," says Quinn *(above)*. "We are leaning more to going to France but if there's enough time between the two he could run in both."

Quinn's own version of the spring double, as opposed to the traditional Lincoln-Grand National double, has been performed by him before.

"In 2008 we ran Blythe Knight in the Champion Hurdle, but he didn't stay, and the Lincoln [11 days later] when he was second carrying 9st 3lb; so it can be done. We'll have to see. If he runs okay we certainly wouldn't rule the Lincoln out.

"The Lincoln's a bit of a cavalry charge and nowadays in these big handicaps you need a horse with a bit of class, which he certainly doesn't lack."

Last year's Buckingham Palace Stakes winner **Highfield Princess** ended her season with a highly creditable sixth of 20 in the British Champions Sprint race at Ascot in

DID YOU KNOW?

John Quinn's 1,000th winner under both codes was Safe Voyage, who scored on Derby day last year.

October and had some high-class sprinters in her wake.

"I'm very happy with her. She had a run in February and we're qualifying her for the fillies' final on Good Friday at the all-weather finals at Newcastle.

"We have a good programme mapped out for her in the second half of the year. After the all-weather finals there's a Group race at Haydock in May, but we can't see a race for her at Royal Ascot, so we're going to use June as, not a break, but an easier time for her, then we're going to roll the dice in the autumn.

"We're thinking about the Goodwood race she ran well in last year [Group 3 Oak Tree] and at York [Group 2 City of York], as well as the Foret in October [Group 1 at Longchamp]. We have also thought about Saudi Arabia next January."

Mr Wagyu was a hardy performer last season, winning five times and finishing second three times in 16 outings from May to October.

"He had a great year but it's going to be trouble for him this year," says Quinn. "He was third in the Ayr Gold Cup off 99. The winner came up the stands' side, the second

Highfield Princess wins the Buckingham Palace Handicap at Royal Ascot; (below) Mr Wagyu comes home in good style to score in the Stewards' Cup consolation

was on the far side, and we were up the middle.

"In an ideal world you'd have preferred to have been one side or the other, but he still ran a massive race.

There is a feeling he might have won, drawn on either wing, but Quinn reckons he still has a workable rating.

"We feel he can be competitive and we feel there's a good race in him. He loves York, Goodwood and Ayr, so that's the way we're thinking.

"He won the Stewards' Cup consolation at Goodwood in a faster time than the Stewards' Cup, so he could go for races like the Stewards' Cup, the Ayr Gold Cup and the big ones at York. If he improves again I think he can win one of those big sprint races. We're ruling nothing out and we're kicking him off in May."

Lord Riddiford is another horse who takes his racing well, winning three times in nine outings last year.

"He's an admirable horse, very good on his day. I was delighted with his comeback run at Wolverhampton off 103."

In late February he ran in the same Lingfield Listed race he won last year, but he failed to repeat the feat. What it meant, however, was his rating dropped to 99, which will help if he returns to Epsom for the Dash in June, a race in which he was fifth last year "not getting the rub of the green".

"He's won twice at Goodwood. He loves the track, so we'll think about that too," adds Quinn.

Imperial Mountain won three out of his four outings as a two-year-old and is described by Quinn as "a very progressive horse who has done nothing but improve".

He adds: "He's a horse with a good future and will more than pay his way. He's rated 85 and I'm sure he'll do well in the summer. He's not slow and won all his races over seven furlongs, but he could get a mile."

As a two-year-old **Titan Rock** was good enough to win a maiden at Glorious Goodwood before finishing a creditable fifth in the Group 3 Acomb Stakes at York's Ebor meeting.

"Last year he won twice, clocking a fast time at Ayr in his final run over seven furlongs before we put him away. He's a big fine horse and I can see him winning a good handicap this year."

Frankenstella won a Haydock handicap in May and six days later was second at Carlisle in her build-up for a crack at the 2m4f Ascot Stakes at Royal Ascot, but had a setback and needed a couple of months off.

"She's back in and we're very happy with her," says Quinn. "She'll definitely get a run in April and then we're thinking of the Chester Cup consolation.

"Last year we were thinking of Royal Ascot but she got a little niggle. This year we're hoping she's good enough again to run at Royal Ascot; it's the place every trainer wants to be going with a chance. She stays very well and could end up a Cesarewitch filly."

First Impression is a dual-purpose five-year-old gelding who was third in a 1m2f handicap at Chester's May meeting and is likely to head back there this season.

He's been placed twice over hurdles already this winter and could be one to pop up at either code.

"I can see him winning a good race on the Flat over one mile two furlongs or three furlongs," says Quinn. "I was pleased with him in February. He ran well at Chester last year and he could be on the wagon for Chester again."

Melody King is "a likeable sort" who won a couple of races last year over five furlongs and is likely to be out early.

"If he improves a bit he could be a good sprinter. If he does, we'll then roll the dice."

Beluga Gold is a three-year-old colt full of promise after running twice at the backend of last season, losing his second start at Doncaster by a short head.

"He's quite a nice horse. He's done well from two to three and could have a spin on

the all-weather before running at Doncaster."

Poet's Magic and **Empirestateofmind** both won three races each last year and the duo are expected to add to stable coffers this season.

"Poet's Magic is a very genuine filly and if she improves again this year she could have a good year," says Quinn.

"Empirestateofmind is very consistent. He won three and it could have been five with a bit more luck.

"He's in the Lincoln but he won't get in. He'll run in the consolation, which should be right up his alley. He's a nice animal and I can see him getting a mile and a quarter."

Moon Over The Sea, who has a good staying pedigree, ran only once last year when fifth over a mile at the Ayr Western Meeting.

"We then put him away. He's done well over the winter and should improve. We like him a lot. He'll do well over staying trips and will be out earlyish."

Truely Aclaimed won once and was second twice in six outings last year in her juvenile campaign, and finished runner-up on her return at Newcastle in January when she made the running, which didn't suit her.

"She's a nice type of filly who will pay her way," says Quinn.

Close Quarter is an unraced Fast Company half-sister to Winter Power, Tim Easterby's brilliant Nunthorpe winner.

"She came to herself only at the backend, so we decided to give her a winter on her back, and she's done fine. We think she's a filly who's up to winning races and if that's the case, she'll be a very valuable horse.

"She'll be out in April when the turf starts. My first aim is to win with her, then we'll see where we go."

Among his two-year-olds, Quinn makes special mention of **Breege**, a filly by Starspangledbanner and three-parts sister to his 2014 Coventry and Prix Morny winner The Wow Signal, "the best horse we've trained"; a colt by Starspangledbanner out of Sunset Dazzle; a Fast Company colt out of Leading Actress; **Signora Camacho**, a three-parts sister to Queen Mary and Prix Robert Papin winner Signora Cabello ("if she's half as good as her three-parts sister, she'll be good"); **Granny Bea**, a filly by Acclamation; and the Kodiac filly **Blooming Robbery**.

Reporting by LAWRIE KELSEY

JOHN QUINN

SETTRINGTON, NORTH YORKSHIRE

RECORD AROUND THE COURSES

	W-R	Per cent	Non-hcp 2yo	Non-hcp 3yo	Non-hcp 4yo+	Hcp 2yo	Hcp 3yo	Hcp 4yo+	£1 level stake
Catterick	40-303	13.2	6-69	3-22	5-15	4-18	9-62	13-117	-58.54
Ayr	32-181	17.7	6-29	1-2	1-3	0-11	7-50	17-86	+36.10
Newcastle (AW)	27-270	10.0	3-50	2-34	0-0	2-35	7-63	13-88	-47.17
Redcar	24-223	10.8	4-77	4-24	8-14	0-17	5-50	3-41	-95.13
Musselburgh	20-141	14.2	5-24	1-2	0-3	0-12	7-41	7-59	-24.85
Thirsk	20-184	10.9	6-49	0-11	0-3	0-13	6-43	8-65	-8.14
Wolverhampton (AW)	20-224	8.9	2-19	2-20	3-18	1-18	3-57	9-92	-92.73
Pontefract	19-163	11.7	2-46	3-12	0-1	1-5	6-44	7-55	+3.86
Beverley	19-201	9.5	10-72	2-11	1-9	1-5	4-56	1-48	-50.91
Chelmsford (AW)	17-90	18.9	2-9	0-1	1-3	1-13	7-29	6-35	-9.73
Haydock	17-103	16.5	1-14	1-5	3-8	2-6	3-27	7-43	-9.01
Hamilton	16-122	13.1	4-20	1-6	0-4	0-7	5-32	6-53	-45.72
Doncaster	16-163	9.8	0-22	0-6	1-11	1-8	7-43	7-73	+11.00
Ripon	14-131	10.7	3-37	2-5	2-5	0-4	2-38	5-42	-8.65
York	14-184	7.6	4-38	0-1	1-11	2-17	2-26	5-91	-44.09
Chester	13-91	14.3	1-10	1-2	3-3	1-7	1-20	6-49	-18.26
Southwell (AW)	10-101	9.9	0-4	0-8	0-2	1-8	4-30	5-49	-50.18
Carlisle	9-89	10.1	2-27	0-1	0-2	0-7	2-25	5-27	-32.17
Epsom	8-40	20.0	0-2	0-0	1-3	0-1	2-8	5-26	+14.70
Lingfield (AW)	8-46	17.4	1-4	1-4	1-4	0-1	1-11	4-22	-11.56
Newcastle	8-84	9.5	2-27	0-4	0-0	0-3	2-20	4-30	-37.67
Goodwood	7-35	20.0	3-4	0-3	0-6	0-2	1-10	3-10	+45.74
Leicester	7-57	12.3	0-10	2-3	0-6	2-8	2-20	1-10	-17.43
Nottingham	7-58	12.1	2-13	0-1	0-2	0-6	3-17	2-19	-0.50
Ascot	4-42	9.5	2-8	0-5	0-8	0-0	0-6	2-15	+22.00
Newmarket	3-30	10.0	0-5	0-2	0-4	0-1	2-5	1-13	-9.00
Kempton (AW)	3-37	8.1	1-3	0-1	0-0	0-7	0-10	2-16	-14.25
Windsor	2-7	28.6	0-2	0-0	0-1	0-0	2-4	0-0	+10.00
Sandown	2-9	22.2	1-1	0-2	0-2	0-0	0-2	1-2	-3.65
Bath	2-16	12.5	1-3	0-0	0-0	0-2	1-4	0-7	+0.75
Wetherby	2-22	9.1	2-5	0-3	0-0	0-0	0-5	0-9	-16.13
Newmarket (July)	2-25	8.0	0-1	0-0	0-0	0-3	1-12	1-9	-17.63
Warwick	1-6	16.7	0-1	0-0	1-2	0-0	0-1	0-2	-2.75
Yarmouth	1-13	7.7	0-1	0-0	0-0	0-2	0-2	1-8	-6.00
Chepstow	1-16	6.2	0-0	0-0	0-0	0-1	1-6	0-9	-10.00
Ffos Las	0-1	0.0	0-0	0-0	0-0	0-0	0-1	0-0	-1.00
Lingfield	0-5	0.0	0-1	0-0	0-0	0-0	0-2	0-2	-5.00
Newbury	0-8	0.0	0-3	0-0	0-2	0-0	0-1	0-2	-8.00
Brighton	0-8	0.0	0-2	0-1	0-0	0-0	0-3	0-2	-8.00

Number of horses racing for the stable **391**

Total winning prize-money **£2,742,093.22**

Hollie Doyle has taken only four rides for the yard in the last five years. Two won, for a profit of £8.50

Promising prospects: Imperial Mountain (below left) and Empirestateofmind

Top sprints all on agenda for Emaraaty

ONE of the major aims this season for Kevin Ryan and assistant-trainer son Adam will be to make **Emaraaty Ana** champion sprinter.

They are hoping the six-year-old gelding can follow in the footprints of their flying mare Glass Slippers, who was retired last year after a career which brought victories at the top level in the Abbaye, Ireland's Flying Five and the Breeders' Cup Turf Sprint.

The 2018 Gimcrack winner Emaraaty Ana finally fulfilled the Ryans' hopes of winning at the top

Emaraaty Ana lands Haydock's Sprint Cup for her delighted team

WINNERS IN LAST FOUR YEARS 79, 58, 65, 76

DID YOU KNOW?
Kevin Ryan's birth was a Golden one in 1967. The Irishman was born in the County Tipperary village of Golden.

level when he landed the Haydock Sprint Cup in September.

After failing to stay a mile in the English and Irish Guineas, he was brought back to sprinting distances and, after being gelded and having a wind operation, he had a long break.

Last year he returned to the track to finish close-up third in two Group 3s, the Abernant and Palace House Stakes, at Newmarket, then finished second in the Group 1 Nunthorpe two weeks before landing the Group 1 Sprint Cup.

"We always thought he was capable of winning a Group 1 and then he ran a huge race in the Breeders' Cup over five furlongs, which didn't suit him. He was fourth and I thought he ran a fantastic race," says Adam.

He'll head to the Al Quoz six-furlong sprint on World Cup night in Dubai on March 26, attempting to halt the Charlie Appleby-Godolphin bandwagon which has dominated it for the last three years.

Emaraaty Ana's major targets in Britain will then be all the top sprints, such as the July Cup, Nunthorpe and Haydock Sprint Cup. And the Breeders' Cup at the end of the year?

"It all depends how the season pans out. It'll be a long old year for him, so we'll see how it goes," says Adam.

Bielsa has always looked as though he had a major race in him and it emerged in September when he landed the Ayr Gold Cup.

"Winning that puts him on a handicap mark of 105, which means you're flirting with Pattern company with him," says Adam.

"He's a very lightly raced horse, so he's the

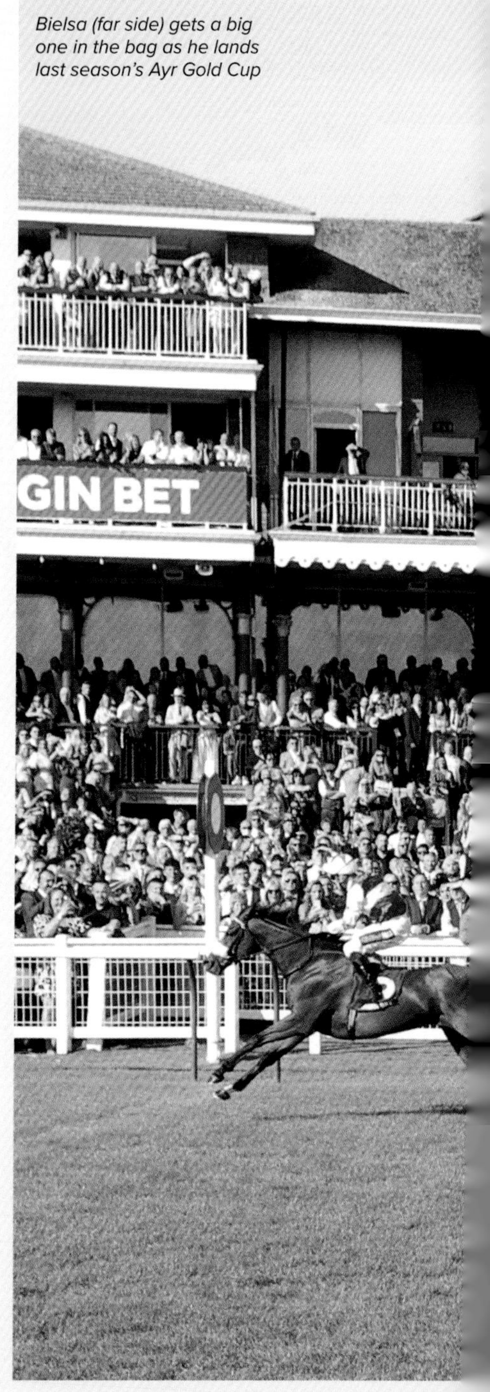

Bielsa (far side) gets a big one in the bag as he lands last season's Ayr Gold Cup

KEVIN RYAN

HAMBLETON, NORTH YORKSHIRE

Backing Sean Davis on all rides for the yard in the last five years has seen a 45% strike-rate and profit of £15.75

RECORD AROUND THE COURSES

	W-R	Per cent	Non-hcp 2yo	Non-hcp 3yo	Non-hcp 4yo+	Hcp 2yo	Hcp 3yo	Hcp 4yo+	£1 level stake
Hamilton	62-289	21.5	14-73	13-39	5-10	8-21	7-68	15-78	-17.41
Wolverhampton (AW)	52-416	12.5	5-65	9-68	4-21	0-33	17-111	17-118	-54.29
Thirsk	49-383	12.8	11-92	6-46	1-9	5-18	11-84	15-134	-14.84
Beverley	47-340	13.8	24-125	4-22	1-14	1-3	10-105	7-71	-25.24
York	46-564	8.2	24-177	2-25	3-44	4-36	8-104	5-178	-200.79
Haydock	44-344	12.8	14-104	4-29	2-29	3-16	14-87	7-79	+75.62
Newcastle (AW)	38-347	11.0	6-62	6-54	0-7	2-24	13-93	11-107	-73.09
Ayr	38-361	10.5	18-96	2-15	0-13	3-22	4-78	11-137	-120.44
Southwell (AW)	37-253	14.6	9-37	8-51	3-15	2-8	4-58	11-84	-68.07
Redcar	35-272	12.9	11-98	6-42	2-6	3-12	12-78	1-36	-67.66
Pontefract	34-248	13.7	9-66	5-38	0-2	3-9	9-77	8-56	-7.23
Musselburgh	31-193	16.1	10-47	2-8	1-6	2-9	6-48	10-75	-21.73
Catterick	29-171	17.0	5-39	4-15	2-6	4-17	7-50	7-44	-3.82
Carlisle	28-177	15.8	12-65	1-7	0-0	3-9	9-55	3-41	-7.29
Doncaster	27-350	7.7	4-84	2-24	3-23	1-21	8-87	9-111	+14.90
Lingfield (AW)	21-150	14.0	3-14	10-33	1-19	1-9	3-31	3-44	-41.25
Ripon	20-226	8.8	3-52	3-19	1-2	0-8	5-61	8-84	-68.43
Chester	19-139	13.7	7-19	1-2	2-12	2-8	5-37	2-61	-33.59
Newmarket (July)	16-125	12.8	4-18	0-6	0-12	0-6	8-55	4-28	+82.83
Chelmsford (AW)	14-100	14.0	0-7	4-17	1-3	1-6	4-27	4-40	-8.43
Newcastle	13-93	14.0	4-27	1-6	0-1	1-4	5-28	2-27	-26.47
Leicester	13-124	10.5	7-31	0-17	0-1	1-5	4-49	1-21	-36.67
Kempton (AW)	12-122	9.8	1-21	1-11	1-4	0-9	5-37	4-40	-47.25
Nottingham	12-124	9.7	3-29	1-11	1-7	2-9	4-47	1-21	-58.13
Newmarket	10-116	8.6	1-21	0-23	4-22	0-4	1-20	4-26	-51.75
Ascot	8-149	5.4	2-22	0-17	2-20	0-1	1-19	3-70	-43.00
Yarmouth	5-29	17.2	2-5	1-2	0-0	0-5	1-12	1-5	-2.08
Epsom	5-41	12.2	1-3	0-0	0-0	0-0	3-10	1-28	-12.75
Wetherby	4-22	18.2	1-3	1-6	0-0	0-0	2-6	0-7	+29.50
Goodwood	4-76	5.3	0-10	0-5	1-7	0-8	2-12	1-34	-34.00
Windsor	3-32	9.4	1-6	1-6	0-0	0-3	0-13	1-4	-5.38
Bath	2-6	33.3	0-0	0-1	0-1	0-1	2-2	0-1	+0.95
Warwick	2-14	14.3	0-2	0-3	0-0	0-0	2-7	0-2	+13.00
Sandown	2-20	10.0	1-7	0-1	1-2	0-0	0-7	0-3	-14.38
Newbury	2-43	4.7	1-20	0-8	0-3	1-1	0-4	0-7	-32.75
Salisbury	1-5	20.0	0-1	1-2	0-1	0-0	0-0	0-1	-1.50
Brighton	0-1	0.0	0-0	0-0	0-0	0-0	0-1	0-0	-1.00
Chepstow	0-5	0.0	0-1	0-1	0-0	0-0	0-2	0-1	-5.00
Lingfield	0-6	0.0	0-1	0-1	0-2	0-1	0-0	0-1	-6.00

Number of horses racing for the stable **763**

Total winning prize-money **£7,163,427.77**

type who'll probably be between the very top handicaps and Pattern company. He could start in something like the Listed Cammidge Trophy at Doncaster. Then there are the top handicaps like the Wokingham, so we'll be quite fluid with him."

In the same Sheikh Obaid ownership as Emaraaty Ana is **Juan Elcano**, winner of the Listed Wolferton Stakes at Royal Ascot last year.

"He was probably a bit unfortunate not to win a Group 2 at York as well," says Adam. "We'll probably work back from Royal Ascot with something like the Wolferton in mind again, then take the same sort of route as last year with him.

"He really showed he was back to his best last year and was unlucky not to have a Group 2 under his belt. It wouldn't be a surprise to see him pick up something along those lines this year."

Last season **Gis A Sub** won a small

Juan Elcano lands the Wolferton Stakes at Royal Ascot and could strike at Group level this season

Pontefract conditions race before a tilt at the Group 2 Richmond Stakes at Goodwood. He was beaten under three lengths in sixth but returned to run a stormer in the Gimcrack in which he finished second to Lusail.

He ended his juvenile campaign with a trip to Chantilly where he was last of six in the Group 2 Criterium de Maisons-Laffitte.

"His run in the Gimcrack was very impressive and you can put a line through his last run; it was too heavy in France. We always felt he would be a better three-year-old and anything he did last year was a bonus.

"There's a good programme now for three-year-old sprinters and this year we'll take in the Commonwealth Cup trials. If he progresses from there, fantastic, and we'll run in the Commonwealth Cup."

The Ryans have had reasonable Classic success down the years: The Grey Gatsby won the 2014 French Derby, Glory Awaits was runner-up in the 2,000 Guineas of 2013, and East was third in the 2019 French 1,000 Guineas.

This year they are triple entered in the French Derby with **Franz**, **Thunder Roar** and **Triple Time**, who is also in the English, Irish and French 2,000 Guineas.

"Triple Time is from a very good family and progressed throughout the year, thriving with every step up in trip from six furlongs to a mile," says Adam.

"He impressed in a Listed win at Haydock and was always a horse who would get better with time. He's grown and strengthened through the winter and he's an exciting horse. He could get ten furlongs, so could be a Dante-type horse too."

Franz won on his only start last season, an October novice stakes race at Haydock, a mile race on soft ground replete with promise for his three-year-old season.

"He's a big colt who took a bit of time to come to hand, but he won really impressively. He's out of a Galileo mare, so was always going to do better as a three-year-old and with time.

"He's certainly filled out through the winter and although he's only lightly raced, we thought we'd put him in the French Derby because he's owned by Haras d'Etreham, who stand his sire Almanzor, and it would be lovely if he could progress in that company for them, especially over there.

"He was a horse with a big frame and will continue to progress throughout this year. He's far from the finished article. His pedigree says that the more time he gets the better he will be."

Thunder Roar had one run at two, finishing second to Hannibal Barca at Salisbury.

"I thought he was unlucky in quite a muddling sort of race. The winner went on to finish fourth in the Vertem Futurity Trophy, so the form has worked out fantastically. He'll be out early and should lose his maiden tag."

Dark Moon Rising won his second start at Beverley, then was just beaten at Haydock stepped up to a mile and finished the season in third in a York nursery.

"He was another one who wasn't the finished article. He was always going to progress as a three-year-old. He could be a nice prospect in handicaps starting off on a mark of 90."

The Cookstown Cafu is from a family the Ryans know well after training a few of the offspring, who always progressed with age.

"We were disappointed with his first run because he'd been showing plenty more at home, but he put that run behind him when he finished fourth at Doncaster and was then a shade unlucky to be caught on the line at York.

"He's a big, scopey horse and off a mark of 79 he should be winning very shortly. He'll certainly get a mile this year."

Hello Zabeel was a late bloomer who made his debut as a three-year-old last year. He was second three times before winning a Carlisle maiden convincingly in the autumn.

"He's from a very good family by Frankel out of a triple Group-winning mare and could possibly be well handicapped off 79, and is one to look forward to. He could be out early so we can get his handicap mark and run him in some better races."

Magical Spirit, who won the Ayr Silver Cup in 2020 and was fourth last year, finished the season unlucky not to win a Doncaster Listed race, losing to King's Lynn by a head.

It meant he finished the year on a mark of 104 and could be similar to Bielsa this year in flirting between Pattern class and the top heritage handicaps.

"We'll be quite fluid with him. As a six-year-old there's still something left in the tank and hopefully he can pick up a big prize this year," says Adam.

Hala Hala Athmani is a half-sister to the stable's Hello Youmzain, winner of the Group 2 Criterium de Maisons-Laffitte on

his third start at two, the Haydock Sprint Cup at three and the Diamond Jubilee at Royal Ascot the following year, earning him a rating of 118.

"She made a very impressive debut at Carlisle. She'd always shown us she was a nice horse at home, and certainly showed that on debut," says Adam.

"She went to Ayr for the Group 3 Firth Of Clyde Fillies' Stakes and finished third. She went to win her race but showed her inexperience and was caught by more experienced horses.

"She was always a big strong filly who we were looking forward to racing at three. Hopefully, she can progress from last year, which was already impressive. She's very exciting."

Sound Reason had a very good season last year, improving from a mark of 69 to 83 after winning twice and being placed four times.

"We thought at the start of the year he was on a fair mark and was a winner waiting to happen. He was another one who was far from the finished article. He's done well over the winter and hopefully can continue his upward trajectory."

The Ryans have "a really nice bunch" of three-year-olds but it's too early to be dogmatic about the 44 juveniles at Hambleton Lodge.

"No buttons have been pressed as yet," says Adam, but he has picked out half a dozen to follow judged on breeding and early signs.

Flying Barty is a Starspangledbanner half-sister to Boonie, a sharp juvenile himself last season for the yard, who won first time out at Beverley in mid-April and went on to finish third in the Windsor Castle at Royal Ascot and the Molecomb at Goodwood.

"She's a nice, strong filly from a family we know well and hopefully can make the same progression Boonie did."

Leap Year Lad is a colt by the first-season sire Havana Grey. He's a nice strong colt and the pedigree says he should be sharp and one for the early season. His sire was a precocious sort."

Sound Reason found plenty of improvement last season and is expected to progress further

"We have a filly by Ardad, who made an unbelievable start to his career last year, out of Juncea. She's a very strong-looking filly who could be quite sharp but also have the scope to progress.

"We also have a colt by Ardad out of the unraced mare Relaxez Vous, who is a nice

strong horse with a good attitude who also has the scope to continue to progress throughout the year."

Anadora was a forward sort for the yard last season, winning at Newcastle first time out in early April before finishing seventh of 15 in the Group 3 Albany at Royal Ascot. She ran with credit throughout the rest of the season, including in a couple of Listed races, without getting her head in front.

"We're hoping her full sister by Havana Gold can follow suit. We're also hoping a Kodiac colt out of Marian Halcombe will be an early sort. He looks a typical Kodiac colt – strong and precocious. He's taking his work very well and all he wants to do is please."

Reporting by LAWRIE KELSEY

Primo leads the way in bid to find the next star

ED WALKER had a record year in 2021, helped by the now-retired European champion sprinter Starman, and this year he's hoping his Upper Lambourn stable houses a replacement for his ace.

To find another gem capable of succeeding the Group 1 July Cup winner will be demanding, but it's a challenge Walker aims to meet head-on.

And he feels he has a trio at his Kingsdown stables "knocking on the door of Group 1 standard" who could be his next star sprinter.

Walker thinks **Primo Bacio** is capable of bursting through the Group 1 door. Although the four-year-old filly won only a York Listed race last season, she is rated 111, only 8lb behind Starman's final mark.

She ran some fine races in defeat after York, finishing unplaced but not far behind the leaders in three Group 1s: the Falmouth, Prix Rothschild and the Sun Chariot.

"She was an impressive Listed winner and then tried at the highest level and was unlucky a couple of times," says

WINNERS IN LAST FOUR YEARS 66, 53, 56, 61

Ed Walker has high hopes for Listed winner Primo Bacio, pictured winning at York

DID YOU KNOW?
Ed Walker worked for Roger Charlton, then four years as assistant to Luca Cumani before taking out a licence in 2010.

Walker, "so we'll try to come back at Group 3 or Group 2 level this season and hopefully continue to fill out her page to the end," says Walker.

"The Duke of Cambridge [Group 2 for fillies and mares over a mile] at Royal Ascot is a major summer target and after that hopefully we'll be aiming her at Group 1s.

"If we don't feel she's capable of winning one over here or in Europe, we could try North America. It depends what her trip is, whether she's just a miler or whether she could stretch a bit further. There are some really good stakes races around, especially in the second half of the season, so that could be an option for her.

"I'm thrilled to keep her in training, she's a really smart filly. She's done very well through the winter, and although she hasn't grown, she's strengthened and filled out and is a much more mature filly."

Second of Walker's trio lining up at the Group 1 door is **Dreamloper**, a five-year-old mare who won the Group 3 Valiant Stakes at Ascot in July, then finished fourth in the Group 2 Hungerford, unplaced in the Group 1 Matron Stakes at Leopardstown, and ended her season with third place in the

Dreamloper: the Valiant Stakes winner has plenty of potential

Great Ambassador (purple colours): "He's a really exciting horse"

Group 1 Sun Chariot and a rating of 109.

"She's a super smart filly who's very good on her day but a little inconsistent. Her major target last season was that new fillies' and mares' mile handicap [Kensington Palace Stakes] at Royal Ascot.

"I thought she was as near a certainty as you can get at Royal Ascot, but she ran an absolute stinker [4-1 favourite, finished 10th of 18].

"I was so disappointed, I didn't know what to do with her; but she's a well-bred filly, so I decided to go on with the plan, which was, if she won, go on to stakes races after the handicap.

"Next race she absolutely dotted up in the Group 3 Valiant. If she'd put in a performance like that at Royal Ascot, she'd have won by half the track; it was very frustrating. But then to get a place in a Group 1 at the end of the season was a real bonus. She ran a huge race.

"She might run in the Group 2 Dahlia Stakes at the Guineas meeting at Newmarket and the Duke of Cambridge could be an option as well. She could be in the same Group races as Primo Bacio, the Falmouth, Sun Chariot, but she could run in the Nassau, an easy ten furlongs at Goodwood – she was doing a lot of good work in the Sun Chariot up that hill at Newmarket.

"She's out of the first filly I trained, Livia's Dream, who never achieved what I kept telling her owner she was capable of. Then in her last race as a five-year-old she won a Listed race at Lingfield. So if Dreamloper won a Group 1, it would be a great story."

Last of the trio of what the trainer hopes will be the "Walker Wonders", is **Great Ambassador**, third in the Stewards' Cup, second in the Ayr Gold Cup, and between

UNIBET
1
2
16
22
KING POWER
UNIBET

those two races winner of a Newmarket handicap and a Listed race at York.

"He's a really exciting horse, a proper sprinter. He's very consistent but he had no luck. In another year he could have won a Wokingham, a Stewards' Cup and an Ayr Gold Cup. The ground and draw was against him, yet he ran unbelievable races in all of them despite that. He's a horse with a very bright future.

"He had a little setback in January, so it might be touch and go whether he'll be ready for the Duke of York, but I would be very disappointed if, past the Duke of York, this horse wasn't running in Group 1s – the Diamond Jubilee, July Cup, Haydock Sprint Cup. I think he's a top-class sprinter. And he's a gelding, so he could travel internationally later on in the year."

Walker is hoping **Popmaster** can also become a stakes sprinter by making the step up from top-end handicapper to Pattern class.

Winner of two all-weather races as a two-year-old, he was just touched off in a couple of six-furlong turf sprints before being gelded.

He was close up in the Palace of Holyroodhouse at Royal Ascot, won twice at Doncaster and Ascot, then was unplaced in the Ayr Gold Cup and the Coral Sprint Trophy at York.

"I wouldn't be surprised if he stepped up to stakes company, but it's hard to know until we try him," says Walker.

"It's tough for sprinters at three, but he'll be tougher and stronger this year. He looks a more substantial horse at four and you'd like to think there's a little more improvement there. He's an exciting sprinter. We'll start him off in handicaps and play it by ear."

Parachute was third in the King George V handicap at Royal Ascot but never seemed to recover from his exertions for the remainder of the season.

"He ran a huge race at Ascot and I was a little disappointed with him after that; whether Ascot left its mark, I'm not sure. He's got more to offer and could be competing in some nice middle-distance handicaps."

American Star was considered good enough to run in the Group 2 Gimcrack after landing a Salisbury maiden, but found the company too hot. She then won a small Newbury nursery, ending the season unplaced in the Group 3 Horris Hill.

"He was bought as a Gimcrack horse and we chanced our arm, but it didn't work. I think he'll get a mile this year as he's strengthened and is a more substantial horse. He has a high rating at 93, which doesn't leave us with much leeway. I think there's more to come from him. But he might be a difficult horse to place."

Kawida is a Listed winner who Walker thinks will stay a mile and a half this season and has entries in the Group 1 Prix Saint-Alary, the Oaks, the French Oaks [Prix de Diane] and the Irish 1,000 Guineas.

"She's a lovely, home-bred filly and we aim high with her this year and see how high we can go. She's done nothing wrong and her form is 2-2-1-1. You only get one shot at these Classic races and as a Listed winner at two I think you've got to treat her as a Classic contender."

Piffle won twice in her first season but a big sales race at Newmarket and a Listed race at Newbury proved beyond her.

However, Walker reports that his mother's filly has wintered very well and strengthened to such an extent that he could pitch her into one of the 1,000 Guineas trials, probably the one nearest home, the Fred Darling at Newbury.

"We'll see how she's working before deciding, but we could chance our arm and try for some black type."

The sprinting filly **Tenaya Canyon** is rated 91 after victory in a big Doncaster handicap and good runs in two Listed races.

"She has a great chance this year of getting some black type and hopefully winning

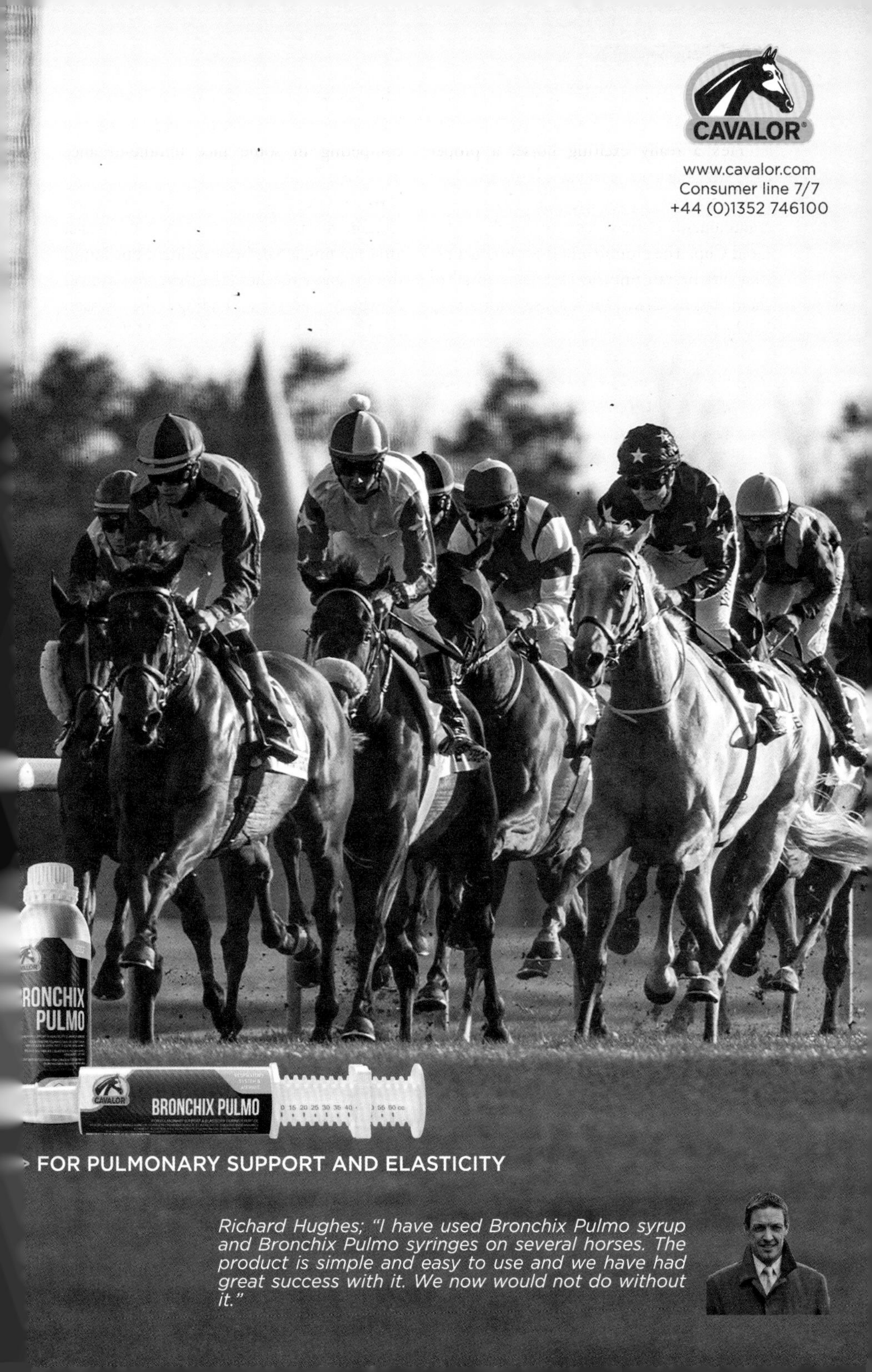
CAVALOR
www.cavalor.com
Consumer line 7/7
+44 (0)1352 746100
BRONCHIX PULMO
BRONCHIX PULMO
FOR PULMONARY SUPPORT AND ELASTICITY
Richard Hughes; "I have used Bronchix Pulmo syrup and Bronchix Pulmo syringes on several horses. The product is simple and easy to use and we have had great success with it. We now would not do without it."

stakes races for her owner-breeder, Whitsbury Manor Stud. She's a very sound filly, very straightforward and won't have to improve a lot to be stakes-winning filly. Her first start will be a five-furlong sprint at Bath."

Bling On The Music is a colt to note, despite disappointing on his only run at two when fifth of eight at Haydock. There were excuses, however, when it was discovered he'd had a setback.

"I was very disappointed and almost relieved when he came back not quite right. But he's made a full recovery and has done exceptionally well from two to three. He's grown a lot, and really stands up and fills the eye. He's very impressive, a gorgeous horse. He'd be my most exciting three-year-old colt. He's got a great presence and is a beautiful mover.

"I don't know how good he is yet but I think he's quite good and I'd be very disappointed and pretty amazed if he wasn't winning his maiden. He'll be targeted at some nice races. He has a great turn of foot, loads of speed for a Sea The Stars.

"I'll be in no rush with him. I think the Classics will come a bit too soon for him, which won't bother me too much because he's a big, immature horse. I think he might even improve at four."

The much-travelled nine-year-old gelding **Stormy Antarctic** has won in every calendar year except 2020 since he began his career in 2015. His 42 outings have taken him to Hong Kong, Germany, Italy, France and Ireland and his nine victories have amassed more than £720,000.

"He's been a great servant and while he's still winning and being competitive in stakes races, as he was last year, we'll carry on.

"He won't be running in handicaps. He won a Listed race last year and was second in three more. If he didn't enjoy his training I'd have retired him by now. The minute he tells me he's had enough, that'll be that. But at the moment the old boy can't wait to get out of his box. I'm going to be fairly fussy about what ground he runs on. He'll only run on soft ground. His optimum distance is nine furlongs."

Glenartney is a very lightly raced four-year-old filly who was fifth in last year's Musidora at York before finishing third in two Listed races.

"She loves soft ground and is definitely a stakes filly. She could travel abroad."

Among the 48 two-year-olds at Kingsdown Stables, Walker has singled out a nap hand of well-bred juveniles.

Top of the list is **USS Constitution**, a colt by US Navy Flag out of an unraced dam who has already produced two winners from three runners.

"This is a very attractive colt by the champion two-year-old and three-year-old sprinter. He's very flashy and I like him a lot. He could be a proper two-year-old and could be one for the Coventry."

The other juveniles are a colt by Gutaifan who "has loads of speed and could be early"; a colt by Acclamation out of Fast Lily, "who looks fast"; a good-looking Oasis Dream colt out of Ruffled, who is "showing up well" and is one of four two-year-olds Sheikh Ahmed has sent to Walker for the first time; and a Dark Angel filly out of Group 3 winner Button Down, a daughter of successful broodmare Oasis Dream. "She's looking sharp," says Walker.

Reporting by LAWRIE KELSEY

Stormy Antarctic: globetrotter is now nine but still showing plenty of enthusiasm

ED WALKER

LAMBOURN, BERKSHIRE

RECORD AROUND THE COURSES

	W-R	Per cent	Non-hcp 2yo	Non-hcp 3yo	Non-hcp 4yo+	Hcp 2yo	Hcp 3yo	Hcp 4yo+	£1 level stake
Kempton (AW)	59-437	13.5	9-92	6-53	3-19	5-28	19-131	17-114	-131.19
Wolverhampton (AW)	45-262	17.2	2-40	10-46	3-13	5-15	13-85	12-63	-62.59
Lingfield (AW)	35-285	12.3	3-49	7-61	2-15	1-10	9-79	13-71	-98.85
Haydock	30-154	19.5	4-19	0-19	0-8	0-3	12-53	14-52	+10.90
Windsor	29-171	17.0	4-40	3-24	1-4	1-3	11-64	9-36	-50.46
Newbury	24-187	12.8	3-50	2-36	0-10	1-4	11-45	7-42	-34.86
Yarmouth	17-97	17.5	2-16	1-5	1-1	1-8	5-44	7-23	+21.28
Chelmsford (AW)	16-146	11.0	0-23	1-22	0-4	1-10	5-42	9-45	-54.40
Newmarket (July)	15-93	16.1	4-21	0-7	1-2	0-1	6-34	4-28	-6.16
Doncaster	15-122	12.3	1-15	2-18	0-8	0-0	7-34	5-47	-40.30
Ascot	14-109	12.8	0-8	1-13	1-11	0-1	10-35	2-41	-29.67
Salisbury	13-97	13.4	2-35	4-17	0-0	0-1	6-32	1-12	-2.92
Redcar	12-48	25.0	3-10	5-11	0-0	3-6	1-20	0-1	+7.64
Newmarket	11-125	8.8	4-32	1-21	1-14	1-6	3-25	1-27	-57.30
Nottingham	10-88	11.4	2-29	0-14	1-4	1-7	4-24	2-10	-18.50
Newcastle (AW)	9-61	14.8	3-14	2-9	0-4	1-7	3-19	0-8	-12.97
Sandown	9-79	11.4	2-13	0-5	1-2	1-4	4-37	1-18	-21.75
Goodwood	9-89	10.1	1-10	2-15	1-9	1-4	4-23	0-28	-43.01
Ffos Las	8-40	20.0	1-5	0-8	0-0	1-3	4-16	2-8	+11.10
York	8-75	10.7	2-11	3-10	2-8	1-3	0-16	0-27	-7.40
Lingfield	6-45	13.3	0-10	3-13	0-0	0-1	3-16	0-5	-25.43
Leicester	6-54	11.1	1-16	0-9	0-0	1-2	3-17	1-10	-13.67
Bath	5-46	10.9	1-5	0-3	0-2	1-5	3-16	0-15	-22.55
Newcastle	4-10	40.0	1-3	0-1	1-1	0-0	0-3	2-2	+22.67
Brighton	4-31	12.9	2-8	1-2	0-0	0-2	1-17	0-2	+4.25
Southwell (AW)	3-20	15.0	1-1	0-4	2-4	0-1	0-6	0-4	-12.22
Pontefract	3-27	11.1	1-3	0-6	0-1	1-3	1-10	0-4	-10.00
Chepstow	3-28	10.7	1-6	1-11	0-1	0-0	0-8	1-2	-5.50
Thirsk	2-13	15.4	1-1	1-4	0-0	0-0	0-5	0-3	-5.09
Musselburgh	1-4	25.0	0-0	0-0	1-1	0-0	0-0	0-3	+3.00
Catterick	1-7	14.3	0-0	0-2	0-1	1-1	0-2	0-1	-4.75
Ripon	1-13	7.7	1-3	0-1	0-0	0-1	0-5	0-3	-10.50
Ayr	1-17	5.9	0-1	0-4	0-2	0-2	1-5	0-3	-13.75
Chester	1-23	4.3	0-3	1-3	0-2	0-1	0-4	0-10	-20.13
Epsom	1-26	3.8	0-5	1-6	0-3	0-1	0-4	0-7	-24.00
Wetherby	0-1	0.0	0-0	0-0	0-0	0-0	0-1	0-0	-1.00
Carlisle	0-3	0.0	0-0	0-2	0-0	0-0	0-1	0-0	-3.00
Warwick	0-4	0.0	0-0	0-3	0-0	0-0	0-0	0-1	-4.00
Hamilton	0-5	0.0	0-0	0-1	0-0	0-0	0-3	0-1	-5.00
Beverley	0-10	0.0	0-1	0-1	0-0	0-0	0-5	0-3	-10.00

Number of horses racing for the stable **403**

Total winning prize-money **£3,084,501.49**

Look out for runners with William Buick on board. His five-year strike-rate is 23% and profit stands at £32.04

THE EXPERTS

VIEW FROM IRELAND ALAN SWEETMAN

Luxembourg heads a huge cast for Classics

THE unbeaten **Luxembourg** heads the list of Irish Classic hopefuls for 2022. In an echo of times past at Ballydoyle, the Camelot colt was bred by Ben Sangster, whose father Robert owned Vincent O'Brien-trained Derby winners The Minstrel and Golden Fleece.

Luxembourg made his debut in low-key surroundings at Killarney in mid-July, winning easily under Michael Hussey. In late September he became O'Brien's 21st winner of the Beresford Stakes, extending the stable's winning sequence in the race to 11.

Despite the stable's prolific Beresford record, not many of O'Brien's recent winners of the 1m Group 2 event have covered themselves with glory. Luxembourg is poised to rectify that trend. He consolidated his tall reputation by landing the odds in the Vertem Futurity at Doncaster, a race won ten years previously by his sire who went on to complete the 2,000 Guineas/Derby double which he will attempt to emulate.

During a 2021 juvenile campaign in which the Ballydoyle team lacked its customary strength in depth, **Point Lonsdale** won four in a row, including the Chesham Stakes at Royal Ascot, before finding Charlie Appleby's Native Trail much too strong in the National Stakes.

Point Lonsdale's victories in the Tyros Stakes and the Futurity Stakes were achieved at the expense of the same limited opponent. Native Trail's subsequent Dewhurst triumph adds collateral substance to his form. He is a brother to the 2019 Derby fourth Broome, a durable colt who belatedly gained Group 1 honours in last year's Grand Prix de Saint-Cloud.

Ballydoyle houses several lightly raced performers who may progress to make the grade at Pattern level. Galileo colt **Star Of India** looked like a sort who will go on to much better things when winning a backend maiden at Leopardstown; Churchill colt **River Thames** did well to beat a twice-raced and shorter-priced stablemate in a maiden at Punchestown in September; **King Of Bavaria**, who landed the 6f Birdcatcher Nursery at Naas off a mark of 95 after a debut maiden win, is expected to mature into a smart three-year-old who will stay further.

Two appearances six months apart were enough to make **Tenebrism** O'Brien's leading juvenile filly in 2021. A daughter of Caravaggio and the 2011 Coronation Stakes winner Immortal Verse, she was out early in the season, scampering to victory in a 5f maiden on soft ground at Naas in the final week of March.

A setback meant she did not run again until sent off at 14-1 in the Cheveley Park at Newmarket in late September. Held up by Ryan Moore, she produced a fine turn of foot to land the 6f Group 1 contest in a style that suggests the Guineas trip will be within her range. Having had only two races, she has the potential to become one of the stars of the season.

If Tenebrism was a revelation in the 6f Group 1 event, **Sacred Bridge**, favourite to extend an unbeaten record, proved a bitter disappointment. The Ger Lyons-trained filly had looked like a Group 1 sprinter in the making when winning the Group 3 Round Tower Stakes at the Curragh in August. Her pedigree gives her a fair chance of staying 1m, but her style of running raises a doubt.

There are no worries on that score about **Discoveries**, the Jessica Harrington-trained filly who avenged a soft-ground defeat in the Debutante Stakes by turning the tables on Agartha in the Moyglare Stud Stakes.

Harrington will plan a three-year-old campaign along the lines followed by her sister Alpha Centauri, whose 2018 Irish 1,000 Guineas triumph was the first of four consecutive Group 1 wins. In common with Alpha Centauri, she is expected to prosper on quick ground.

By virtue of having finished a short-head second to Discoveries in a 7f Curragh maiden, **Tuesday** can be rated a bright prospect for Ballydoyle, although it is concerning she did not appear again after that June debut. More encouragingly, the sister to the trainer's 1,000 Guineas and Oaks winner Minding has retained a prominent position in ante-post markets for the Classics.

A possible dark horse among the Ballydoyle fillies is the impeccably bred **Toy**. A half-sister to four Group 1 winners, including Gleneagles and last season's Prix de Diane heroine Joan Of Arc, she was second in a 24-runner maiden at the Curragh in October.

Joseph O'Brien's Moyglare runner-up **Agartha** was beaten in four maidens, including behind Sacred Bridge at Naas, before winning the Group 3 Silver Flash Stakes at Leopardstown and the Group 2 Debutante Stakes at the Curragh. She was fourth in the Prix Marcel Boussac when stepped up to 1m for the first time and appeals as a tough filly who should continue

to make her presence felt at Pattern level.

Form involving Agartha received an early 2022 boost when Silver Flash runner-up **Juncture** trounced the opposition in the Listed Patton Stakes over 1m at Dundalk. The Dark Angel filly is held in good regard by Ger Lyons, as is the same sire's **Dr Zempf**, the Phoenix Stakes runner-up who failed to produce his best form in the Middle Park in which the tough and consistent **Castle Star** finished second for Fozzy Stack.

Lyons experienced another reverse on British soil when impressive Blenheim Stakes winner **Straight Answer** flopped in the Dewhurst. However, his yard is increasingly influential domestically, and he has high hopes for the Kodiac colt, as well as for Listed-winning filly **Panama Red** and **Atomic Jones**, a Wootton Bassett colt who was unbeaten in two starts at two. Atomic Jones showed a good attitude when mastering Ballydoyle's subsequent Criterium de Saint-Cloud runner-up **Stone Age** in a 1m Group 2 event at Leopardstown's Irish Champion Stakes meeting.

Donnacha O'Brien, whose 2021 season was relatively quiet after a productive 2020, has prospects of high-level success with the Vertem Futurity runner-up **Sissoko** and **Piz Badile**, a promising second behind Dermot Weld's useful colt **Duke De Sessa** in the Group 3 Eyrefield Stakes at Leopardstown.

Emerging force Paddy Twomey has a fine standard-bearer in the filly **Limiti Di Greccio**, whose Listed juvenile form makes good reading.

Veteran trainer Jim Bolger, who enjoyed a fine 2021 campaign, needs to elicit improvement from the likes of **Boundless Ocean** and **Manu Et Corde** if they are to make an impression on the three-year-old Pattern scene.

Straight Answer (left): carries high hopes for his trainer Ger Lyons, who could also do well with Panama Red (above)

ANTE-POST ANALYSIS NICK WATTS

Coroebus can roll back the years for Godolphin

2,000 GUINEAS

Godolphin haven't been players in the 2,000 Guineas for a long time now. Dawn Approach won in their silks in 2013, but before that you had to go back to the Saeed bin Suroor-trained Island Sands in 1999 for their previous victory.

It's not a pretty record, but Charlie Appleby is doing his best to make Godolphin relevant again in the Classics, and it has worked in the Derby. This is the year it could be the first colts' Classic that goes their way.

Appleby has strength in depth here, with Native Trail and Coroebus likely to go up against the Ballydoyle duo of Luxembourg and Point Lonsdale.

The current odds favour Native Trail, but **Coroebus** appeals more at a general 5-1. Unlike his stablemate, he has been beaten, but he really shouldn't have been.

That one loss on his record came in the Group 2 Royal Lodge Stakes at Newmarket where he showed a blinding turn of foot to hit the front, only to get worn down close home by Royal Patronage. That was an eyecatching effort, however, and a subsequent easy win in the Group 3 Autumn Stakes meant he headed into winter quarters on a positive note.

He possesses a strong turn of foot, possibly more so than Native Trail, and we know he handles the track as two of his three runs as a two-year-old came on the Rowley Mile course.

DERBY

O'Brien's **Luxembourg** is interesting and, while he divided opinion slightly as a two-year-old, he has a big fan here. He never came close to defeat in three runs as a juvenile, progressing from a win at Killarney to the Group 2 Beresford Stakes at the Curragh and Group 1 Vertem Futurity at Doncaster in quick succession.

I fancy him to win the Derby. It could be that in the Guineas he runs the perfect Epsom trial by finishing well into third or fourth – typical of an O'Brien preparation.

He can be backed at 4-1 to win the Epsom Classic, so the market isn't quite sold on him yet even if he is favourite. If you wanted one at a bigger price who could emerge as a candidate come June then you could do worse than have a look at **El Bodegon**.

A brother to multiple Group 1 winner Best Solution, the James Ferguson-trained colt got better as he was upped in trip last season.

He started off over six furlongs at Windsor in July, then won races over 7f, 1m1f and a Group 1 over 1m2f on his final start of the campaign. That final victory was achieved in the Criterium de Saint-Cloud, in which he easily beat off O'Brien's Stone Age with Appleby's Goldspur in third.

A confirmed stayer, El Bodegon could be interesting if he went to Chester for a trial, or perhaps the win-and-you're-in race at Epsom.

1,000 GUINEAS

Even if the Luxembourg team have to put up with a narrow defeat in the 2,000 Guineas, they could make up for it a day later in the fillies' equivalent with **Tenebrism**.

It almost goes without saying that a Ballydoyle filly is beautifully bred, but she really is, by Caravaggio out of Marois and Coronation Stakes winner Immortal Verse.

She had a slightly odd season as a two-year-old. She won both of her races, but one was in March and the other in late September. She was sent off at 7-2 and 14-1 suggesting she hadn't been showing a huge amount at home – but those are the horses you want to be with – the ones who bring it to the track.

She hosed up on her debut at Naas but then suffered a setback which kept her off the track for 181 days before she reappeared in the Group 1 Cheveley Park.

That was not the best preparation for the Newmarket test, and one that would be too much for most horses, but Tenebrism took it in her stride, finishing very strongly to beat Flotus by a length with Sandrine well held in third.

It was a stunning display considering her absence, and she has to be a huge player in the Guineas with the step up to a mile looking certain to suit.

Tenebrism: put up a fine performance in the Cheveley Park and has Classic appeal

OAKS

Tenebrism doesn't appeal as an Oaks filly, but there are a couple who catch the eye at this early stage.

First up is the William Haggas-trained **Golden Lyra**. She would have gone into many notebooks when hosing up on her debut in a 7f novice event at Newmarket in October, winning by five lengths on ground that wouldn't have suited.

Her pedigree screams middle distances as she is by Lope De Vega out of a sister to Sea The Moon. And, while she is still very much an unknown quantity, the 25-1 available will soon vanish if she hits the ground running this season.

The Ed Walker-trained **Kawida** is also interesting at 40-1. She is more experienced, having raced four times last season, winning twice including a Listed event at Newmarket on her final start of the season. She, too, is bred for an Oaks trip and could find untold improvement when venturing up to 1m4f.

ST LEGER

Have a look at **Frantastic** – currently 33-1 – for the final British Classic. This Derby entry won a novice event at Newcastle on the second of two starts last year and is a brother to Cracksman, who would have stayed a Leger trip. He might not be forward enough to contest a Derby, but races like the Bahrain Trophy, Gordon Stakes and Great Voltigeur all look better fits for him time-wise before a potential date at Doncaster in September.

Ten winners from Big Bard to Ruby Cottage

BIG BARD Gary Moore

Gary Moore's stable has never housed a stronger team, and the four-year-old Big Bard looks likely to play his part in a potentially lucrative 2022 campaign. A big gelding with stacks of physical scope, Big Bard found his niche in 6f handicaps last term, winning Class 6 events at Chelmsford and Brighton with rampant authority. He went off too hard in front when well beaten off his revised mark of 70 on a return visit to Chelmsford, and that run can be swiftly erased from memory. It will be a big disappointment if he doesn't progress into an 80+ horse this summer.

BOLLIN MAY Tim Easterby

This daughter of Mayson showed more than enough in six starts as a juvenile to suggest she will enjoy a rewarding three-year-old season. Runner-up in a Beverley maiden over 5f, Bollin May bettered that form when an excellent fifth behind Allayaali in a valuable fillies' nursery at Doncaster's St Leger meeting in September. She wasn't ridden to best advantage on her subsequent start at Pontefract and, as a result, starts 2022 on an eminently workable mark of 68. Her breeding suggests some cut in the ground will always suit.

DE VEGAS KID Tony Carroll

Tony Carroll's Brighton record-holder Pour La Victoire is well into retirement now, but former stablemate De Vegas Kid could take over from him this year in terms of prolific scoring at the seaside track. Already a four-time winner on Race Hill, the eight-year-old ended 2021 out of form, but that has resulted in a dramatic drop in his handicap mark. Taking into account the fact he started his Brighton campaign last term off a mark of 77, De Vegas Kid ought to be able to win multiple handicaps at his beloved venue from a starting point 11lb below that rating. He is best in a strongly run mile on firm ground. The Brighton Mile in August is the likely big target.

HELM ROCK Daniel & Claire Kubler

Helm Rock ultimately failed to build on two early-summer Carlisle wins during his three-year-old campaign, but showed enough in four subsequent defeats to suggest he can develop into a useful mile handicapper at four. Interestingly, he was backed from 7-1 to 3-1 favourite for a Class 5 Newmarket handicap on good ground in late October prior to being withdrawn, having unseated his rider on the way to the start. He is a big horse with lots of physical scope for further improvement.

KING VIKTOR Brian Ellison

King Viktor's running style suggests he won't fulfil his potential until sent over 2m, so the fact he could win three times last term at trips between 1m3f and 1m6f augurs very well for his future. A strong galloper who

takes time to engage top gear, he finds plenty off the bridle, and a track with a long straight should always suit him best. Brian Ellison does particularly well with this type of handicapper, and he'll be confident of exploiting King Viktor's mark of 65 early on in the season.

KINGMANIA Chris Wall

Kingmania looked like developing into a Britannia type early last summer following comfortable 7f wins at Leicester and Doncaster, but she missed the Royal meeting and signed off her campaign early with a defeat at Newmarket's July meeting. At the time, I considered she wasn't given the best of rides that day, but the fact she failed to reappear suggests something may have been amiss. Kingmania is a classy filly with a high cruising speed and sharp turn of foot. She promises to be even better when stepped up to a mile in 2022.

LA TRINIDAD Roger Fell

La Trinidad made the anticipated progress from three to four, and landed back to back York handicaps in the summer. He clearly goes particularly well on the Knavesmire, and six of his seven races in 2021 were at York. A strong traveller with a good turn of foot, La Trinidad starts 2022 only 6lb higher than at the beginning of last season, and there seems no obvious reason why he won't pay his way once again. He goes particularly well on good to firm, and I think his best trip may turn out to be 1m1f.

LADY NECTAR Ann Duffield

Lady Nectar looked set for a highly successful

season in 6f handicaps in the north after toying with her Thirsk rivals first time out last term. However, she failed to add to her tally in five subsequent starts, leaving the impression she wasn't quite right. I thought she was destined for something like Ayr's Bronze or Silver Cup after that impressive Thirsk win, and there is still plenty of time for her to reach that level at the age of five. A strongly run, big-field 6f on top of the ground suits the mare ideally.

RODRIGO DIAZ David Simcock

Bought halfway through the 2021 campaign as a prospective Melbourne Cup horse, Rodrigo Diaz didn't travel to Australia last winter, but that valuable race is likely to be firmly on the agenda this year. He'll also be of significant interest in Group races over 2m-plus in Britain after a highly progressive four-year-old campaign which saw him land a Doncaster handicap and finish runner-up to Hukum in the Group 3 Geoffrey Freer Stakes at Newbury. Staying is his game, and he remains unexposed at those trips.

RUBY COTTAGE Malcolm Saunders

There are ample opportunities during a firm-ground summer at Bath for sprinters, and Ruby Cottage, who won two handicaps there last season, looks likely to improve again as a four-year-old. Since sent handicapping, her Bath form figures read 3122216, and you can put a line through that last one as she was probably over the top by then after a busy spell. Closely related to six-time scorer Coronation Cottage, who was also trained by Malcolm Saunders, the four-year-old has plenty more to give at Bath this year.

Rodrigo Diaz (green cap): the highest profile of the ten to watch this season but still unexposed at staying distances; (below) La Trinidad seems well treated by the handicapper

NAMES TO MAKE IT PAY PAUL KEALY

Ten horses to focus on throughout the season

ANTARAH

Antarah created a big impression at Newcastle when sauntering to a last-to-first success at Newcastle at odds-on under Jim Crowley, and there will be little doubt what distances he will be campaigned at as a three-year-old.

A son of Sea The Stars out of a dam who won over 1m2f, it will be middle distances all the way for Antarah, who looks a hot prospect. Again, it's hard to work out exactly what he did at Newcastle because the time was particularly poor, but in some respects that makes it even more impressive that he was able to come from the back because those in front ought to have had plenty in the locker yet.

The Gosdens are renowned for starting some serious horses on the all-weather (the likes of Enable, Jack Hobbs, Persuasive and Without Parole all made winning debuts on artificial surfaces and there have been many more) and there's no reason the MO is going to change now.

Antarah could well be another top prospect and we can expect to see him in a Derby trial in the spring, possibly starting in Sandown's Classic Trial, a race the stable has won nine times, including in 2014 with Western Hymn, yet another late-season all-weather debut winner as a juvenile.

ATOMIC JONES

If Ger Lyons is right we should be hearing plenty about Atomic Jones this coming season. He is a son of Richard Fahey's champion French two-year-old Wootton Bassett, whose standing as a stallion just continues to rise (he stood for €6,000 in 2012, but has spent the last two seasons with Coolmore and is now at €150,000).

Atomic Jones has won both outings in photo-finishes, starting with a Curragh maiden over 7f in June. That race didn't work out brilliantly, but it didn't matter to Atomic Jones, who returned after 11 weeks off to land the Group 2 Champions Juvenile Stakes over a mile by a head from the Aidan O'Brien-trained Stone Age, who finished second in the Group 1 Criterium de Saint-Cloud two starts later.

That was a fine start from a horse whose trainer was surprised he even managed to get him to the track as a juvenile. "He's a huge big baby and I didn't expect to be running him this year, never mind winning two," Lyons said after the Leopardstown success.

A mile is likely to be very much a minimum for him as a three-year-old, so it's no surprise to see an Irish Derby entry alongside one for the 2,000 Guineas at Newmarket.

AUDIENCE

Didn't make his debut until the last week of October, but this Cheveley Park-bred son of Iffraaj left a fair impression when streaking away to win his maiden by the best part of four lengths at Newmarket.

A half-brother to 6f Group 3 winner Dark Lady, Audience was not particularly strong in the market (15-2) and saw plenty of daylight on the outside early, but he looked very straightforward and fairly cruised through the race before drifting to the stands' rail and sprinting clear.

What the form is worth is questionable as the Charlie Appleby-trained runner-up Yantarni has been beaten at odds-on twice since and been gelded, but Audience was clearly in a league of his own and is an exciting prospect, although what the targets will be remain to be seen.

Both sire and dam's sire (Oasis Dream) were quick, so a drop to sprinting would not be a total surprise, but he clearly got 7f well on his debut and perhaps the Jersey Stakes would be an ideal early season target for John and Thady Gosden.

COROEBUS

Coroebus is the first of the more established three-year-olds as he has only stablemate Native Trail ahead of him in the betting for the 2,000 Guineas. It's true that Native Trail has his measure on racecourse performance (and on the clock) so far, but this son of Dubawi looked very much a work in progress as a juvenile and he made his debut two months later than his dual Group 1-winning rival.

Following a July Course success at Newmarket in August, Coroebus was not seen again until the Group 2 Royal Lodge Stakes on the Rowley Mile course in late September and, having been supported into favouritism, he looked to be in the process of putting up a massive performance before getting tired and being collared by Royal Patronage late on. This was simply a case of horse and jockey learning on the job, though,

Coroebus powers to victory in the Autumn Stakes

with William Buick sending him on a long way from home.

Having taken it up just inside the two-furlong pole, Coroebus had quickened into a four-length lead with a furlong to run, but he tied up late having traded at the minimum 1.01 on Betfair. There was no mistake next time, though, with Buick producing a more controlled performance in the Autumn Stakes a couple of weeks later and Coroebus won by an easy two lengths.

Out of a half-sister to dual Dubai World Cup winner Thunder Snow, he is more likely to stay the Derby trip than Native Trail, although he would be far from guaranteed to do so. He looks a potential top-notcher over 1m2f, though, even if he doesn't prove quick enough for the Guineas.

DISCOVERIES

If Discoveries improves in the same manner as her two most illustrious siblings from two to three, we could be in for something special as on juvenile form she's a little bit better than both of them.

The Jessica Harrington-trained filly is a sister to Alpha Centauri, who won the Irish 1,000 Guineas, Coronation Stakes, Falmouth and Prix Jacques le Marois; and a half-sister to Alpine Star, who won the Coronation Stakes and was beaten less than a length when second in three other Group 1s, including to the likes of Palace Pier and Tarnawa.

She clearly has some footsteps to follow, but the signs are good as she started to show massive improvement during the autumn and, after being beaten four and a half lengths when third to Agartha in the Debutante Stakes at the Curragh in August, she reversed that form with a three-quarter-length success in the Group 1 Moyglare over the same filly the following month.

Neither of her top-class siblings managed to win at Group 1 level as juveniles (Alpine

Goldspur (right): Classic potential

Star didn't run in one, but Alpha Centauri was only fifth in the Moyglare), so Discoveries was already ahead of the curve by the autumn.

Harrington did not want her doing too much at two, though, and she was immediately put away for the season and, in certain respects, forgotten about in terms of ante-post markets. It remains to be seen whether her trainer can get her to the 1,000 Guineas at Newmarket as both Alpine Star and Alpha Centauri failed to get there, but if she does this filly would be a massive threat to Inspiral and Tenebrism, neither of whom are guaranteed to get a mile as three-year-olds, and quotes of 16-1 will be a distant memory.

GOLDSPUR

The talent at Charlie Appleby's disposal is incredible these days, and if neither Native Trail nor Coroebus turn out to be Derby colts, this one, by Dubawi out of Lancashire Oaks winner Pomology, could be.

Goldspur began his career with a sparkling success at Sandown by six and a half lengths in September, a victory which came on very soft ground. It was a lot quicker when he won the Group 3 Zetland Stakes at Newmarket a month later, though, with a battling victory by a head from Unconquerable.

That form was just about franked in the Criterium de Saint-Cloud next time, although it was only good enough for the pair to finish third and fifth to the James Ferguson-trained El Bodegon. It might not be wise to hold that against him, though, as Appleby was getting some quick experience into the horse, who was having his third run in the space of six weeks and it was just two weeks after that head to head at Newmarket.

Everything about Goldspur screams stamina, and if he doesn't quite have the class for the Derby, it's easy enough to see him being campaigned with the St Leger in mind.

MUJTABA

An older horse, but an interesting one considering Shadwell's decision to downsize and focus on quality rather than quantity following the sad death of Shadwell founder Hamdan Al Maktoum last March.

That connections decided to keep in training a horse who had been gelded in April and didn't make his three-year-old debut until late August was a tip in itself and Mujtaba could not have made a better start when he did get going.

Well backed on his debut at Chepstow, he ran out a comfortable winner at a shade of odds-on and didn't need to improve on that to follow up in weak company at Chester the following month. Somewhat surprisingly he was a bit weak in the market for his handicap debut off a mark of 90 at Redcar in October, but he was always travelling over his rivals and won again, by a commanding two and a quarter lengths.

Trainer William Haggas has him in the Lincoln, which this year takes place just a week after Cheltenham, and it is a race he likes to target with a decent performer. Haggas has won it four times and his last two winners were subsequent multiple Group scorers Penitent and Addeybb, the latter having won four times in the highest class.

Whether Mujtaba can follow suit remains to be seen, but a revised handicap mark of 98 (8lb higher than at Redcar) is likely to underestimate his ability by some way.

Star Of India: won his sole start at two and is full of potential

SPIRIT CATCHER

Mark Johnston, operating from this year under a joint licence with son Charlie, is renowned for improving three-year-old handicappers, many of them middle-distance performers. Spirit Catcher might be a little different given he's a half-brother to Prix de l'Abbaye winner Wizz Kid, but he could prove to be quite decent in handicaps from 7f-plus.

He was a late starter for Johnston, winning a Redcar novice by an easy four lengths from some admittedly moderate rivals, and he was then beaten a neck when odds-on favourite for a three-runner contest at Chelmsford, although he came out best at the weights given he was conceding 7lb to the winner. Spirit Catcher was a little bit too keen from the front in the early stages, so can be rated better than that and a starting handicap mark of 87 looks fair.

His sire, Prix du Jockey Club winner New Bay, who was third in Golden Horn's Arc, has started his career as a stallion very well

and promises to get plenty who improve with age.

What distance Spirit Catcher will end up getting remains to be seen, but there's plenty of talent there if he can be taught to settle, and he could turn into a useful handicapper at a mile and perhaps one for the Britannia at Royal Ascot.

STAR OF INDIA

Futurity winner Luxembourg was the big hope for Aidan O'Brien at the end of the 2021 campaign, but you just know he is going to unleash some top-class performers who didn't show their hands to any serious extent at two. Indeed, O'Brien ran far fewer two-year-olds last season than he has in any campaign since 2015, and that was a year in which The Gurkha won the French Guineas and Sussex Stakes having been unraced at two, while US Army Ranger, also unsighted at two, ended up favourite for the Derby (second to Harzand).

It is impossible to single out any he has yet to race, but he certainly has a few worth a second look after just one outing. One of those is undoubtedly Star Of India, who is a half-brother to Sudirman who won the Group 1 Phoenix Stakes over 6f at two. However, Star Of India was described as a "grand staying type" by Seamie Heffernan after winning over 7f on his Leopardstown debut in October, and he is a brother to Roman Empire, who was second to Mohaafeth in last season's Hampton Court Stakes at Royal Ascot (before being sold to Hong Kong and now racing as S J Tourbillon).

The form of his maiden has yet to be really tested as only one of the first five home has run since (third has been second in maidens twice more), but there was a lot to like about the way Star Of India pulled clear in the final furlong and there's little doubt we will see him in a Derby trial somewhere along the way.

TOY

Toy hasn't set the ante-post markets alight yet, but if she lives up to her pedigree we can expect her to start making waves soon enough. Of course, a cracking pedigree is by no means a guarantee of success, but when you're a daughter of You'resothrilling you are expected to be contesting top company at some stage.

This is the eighth pairing between Galileo and You'resothrilling and you can understand why they keep going back as not only are the previous seven all winners, they all finished in the first four in at least one European Classic, with the pick of the crop dual Guineas winners Gleneagles.

Toy has plenty to live up to then, and she has only run once, right at the end of last season. She showed plenty in finishing second of 24 in a soft-ground maiden at the Curragh. Her family is renowned for being tough and it has to be encouraging the way she put her head down and battled. She'll leave this form well behind.

TUESDAY

Another once-raced filly trained by Aidan O'Brien, but this one has had problems as she hasn't raced since her debut in June. Tuesday showed plenty at the Curragh, though, going down by only a short head to subsequent Moyglare winner Discoveries.

Assuming O'Brien can get her back on track, this Irish 1,000 Guineas and Oaks entry can be expected to come into her own this season.

Like so many of the Coolmore crew, she has a pedigree to die for, being a sister to two Classic-winning fillies in Empress Josephine and, more notably, Minding. She's playing catch-up now, but has to be a name to look out for.

TWILIGHT SPINNER

An older sprinter who can be expected to hit the ground running if we get some soft ground in the spring.

Twilight Spinner showed bags of promise in three starts for David O'Meara last season, winning the last two of them on easy ground. She won her side by just over 14 lengths when off the mark in a maiden at Ripon in May and, despite being surprisingly weak in the market on heavy ground at Haydock next time, she stormed home by six and a half lengths from the 100-rated Ventura Diamond in Listed company.

Things didn't go right for Twilight Spinner following a sale and a switch to Joseph O'Brien, for whom she managed only one run, a five-length second to Art Power over six furlongs at the Curragh in September.

That effort came on good ground, and she was clearly being prepared for some late-season action in soft-ground sprints. Indeed, she had five-day entries for a few, including the Champions Sprint, but never made the track.

Hopefully she will make up for lost time this season.

VIEW FROM FRANCE SCOTT BURTON

French hearts ready to melt for Raclette

IN 2021 much of France's lucrative prize-money went for export, along with the majority of its most prestigious trophies.

An early look at Classic entries in both France and Britain might lead you to conclude that – at least if you were to take the 1,000 and 2,000 Guineas as a marker – it will be another tough year.

The Andre Fabre-trained Rebel Path and Topgear from the Fabrice Chappet yard are the sole representatives among the colts.

The picture for the 1,000 Guineas is slightly rosier, with Zellie and Fleur D'Iris engaged by the 31-time champion, along with Malavath for Francis Graffard and the Stephane Wattel-trained pair Rosacea and Who Knows.

Entries made on March 1 might quickly look out of date by the beginning of May and the early weeks of the turf season are likely to reveal plenty of promising performances in established trials and conditions races.

In terms of Classic potential the obvious starting point are the two Group juvenile races staged on Arc day last October, which for the third consecutive year took place on very testing ground.

If you go back to the initial entries for the Marcel Boussac and the Jean-Luc Lagardere – made last August – the small number of French horses engaged at Newmarket makes sense.

Only 25 of the 60 fillies given an entry in the Boussac were trained in France, while just 13 of the 54 horses in the Lagardere were home chances.

Fabre has not made a huge priority of the Boussac down the years and **Zellie** was just his second winner of the race, 26 years on from Daniel Wildenstein's Miss Tahiti.

A Wootton Bassett daughter of a Nathaniel mare, Zellie made six starts at two, three of them in the colours of the trainer's daughter, Lavinia Fabre. Purchased privately by the Qatar-based Al Wasmiyah Farm, Zellie showed a smart turn of foot to come from off the pace to get to Times Square before essentially outstaying her rival.

Fabre looked to have an extremely strong hand going into the race but elected not to risk the unbeaten **Raclette** on the holding Longchamp turf.

A Juddmonte homebred by Frankel out of the dual US Grade 1 winner Emollient, Raclette looked as exciting as any two-year-old filly in Europe, brushing aside the opposition at Deauville and then Chantilly.

Fabre considered a trip to Newmarket to test her suitability for the Rowley Mile but a storm in Chantilly on the day she was set to work scuppered that plan and Raclette was put away for the season.

She remains hugely exciting and the choice not to give her a 1,000 Guineas entry may be more a reflection of her inexperience and of Fabre's conviction that she will be a horse for middle distances this season; the Poule d'Essai des Pouliches offers her better timing with a view to the Diane.

Agave could be an interesting filly to watch for the same connections on the basis of her sole appearance when winning the often informative Prix de la Cascade at Longchamp.

She is by Dubawi out of the Champs Elysees mare Contribution – herself a sister to none other than Enable – and is entered in the Pouliches, the Saint-Alary and the Diane.

The yard also ran Godolphin's **Fleur D'Iris** in the Boussac, where her defeat of Zellie in the Prix d'Aumale was comprehensively reversed, and – along with another beaten filly from Longchamp, **Who Knows** – she was again unplaced when turned round 13 days later for the Prix Miesque.

Potentially of more interest is **Acer Alley**, who showed a real turn of foot to run down the colts over seven furlongs in the Prix a Rochette and can be readily forgiven for not reproducing that on Arc day.

And as noteworthy as any of the Boussac runners could be runner-up **Times Square** *(above)*, who was deliberately kept fresh by trainer Christophe Ferland after finishing third to a pair of smart colts at Deauville in August, and who had daylight back to the rest of the field at Longchamp.

If she takes after her sire Zarak then there could be plenty more to come at three and Ferland has already spoken of a comeback run in the Prix de la Grotte with a view to the Pouliches.

Stablemate **Accakaba** is more speedily bred and was far from disgraced when fourth in the Prix Jean-Luc Lagardere, Ferland pitching her in against the colts but over seven furlongs.

A seasonal debut in the Prix Imprudence over a straight seven furlongs at Deauville could be first up as Ferland and the Wertheimer Brothers seek to establish her chances of staying the turning mile of the Pouliches.

Hopes of a French-trained Classic colt to emerge from the Lagardere rest squarely with **Ancient Rome**, a close-up third to Angel Bleu at Longchamp before being beaten by the same rival in the Criterium International three weeks later.

Powerfully built even as a juvenile, Coolmore's War Front son of Prix de Diane third Gagnoa might not be one to give up on when confronting better ground again, while his early closing entries span the distance range all the way up to the mile and a half of the Grand Prix de Paris.

Godolphin's Iffraaj colt **Rebel Path** ran twice over six furlongs last summer, going down to fellow Guineas entry Topgear before defeating Malavath on his second start.

It is worth remembering that most of Fabre's Guineas runners have been given some previous experience of the Rowley Mile.

The exception was Territories, who was supplemented in 2015 in part due to a paucity of Godolphin candidates stabled with Charlie Appleby and Saeed bin Suroor, which is a situation that looks unlikely to be repeated in 2022.

All told, unless Rebel Path crops up at the Craven Meeting, it would be a surprise to see him line up in the Guineas.

Indeed, this is a pertinent moment to point out that the only juvenile runner sent by Fabre to his favourite course in Britain last autumn was **Trident**, who has since been sold to Hong Kong.

Ancient Rome aside, the two end-of-season Group 1s run at Saint-Cloud offered limited hope on the home front.

Indeed, were Ralph Beckett to send Angel Bleu to Longchamp for the Poule d'Essai des Poulains, it would be in the knowledge that only Ancient Rome and Trident among French-trained colts achieved a rating of 110 in the European two-year-old classification.

Jean-Claude Rouget was notably quiet over Arc weekend at the end of what he publicly warned was something of a rebuilding year, and a number of his three-year-olds kept away from the bright lights may come forward in the early months of this season.

Rouget will be as keen as any to find a gem from the first three-year-old runners by his European Champion Almanzor, with France Galop listing six of the stallion's progeny as being in his care; **Lassaut** might be the pick according to entries.

Another former Rouget inmate, Zelzal, is responsible for **Caracal**, who won a Bordeaux maiden on his sole start last season, while a second Al Shaqab colt to monitor is **Welwal**, whose sole defeat in three starts came at the hands of the much-vaunted Raclette.

The Aga Khan's **Vadeni** lost his unbeaten record with a somewhat muted display in the Prix de Conde, although the fact his conqueror El Bodegon went on to Group 1 success offers some mitigation, while 1m1f on soft ground may not have been the ideal combination of circumstances at that stage of his development.

Among the Rouget fillies, **Zelda** was three from four last year in the colours of former NBA star Tony Parker's Infinity Nine Horses, rounding off with a straightforward Listed success at Chantilly (Parker also has Classic hopes with **Mangoustine**, who has moved this year to the resurgent Mikel Delzangles).

As a Dubawi daughter of the Aga Khan's three-time Group 1 winner Ervedya, **Erevann** boasts the bluest of blood and her winning debut for Rouget in a well-contested maiden at Deauville last October promised much.

This year will mark a new departure for the famous emerald green silks following the retirement of one of French racing's true greats, Alain de Royer-Dupre. Francis Graffard will continue to operate his own yard in parallel with His Highness' Aiglemont complex and has exciting three-year-old fillies to run from both.

Ebba will bid to keep up the remarkable record of her dam Ebiyza, whose first two runners Edisa and Ebaiyra have both won at Group level.

Ebba made a good impression on her sole start for Royer-Dupre at Fontainebleau last backend and holds entries in the Saint-Alary and the Diane.

Malavath provided a huge thrill for her connections when Graffard stepped her up from a Group 2 win over six furlongs to finish runner-up at a mile in the Breeders' Cup Juvenile Fillies' Turf at Del Mar.

Raced five times at two and by Mehmas, it would be easy to dismiss Malavath's chances of progressing again this year. But she is reportedly a far from extravagant worker who saves her efforts for race day and it wouldn't be the least bit surprising to see her take another step forward during the spring.

Final word for the three-year-olds goes to **Rosacea**, who swept past her rivals in devastating fashion to claim the Group 3 Prix des Reservoirs in October.

Wattel was unable to conceal his enthusiasm afterwards and the daughter of Soldier Hollow looks every inch a Group 1 filly, while owner/breeder Jurgen Winter will be unafraid to take on the best of Britain and Ireland on their home patch sooner or later.

Turning to the older brigade, one horse who did plenty of travelling last season was **Suesa**, who made consecutive starts in the Commonwealth Cup, the King George Stakes at Goodwood and the Nunthorpe.

Europe's sprint programme will almost oblige trainer Francois Rohaut and owner George Strawbridge to consider another extensive campaign.

On her very best day she may be the Old World's best chance of repelling the likes of Home Affairs and Nature Strip reportedly heading up from Australia for Royal Ascot.

With Covid restrictions on travelling staff hopefully a thing of the past, at least Rohaut will be able to prepare Suesa in a more conventional manner and if you were betting on which division might produce a French-trained champion of Europe, sprinting might easily be favourite.

Marianafoot retains the potential to add to his Prix Maurice de Gheest success for trainer Jerome Reynier, who will also welcome back fellow seven-year-old **Skalleti** *(left)* in the orange and silver hoops of owner Jean-Claude Seroul.

Bubble Gift emerged quietly as among France's best middle-distance horses last term and can enjoy another profitable year under the careful stewardship of Delzangles.

Just when we were about to give up hope of a British Group 1 winner for French trainers in 2021, **Sealiway** popped up in the Champion Stakes to hold off the steeply progressive Dubai Honour, with several of the boys of summer such as Mishriff and Adayar readily turned away.

With the three members of the Rossi training clan now suspended indefinitely pending legal charges, Graffard has inherited Sealiway.

A trip to the Saudi Cup ended up in a no-show as the son of Galiway refused to face the dirt kickback – in common with virtually every other European challenger – but a return to turf should prove the ticket and should he add to his Group 1 wins at two and three, Sealiway could be a serious stallion prospect for the Chehboub family.

Graffard enjoyed more luck in Riyadh with **Ebaiyra**, who enhanced her fine Group-race record when finishing third behind Japan Cup runner-up Authority.

She filled the same place in the Hong Kong Vase in December and more globetrotting could be on the agenda now the decision has been made to keep her in training following her Saudi showing.

Standing in his way at middle distances could be **Mare Australis**, who progressed rapidly during the spring in 2021 and sprang a minor surprise in the Prix Ganay.

At the time Fabre saw him as a horse to be aimed at the Arc, a hope that was derailed by injury. Having spent extended time back in Germany with his breeders at Gestut Schlenderhan, hopefully patience will pay off with this son of Australia.

Another colt who made a splash in the spring only to disappear from view is **Fenelon**, who showed plenty of raw power and talent in two wins, while having something of the teenage delinquent about him.

Nicolas Clement was forced to play the long game after the son of Fastnet Rock got cast in his box the morning of the Prix du Lys but there is every hope that Fenelon could develop into a candidate for top honours at a mile and a half.

GLOBAL CHALLENGE NICHOLAS GODFREY

Overseas stars who could be big players in top British races

CAMPANELLE *Wesley Ward (USA)*

4f Kodiac - Janina

Completing a Royal Ascot hat-trick will be a primary target for this top-class Irish-bred filly, who won the Queen Mary in fine style as a two-year-old before needing the assistance of the stewards in last year's Commonwealth Cup. Even if the latter did involve a controversial decision to demote Dragon Symbol, the performance demonstrated Campanelle's ability to act both in pretty testing conditions and over 6f – neither of which are traits generally associated with Wesley Ward's formidable team. She had the blinkers reapplied, by the way.

As such, the Platinum Jubilee appeals as an option, not least because the stable has other likely suspects for the King's Stand. Presumably Campanelle might stick around for a longer European campaign, as she did in both 2020 (won G1 Prix Morny) and 2021, though her most recent campaign did not finish well when fly-leaping and giving Frankie Dettori a whack in the face at Deauville, where she was last of 12 in the Maurice de Gheest; she was also beaten back in the States as hot favourite for her Breeders' Cup prep.

Golden Pal (left): dual Breeders' Cup winner could run at Royal Ascot

EFFORIA *Yuichi Shikato (JAP)*
4c Epiphaneia - Katies Heart

Japan's four winners on the Saudi Cup undercard offered another example of their towering status on the global stage. Even the Breeders' Cup has now fallen within Japan's ambit – but the Prix de l'Arc de Triomphe remains elusive.

After his Horse of the Year campaign as a three-year-old, the outstanding Efforia would surely be a major contender in Paris. Due to start the season in the G1 Osaka Hai on April 3, the son of Japan Cup winner Epiphaneia has been beaten only once in seven career starts, and that was when he was touched off by Shahryar in the Tokyo Yushun (Japanese Derby).

Having won the Satsuki Sho (2,000 Guineas), Efforia was odds-on in Tokyo and caught only in the final stride. He put matters right in no uncertain terms on his last two starts, returning after a five-month layoff to thwart a pair of superstars in Contrail and Gran Alegria in the Tenno Sho (Autumn) before rounding off a brilliant season in the Arima Kinen (Grand Prix) at the end of the year. Japanese middle-distance form is the best in the world, and Efforia starts 2022 in pole position.

GOLDEN PAL *Wesley Ward (USA)*
4c Uncle Mo - Lady Shipman

Dual Breeders' Cup winner Golden Pal is the superstar name on a mighty list of older horses who could represent Wesley Ward at Royal Ascot in 2022. There won't be many faster horses on show at the royal meeting: he had the Breeders' Cup Turf Sprint won as soon as he rocketed out of the gate at Del Mar. Ward has often described Golden Pal as the best he's ever trained, unbeaten at home since his debut in the States, where the turning tracks allow him to make the most of his abundant early toe.

However, he's been beaten both times in England, albeit only on unsuitably softish ground at Ascot as a two-year-old when he only just failed to last out and was caught by The Lir Jet in the Norfolk. While he missed Royal Ascot last term after a setback, his return to England for the Nunthorpe Stakes was puzzling as he seemed to be travelling easily on the lead only to fall into a heap when challenged inside the final furlong. Frankie Dettori said he seemed to be waiting for a turn, and he won't get that in the King's Stand Stakes.

HAPPY CRAF *Allan Smith (Bahrain)*
4f Mastercraftsman - Alegre Roma

Allan Smith, the 16-time Bahraini champion trainer, has always hankered for another victory back at home, a feat the Essex-born expat achieved plenty of times when he was based in Belgium in the 1980s and '90s. Now the veteran handler may finally have the right horse in the shape of Happy Craf, an Argentine-bred filly with whom he landed a couple of legs of the new Bahrain Turf Series over 7f at Sakhir over the winter.

Bizarrely, Happy Craf was rated too high in the handicap to compete in the last round in February but she had already done enough to secure the overall series victory. By that stage, she was already in quarantine ready for a crack at prizes in Britain during the summer, when Uruguayan jockey Edinson Rodriguez, her regular partner in Bahrain, is expected to travel with her.

Allan Smith said: "She's a lovely mare, such a big girl and full of power, and she's just gone from strength to strength. Going over to the UK she'd be stationed with my son Martin in Newmarket and we'll hopefully pick up a Group 3 or Listed race for fillies and mares and then she'll go off to stud."

HOME AFFAIRS *Chris Waller (AUS)*
3c I Am Invincible – Miss Interiors

It's been a while since Australia-trained sprinters bestrode Royal Ascot like colossi; in fact, they haven't had a winner for a decade since Black Caviar in 2012 (although Merchant Navy was a recent ex-Aussie).

That could be about to change with Waller-trained stablemates Home Affairs and Nature Strip both earmarked for a trip to England. Carrying the Coolmore colours, Home Affairs is the new kid on the block and he looked top drawer when slamming three-year-old rivals in the G1 Coolmore Stud Stakes at Flemington over 6f in October.

Returning nearly four months later, he produced a career-best against older horses in the Black Caviar Lightning Stakes over 5f at the same venue, holding off odds-on Nature Strip and a group of the nation's top older sprinters. While there were mitigating circumstances for the touched-off runner-up, who missed the break, it was noticeable that top jockey James McDonald had deserted his old sparring partner to ride the younger horse.

Chris Waller said: "He raced against the young horses and dominated last preparation and now he's come back and beaten the best at weight-for-age so it's pretty exciting going forward."

NATURE STRIP *Chris Waller (AUS)*
7g Nicconi – Strikeline

Multiple G1 winner went into the second half of his Sydney campaign as world's #1 sprinter with career record featuring seven top-level successes – plus the most recent running of the Everest, the world's richest turf race at Randwick. Now seven, he also won the Darley Sprint Classic in Melbourne to complete his best-ever spring campaign down under, after which he topped the sprint list in the Longines World Racehorse Rankings for 2021 with a mark of 124.

Although Nature Strip was beaten on his first two autumn starts, there were obvious excuses. He missed the break and yet still only just failed to beat younger stablemate Home Affairs in the Lightning Stakes, and then he couldn't handle a heavy track at Randwick in a G2 event won by top sprinter Eduardo. Next up was his bid to complete a

Pizza Bianca: Royal Ascot would be the dream for his celebrity owner

hat-trick in Sydney's most prestigious sprint, the TJ Smith Stakes, at The Championships, after which a final decision on Royal Ascot was expected.

Lightning Stakes fourth Swats That has also been mentioned in Royal Ascot dispatches.

Rod Lyons (senior part-owner) said: "We've got our hearts set on going – it'll be up to Chris but so long as he races really well and he pulls up well after the TJ, we intend to be heading to Royal Ascot. The boys and girls are all looking forward to it – that's our aim, our long-term goal."

PIZZA BIANCA *Christophe Clement (USA)*
3f Fastnet Rock - White Hot

Pizza Bianca's owner, the celebrity chef Bobby Flay, was talking about a trip to Royal Ascot almost as soon as she crossed the line to give her trainer Christophe Clement his first Breeders' Cup success in last year's Juvenile Fillies' Turf at Del Mar.

The Coronation Stakes would surely provide the target for the daughter of Fastnet Rock – no stranger to Ascot success as a sire – who was given a sublime ride by Jose Ortiz at Del Mar, who weaved a passage through the field from the rear before beating French-trained Malavath by a half-length.

Also a staying-on second to Godolphin's Wild Beauty on her previous outing in the G1 Natalma at Woodbine, she is bred to do better with time and possibly distance, her dam being closely related to Derby winner Pour Moi. As her usually reticent trainer suggested she was top class at two, it bodes especially well for a bright future.

Bobby Flay (owner-breeder) said: "I'm a dreamer, and believe that when they are good these horses can take you all over the world, so maybe Ascot where I've had a second before."

TIZ THE BOMB *Ken McPeek (USA)*
3c Hit It A Bomb - Tiz The Key

Kenny McPeek is an American pioneer, having saddled runners in the UK well before Wesley Ward found his way to Royal Ascot. The Classics have long been on his radar, but he will be hoping that Tiz The Bomb's proposed trip to Epsom is slightly more positive than when he brought Daddys Lil Darling to the Oaks in 2017 when the

filly bolted on the way to the start and had to be withdrawn.

This year's McPeek representative won three times as a two-year-old (including a G2 at Keeneland) before being beaten a running-on length and a half by Godolphin's Modern Games in the Breeders' Cup Juvenile Turf. Any thoughts of a run down the US Triple Crown trail were scotched when he was down the field behind Kentucky Derby hope White Abarrio on his seasonal debut at Gulfstream Park but he duly regained the winning thread next time in stakes company on a synthetic surface at Turfway Park.

Ken McPeek said: "He may run in the 2,000 Guineas first and then come back in the English Derby. We are really excited about it. He's a top-level grass horse. His second in the Breeders' Cup would justify that he's good enough and we are working on a plan to get him there. He won at Kentucky Downs, which is equivalent to a European turf course with the uphill and downhill so he should be able to handle the contours of Epsom."

TWILIGHT GLEAMING *Wesley Ward (USA)*
3f National Defense - Thames Pageant

Hardly a surprise that a return to Royal Ascot was nominated straight away for Twilight Gleaming amid post-race celebrations after she became a third winner of the Breeders' Cup Juvenile Turf Sprint for Wesley Ward. Displaying all the early speed so often associated with her barn's representatives, this Irish-bred filly (purchased at Goffs Orby Sale) was the speed of the speed at Del Mar, burning off One Timer before holding on from Railway Stakes winner Go Bears Go by a half-length.

After bolting up in a maiden at Belmont Park, she'd tried the same tactics in the Queen Mary, only to get collared by a stronger stayer on the day in Quick Suzy, but a subsequent Listed win on unfavourable soft ground in France showed a gritty side to her that ought to stand her in good stead for her three-year-old campaign.

Wesley Ward said: "I will see how she progresses and I imagine either the King's Stand or the Commonwealth Cup will be on her agenda. I knew she was fast – she won at Belmont on the grass and finished second in the Queen Mary. Then we knew we had something special."

VERRY ELLEEGANT *Chris Waller (AUS)*
6m Zed – Opulence

Melbourne Cup heroine took her career record to 11 G1 wins in February at Randwick when she held off She's Ideel to win a heavy-ground Chipping Norton Stakes. As the mile is short of her optimum, that was no shabby effort, showcasing her famous battling qualities. "She fights like a tiger," said her adoring trainer Chris Waller, who added that she is "freakish".

Few would argue given a CV that shows her to have danced every dance across several seasons, never looking better than during the Melbourne spring carnival in 2021 when she followed up a close third in the Cox Plate with an impressive four-length victory in the Melbourne Cup.

With testing conditions right up her street, the six-year-old's owners have long since mooted the idea of a trip to Europe for the Arc de Triomphe. First, though, comes a third crack at Randwick's Queen Elizabeth Stakes, where she's gone head-to-head with Addeybb in the last two years.

Brae Sokolski (part-owner) said: "The Arc is absolutely on her agenda – we feel it is the ultimate challenge. I've told Chris not to pencil it in on the calendar but to use a texta marker!

"We are not perturbed at all taking on Europe's best on home soil. Our focus is the Sydney autumn carnival, then we want to give her a spell before deciding on her campaign structure for the Arc."

THIS SEASON'S KEY HORSES

By Dylan Hill

A Case Of You (Ire)

4 b c Hot Streak - Karjera (Key Of Luck)

Adrian McGuinness (Ire) — Gary Devlin

PLACINGS: 311/10103215-1 — RPR **119**

Starts	1st	2nd	3rd	4th	Win & Pl
12	6	1	2	-	£335,275

Date	Course	Race	Prize
2/22	Dund	6f stand	£8,429
10/21	Lonc	5f Gp1 heavy	£178,563
5/21	Naas	6f Gp3 3yo soft	£26,339
3/21	Dund	6f 3yo stand	£7,112
10/20	Curr	6½f Gp3 2yo soft	£25,000
9/20	DRoy	7f Mdn Auct 2yo soft	£11,500

Flourished when dropped back to 5f last autumn and gained a dramatic last-gasp victory in the Prix de l'Abbaye, building on a half-length second in the Flying Five; was set to travel to Dubai after a winning reappearance at Dundalk; seems most effective with plenty of cut.

Adayar (Ire)

4 b c Frankel - Anna Salai (Dubawi)

Charlie Appleby — Godolphin

PLACINGS: 41/221145- — RPR **129+**

Starts	1st	2nd	3rd	4th	Win & Pl
8	3	2	-	2	£1,453,831

Date	Course	Race	Prize
7/21	Asct	1m4f Cls1 Gp1 gd-fm	£496,213
6/21	Epsm	1m4f Cls1 Gp1 3yo gd-sft	£637,988
10/20	Nott	1m½f Cls4 Mdn 2yo soft	£7,763

Became the first horse to win the Derby and King George in the same year since Galileo with his famous double last season; only fourth in the Arc (faded late having made the running) and well beaten in fifth under similar front-running tactics in the Champion Stakes.

Addeybb (Ire)

8 ch g Pivotal - Bush Cat (Kingmambo)

William Haggas — Sheikh Ahmed Al Maktoum

PLACINGS: 03/41212/11211/2126- — RPR **121**

Starts	1st	2nd	3rd	4th	Win & Pl
24	12	5	2	2	£3,554,183

Rating	Date	Course	Race	Prize
	4/21	Rand	1m2f Gp1 good	£1,367,697
	10/20	Asct	1m2f Cls1 Gp1 soft	£425,325
	9/20	Ayr	1m2f Cls1 List gd-sft	£15,737
	4/20	Rand	1m2f Gp1 soft	£674,339
	3/20	Rose	1m2f Gp1 gd-sft	£216,402
	8/19	Hayd	1m2½f Cls1 Gp3 heavy	£35,727
	6/19	Asct	1m2f Cls1 List soft	£56,710
	4/18	Sand	1m Cls1 Gp2 gd-sft	£56,710
99	3/18	Donc	1m Cls2 97-107 Hcap soft	£62,250
93	9/17	NmkR	1m1f Cls2 65-93 Hcap gd-sft	£18,675
88	7/17	Asct	1m Cls3 74-88 3yo Hcap good	£9,704
	6/17	Hayd	1m Cls4 Mdn 3yo gd-sft	£4,690

Veteran 1m2f specialist who won a fourth Group 1 in last season's Queen Elizabeth Stakes at Randwick in Australia but failed to match best form in just two runs back in Europe; no match for St Mark's Basilica in the Eclipse and only sixth when defending Champion Stakes crown.

Agartha (Ire)

3 b f Caravaggio - Arya Tara (Dylan Thomas)

Joseph O'Brien (Ire) — Scott C Heider

PLACINGS: 33221124- — RPR **108**

Starts	1st	2nd	3rd	4th	Win & Pl
8	2	3	2	1	£158,383

Date	Course	Race	Prize
8/21	Curr	7f Gp2 2yo soft	£52,679
7/21	Leop	7f Gp3 2yo good	£26,339

Dual Group winner last season, most notably in the Debutante Stakes, relishing switch to front-running tactics after four placed efforts in maidens; came up short at Group 1 level, finishing second in the Moyglare and fourth in the Prix Marcel Boussac.

Al Aasy (Ire)

5 b g Sea The Stars - Kitcara (Shamardal)

William Haggas — Shadwell Estate Company

PLACINGS: 3/5116/112248- — RPR **122+**

Starts	1st	2nd	3rd	4th	Win & Pl
11	4	2	1	1	£210,698

Date	Course	Race	Prize
5/21	Newb	1m4f Cls1 Gp3 gd-sft	£56,710
4/21	Newb	1m4f Cls1 Gp3 good	£25,520
7/20	NmkJ	1m5f Cls1 Gp3 3yo gd-sft	£23,081
6/20	NmkR	1m4f Cls5 3yo soft	£3,493

Frustrating but hugely talented middle-distance performer; won two 1m4f Group 3 races by wide margins at Newbury last season but narrowly beaten the next twice, including in the Coronation Cup, appearing to duck the issue; disappointed twice after a gelding operation.

Al Suhail

5 b g Dubawi - Shirocco Star (Shirocco)

Charlie Appleby — Godolphin

PLACINGS: 2132/01/3036131- — RPR **117**

Starts	1st	2nd	3rd	4th	Win & Pl
13	4	2	4	-	£152,792

Date	Course	Race	Prize
10/21	NmkR	7f Cls1 Gp2 gd-sft	£68,052
9/21	Hayd	7f Cls3 gd-fm	£8,370
7/20	NmkJ	1m Cls1 List 3yo gd-sft	£14,461
8/19	Yarm	7f Cls4 2yo gd-fm	£4,852

Comfortable winner of the Challenge Stakes at Newmarket on final run last season, gaining an overdue win at Group level having finished second or third four times previously; possibly flattered having enjoyed the run of the race in front; effective at 7f-1m.

Albaflora

5 gr m Muhaarar - Almiranta (Galileo)

Ralph Beckett — Miss K Rausing

PLACINGS: 12622/145322- RPR **115**

Starts	1st	2nd	3rd	4th	Win & Pl
11	2	5	1	1	£295,519

5/21	Asct	1m4f Cls1 List soft	£20,983
6/20	Hayd	1m2f Cls5 Mdn good	£3,493

Developed into a smart middle-distance mare last season, running away with a Listed race at Ascot by seven lengths and beaten a short head on Champions Day at Ascot, although largely disappointing in between.

Albahr

3 ch g Dubawi - Falls Of Lora (Street Cry)

Charlie Appleby — Godolphin

PLACINGS: 31111-5 RPR **108**

Starts	1st	2nd	3rd	4th	Win & Pl
6	4	-	1	-	£173,678

9/21	Wood	1m Gd1 2yo good	£137,931
8/21	Sals	1m Cls1 List 2yo good	£24,385
7/21	Hayd	7f Cls5 2yo gd-fm	£3,780
6/21	Hayd	7f Cls4 2yo gd-fm	£4,347

Won final four races last season, all at odds-on; gained biggest domestic win in a Listed race at Salisbury and easily added a Grade I in Canada before getting trapped in the stalls at the Breeders' Cup; disappointed on return at Meydan and being a gelding limits opportunities.

Alcohol Free (Ire)

4 b f No Nay Never - Plying (Hard Spun)

Andrew Balding — J C Smith

PLACINGS: 121/1513168- RPR **121**

Starts	1st	2nd	3rd	4th	Win & Pl
10	5	1	1	-	£1,016,503

7/21	Gdwd	1m Cls1 Gp1 soft	£567,100
6/21	Asct	1m Cls1 Gp1 3yo heavy	£242,081
4/21	Newb	7f Cls1 Gp3 3yo good	£25,520
9/20	NmkR	6f Cls1 Gp1 2yo good	£124,762
8/20	Newb	6f Cls5 2yo gd-sft	£3,493

Three-time Group I winner who beat the boys in last season's Sussex Stakes, adding to wins in the Coronation Stakes and the 2020 Cheveley Park; didn't stay 1m2f in the Juddmonte International before disappointing in the QEII Stakes.

Aldaary

4 ch g Territories - Broughtons Revival (Pivotal)

William Haggas — Shadwell Estate Company

PLACINGS: 11/1355711- RPR **119+**

Starts	1st	2nd	3rd	4th	Win & Pl
9	5	-	1	-	£199,728

109	10/21	Asct	1m Cls2 101-111 Hcap gd-sft	£103,080
103	10/21	Asct	7f Cls2 98-107 Hcap heavy	£64,425
93	5/21	Asct	7f Cls2 86-100 3yo Hcap gd-sft	£10,823
	10/20	Leic	6f Cls4 2yo heavy	£5,111
	10/20	Yarm	6f Cls4 2yo soft	£5,111

Landed a big handicap double at Ascot last autumn, including the Balmoral under a big weight, bouncing back to form having won first three career starts; hadn't been quite as effective on quicker ground through the summer (all five wins on good to soft or softer).

Alenquer (Fr)

4 b c Adlerflug - Wild Blossom (Areion)

William Haggas — M M Stables

PLACINGS: 12/11329-1 RPR **116**

Starts	1st	2nd	3rd	4th	Win & Pl
8	4	2	1	-	£470,993

2/22	Ling	1m2f Cls1 Gp3 stand	£62,381
6/21	Asct	1m4f Cls1 Gp2 3yo heavy	£98,335
4/21	Sand	1m2f Cls1 Gp3 3yo good	£25,520
8/20	Newb	7f Cls5 Mdn 2yo soft	£4,140

Quickly proved a smart middle-distance colt last season, winning Sandown's Classic Trial and the King Edward VII at Royal Ascot; couldn't land a blow in three runs at Group I level, though ran on well when a six-length second in the Juddmonte International; has since won the Winter Derby.

Alpinista

5 gr m Frankel - Alwilda (Hernando)

Sir Mark Prescott — Miss K Rausing

PLACINGS: 164/4122/11111- RPR **119**

Starts	1st	2nd	3rd	4th	Win & Pl
12	7	2	-	2	£425,436

11/21	Muni	1m4f Gp1 gd-sft	£84,821
9/21	Colo	1m4f Gp1 good	£62,500
8/21	Hopp	1m4f Gp1 good	£89,286
7/21	Hayd	1m4f Cls1 Gp2 soft	£65,217
4/21	Gdwd	1m4f Cls1 List gd-fm	£22,684
8/20	Sals	1m2f Cls1 List firm	£20,132
7/19	Epsm	7f Cls4 Mdn 2yo good	£4,787

Enjoyed a fairytale campaign last season when winning all five races, the last three at Group I level in Germany including a win over subsequent Arc hero Torquator Tasso; gained biggest win on home soil when landing the Lancashire Oaks at Haydock.

Ancient Rome (USA)

3 b c War Front - Gagnoa (Sadler's Wells)

Andre Fabre (Fr) — Tabor, Smith, Magnier & Westerberg

PLACINGS: 211132- RPR **113**

Starts	1st	2nd	3rd	4th	Win & Pl
6	3	2	1	-	£159,616

9/21	Lonc	1m Gp3 2yo gd-sft	£35,714
8/21	Deau	7½f 2yo gd-sft	£15,179
7/21	Deau	7½f 2yo heavy	£12,054

Last year's leading two-year-old colt in France according to Racing Post Ratings despite two defeats when favourite in Group I races; had landed a Group 3 impressively over a mile and did better still when stepped back up to that trip to run Angel Bleu to a head at Saint-Cloud.

Angel Bleu (Fr)

3 b c Dark Angel - Cercle De La Vie (Galileo)

Ralph Beckett — Marc Chan

PLACINGS: 31102111- — RPR **114+**

Starts	1st	2nd	3rd	4th	Win & Pl
8	5	1	1	-	£440,072

	Date	Course	Race	Prize
	10/21	StCl	1m Gp1 2yo v soft	£127,545
	10/21	Lonc	7f Gp1 2yo heavy	£204,071
	7/21	Gdwd	7f Cls1 Gp2 2yo soft	£85,065
	5/21	Pont	6f Cls2 2yo soft	£9,682
	4/21	Sals	5f Cls4 2yo gd-fm	£4,266

Tough and classy two-year-old last season, flourishing at the end of a busy year with a Group 1 double in France, both on very soft/heavy ground; seemingly less effective on a quicker surface and more likely to head back to France in pursuit of Classic honours.

Anmaat (Ire)

4 b g Awtaad - African Moonlight (Halling)

Owen Burrows — Shadwell Estate Company

PLACINGS: 2/132112- — RPR **108+**

Starts	1st	2nd	3rd	4th	Win & Pl
7	3	3	1	-	£58,472

	Date	Course	Race	Prize
94	9/21	Donc	1m2f Cls2 83-98 Hcap gd-fm	£16,200
86	8/21	Bath	1m2f Cls3 74-92 Hcap good	£6,281
	5/21	Ling	1m Cls5 3yo stand	£3,024

Sharply progressive handicapper last season and very nearly landed a major plunge in the Cambridgeshire, travelling best before being worn down by a late closer; had won two 1m2f handicaps prior to that and should have more to come, perhaps even in Group company.

Antarah (Ire)

3 ch c Sea The Stars - Adool (Teofilo)

John & Thady Gosden — Shadwell Estate Company

PLACINGS: 1- — RPR **93+aw**

Starts	1st	2nd	3rd	4th	Win & Pl
1	1	-	-	-	£3,672

	Date	Course	Race	Prize
	10/21	Newc	1m Cls5 2yo stand	£3,672

Tore apart what looked a useful field of maidens at Newcastle on sole start last season, quickening clear of two previous runners-up with huge gap back to fourth; bred for middle distances and potentially smart.

Aratus (Ire)

4 b g Free Eagle - Shauna's Princess (Soviet Star)

Clive Cox — Adrian Butler

PLACINGS: 21/111- — RPR **106+**

Starts	1st	2nd	3rd	4th	Win & Pl
5	4	1	-	-	£50,666

	Date	Course	Race	Prize
98	8/21	Gdwd	7f Cls2 88-111 Hcap good	£25,770
94	8/21	Newb	7f Cls3 85-94 Hcap good	£10,308
	7/21	Donc	7f Cls5 gd-fm	£3,672
	11/20	Kemp	7f Cls4 Mdn 2yo std-slw	£9,704

Exciting prospect who has won all four races since a losing debut, including three last season; bridged a step up to Class 2 company when completing the four-timer in a 7f handicap at Goodwood before missing a subsequent target due to heavy ground; should get a mile.

Arecibo (Fr)

7 b g Invincible Spirit - Oceanique (Forest Wildcat)

Robert Cowell — T W Morley

PLACINGS: 585442477/161224843- — RPR **115**

Starts	1st	2nd	3rd	4th	Win & Pl
48	6	9	5	9	£282,091

	Date	Course	Race	Prize
99	5/21	NmkR	5f Cls2 80-99 Hcap soft	£10,800
91	4/21	NmkR	5f Cls3 72-91 Hcap good	£6,750
91	7/19	Ayr	5f Cls3 69-91 Hcap gd-fm	£9,704
	4/18	Fntb	6f 3yo gd-sft	£15,487
	3/18	Chan	6½f 3yo stand	£12,389
	7/17	MsnL	5½f 2yo soft	£11,538

Enjoyed a remarkable run of form early last season, winning two 5f handicaps at Newmarket after starting on a mark of 91 and finishing second in the King's Stand at Royal Ascot; form tailed off following a close second in a Group 3 at Sandown in July.

Art Power (Ire)

5 gr h Dark Angel - Evening Time (Keltos)

Tim Easterby — King Power Racing Co

PLACINGS: 31/111644/6348514- — RPR **120+**

Starts	1st	2nd	3rd	4th	Win & Pl
15	5	-	2	4	£257,334

	Date	Course	Race	Prize
	9/21	Curr	6f Gp3 good	£26,339
	7/20	Naas	6f Gp3 3yo yld-sft	£25,000
97	6/20	Asct	5f Cls2 83-104 3yo Hcap gd-sft	£22,642
	6/20	Newc	6f Cls5 std-slw	£3,493
	10/19	York	5f Cls3 2yo soft	£9,704

Yet to win above Group 3 level but has proved himself a high-class sprinter during the last two seasons, regularly knocking on the door in top races; beaten less than two lengths in the Diamond Jubilee Stakes, July Cup and Sprint Cup; seems better over 6f than 5f.

Artistic Rifles (Ire)

6 b g War Command - Chatham Islands (Elusive Quality)

Edward Bethell — Zaro Srl

PLACINGS: 1167078/3411/311011- — RPR **113**

Starts	1st	2nd	3rd	4th	Win & Pl
24	9	-	3	2	£128,874

	Date	Course	Race	Prize
	9/21	Hayd	1m Cls1 Gp3 gd-fm	£45,368
96	7/21	Haml	1m½f Cls2 84-103 Hcap gd-fm	£15,462
88	4/21	Ripn	1m Cls3 76-90 Hcap gd-fm	£6,443
86	3/21	Donc	1m Cls2 73-94 Hcap good	£23,193
85	9/20	Rdcr	1m Cls4 73-86 Hcap good	£5,822
	6/20	Siro	1m1f good	£4,321
83	6/19	Donc	1m Cls4 75-85 3yo Hcap gd-fm	£5,531
77	5/19	Donc	1m Cls3 77-93 3yo Hcap gd-fm	£7,763
72	10/18	Catt	7f Cls3 72-88 2yo Hcap good	£9,338

Hugely progressive miler last season, winning four out of five races on turf; kicked off by winning the Spring Mile at Doncaster and added two more handicaps before successfully stepping up to Group 3 level at Haydock (possibly flattered by dictating steady gallop).

Atomic Jones (Fr)

3 b/br c Wootton Bassett - Loyale (Turtle Bowl)

Ger Lyons (Ire) — Sean Jones, David Spratt & Mrs Lynne Lyons

PLACINGS: 11- — RPR **105**

Starts	1st	2nd	3rd	4th	Win & Pl
2	2	-	-	-	£74,540

9/21	Leop	1m Gp2 2yo good	£65,848
6/21	Curr	7f Mdn 2yo gd-fm	£8,692

Unbeaten in both runs as a two-year-old last season, culminating in a Group 2 at Leopardstown (form suspect with very little covering first six); described as a "big, huge baby" by his trainer and expected to prove much better as a three-year-old over a mile and beyond.

Audience

3 b c Iffraaj - Ladyship (Oasis Dream)

John & Thady Gosden — Cheveley Park Stud

PLACINGS: 1- — RPR **90+**

Starts	1st	2nd	3rd	4th	Win & Pl
1	1	-	-	-	£5,400

10/21	NmkR	7f Cls4 2yo good	£5,400

Clearcut winner of a 7f novice at Newmarket on sole start last season, storming clear by three and three-quarter lengths; not certain to get a mile on pedigree but looks capable of stepping up to a much higher grade.

Baron Samedi (red star): huge improver last season and might have more to give

Baaeed

4 b c Sea The Stars - Aghareed (Kingmambo)

William Haggas — Shadwell Estate Company

PLACINGS: 111111- — RPR **127+**

Starts	1st	2nd	3rd	4th	Win & Pl
6	6	-	-	-	£949,336

	Date	Course	Race	Prize
	10/21	Asct	1m Cls1 Gp1 gd-sft	£623,810
	9/21	Lonc	1m Gp1 gd-sft	£229,580
	7/21	Gdwd	1m Cls1 Gp3 3yo gd-sft	£56,710
	7/21	NmkJ	1m Cls1 List 3yo gd-fm	£29,489
	6/21	NmkJ	1m Cls4 3yo gd-sft	£4,860
	6/21	Leic	1m Cls4 Mdn gd-fm	£4,887

Unbeaten in six races (all over a mile) after a breathtaking three-year-old campaign last season; gained first Group 1 victory in the Prix du Moulin before claiming the scalp of chief rival Palace Pier by a neck in a thrilling Queen Elizabeth II Stakes; could stay further.

Baron Samedi

5 b g Harbour Watch - Dame Shirley (Haafhd)

Joseph O'Brien (Ire) — Lech Racing

PLACINGS: 000/5811111/11536-4 — RPR **118+**

Starts	1st	2nd	3rd	4th	Win & Pl
16	7	-	1	1	£420,695

	Date	Course	Race	Prize
	6/21	Belm	2m Gd2 yield	£160,584
	4/21	Navn	1m6f Gp3 good	£26,339
	10/20	Lonc	1m3f Gp2 heavy	£48,885
97	9/20	List	1m4f 78-101 Hcap heavy	£20,000
79	9/20	Navn	1m2f 72-92 Hcap gd-yld	£5,500
73	9/20	DRoy	1m4½f 45-73 3yo Hcap soft	£4,500
65	8/20	Cork	1m2f 57-69 3yo Hcap heavy	£5,000

Remarkable success story in 2020, when graduating from 65-rated handicapper to Group 2 winner, and maintained progress over staying trips last season, notably with a second win at that level in the US; fine third in the Irish St Leger back home.

Bay Bridge

4 b c New Bay - Hayyona (Multiplex)

Sir Michael Stoute | James Wigan

PLACINGS: 34/1111- | RPR **117+**

Starts	1st	2nd	3rd	4th	Win & Pl
6	4	-	1	1	£76,131

	10/21	NmkR	1m2f Cls1 List good	£29,489
105	10/21	York	1m2½f Cls2 93-107 Hcap gd-sft	£15,462
90	5/21	Newb	1m2f Cls2 81-101 3yo Hcap gd-sft	£25,770
	4/21	Newc	1m2f Cls4 3yo std-slw	£4,347

Won all four races last season, punctuated by a long mid-season absence (missed Royal Ascot with injury when favourite for the King Edward VII); returned with a handicap win at York before narrowly winning a 1m2f Listed race at Newmarket; should stay 1m4f.

Bayside Boy (Ire)

3 b c New Bay - Alava (Anabaa)

Roger Varian | Teme Valley & Ballylinch Stud

PLACINGS: 12133- | RPR **114**

Starts	1st	2nd	3rd	4th	Win & Pl
5	2	1	2	-	£165,966

9/21	Donc	7f Cls1 Gp2 2yo gd-sft	£71,336
7/21	Newb	7f Cls4 2yo good	£5,400

Smart and consistent two-year-old last season; gained a notable scalp when edging out Reach For The Moon in the Champagne Stakes and acquitted himself well when twice third at Group 1 level in the Dewhurst and Vertem Futurity Trophy; should stay beyond a mile.

Beauty Inspire (Ire)

3 ch c Mehmas - Darwell (Zamindar)

Ger Lyons (Ire) | Beauty Stable Partnership

PLACINGS: 11- | RPR **102+**

Starts	1st	2nd	3rd	4th	Win & Pl
2	2	-	-	-	£35,031

7/21	Curr	6½f Gp3 2yo good	£26,339
6/21	Curr	6f Mdn 2yo good	£8,692

Impressive winner of both starts last season, hacking up on debut before comfortably landing odds of 1-2 in a Group 3 back at the Curragh; had Group 1 targets on agenda only to miss the rest of the season; looks a sprinter on pedigree.

Believe In Love (Ire)

5 b m Make Believe - Topka (Kahyasi)

Roger Varian | Koji Maeda

PLACINGS: 52/622111131/71625- | RPR **112+**

Starts	1st	2nd	3rd	4th	Win & Pl
16	6	4	1	-	£177,573

	7/21	Leop	1m6f Gp3 good	£34,241
	10/20	StCl	1m6f Gp3 heavy	£26,695
97	8/20	NmkJ	1m6f Cls2 88-97 Hcap soft	£9,704
88	8/20	NmkJ	1m6f Cls2 81-96 Hcap gd-fm	£9,704
80	7/20	Gdwd	1m4f Cls3 70-91 Hcap good	£10,997
76	3/20	Kemp	1m3f Cls4 63-80 3yo Hcap std-slw	£6,469

Smart staying mare who has won 1m6f Group 3 races in each of the last two seasons and came close to a Group 1 victory when beaten a short neck by Loving Dream in last season's Prix de Royallieu; has produced best form with plenty of cut but has also won on good to firm.

Berkshire Rocco (Fr)

5 ch g Sir Percy - Sunny Again (Shirocco)

Andrew Balding | Berkshire Parts & Panels

PLACINGS: 4413/22421/220- | RPR **108**

Starts	1st	2nd	3rd	4th	Win & Pl
12	2	5	1	3	£311,687

10/20	Asct	1m6f Cls1 List 3yo soft	£22,684
8/19	Ches	7f Cls4 2yo good	£5,852

Developed into a smart stayer in 2020, finishing second in the St Leger and Queen's Vase before winning a Listed race at Ascot; disappointing in three runs last season, punctuated by a long layoff through the summer; since been gelded.

Berkshire Shadow

3 gr c Dark Angel - Angel Vision (Oasis Dream)

Andrew Balding | Berkshire Parts & Panels No1 Fanclub

PLACINGS: 11274- | RPR **109**

Starts	1st	2nd	3rd	4th	Win & Pl
5	2	1	-	1	£123,929

6/21	Asct	6f Cls1 Gp2 2yo gd-fm	£59,200
4/21	Newb	5f Cls4 Mdn 2yo good	£4,266

Clearcut winner of last season's Coventry Stakes at Royal Ascot; failed to win again but confirmed himself a smart two-year-old when second in the Vintage Stakes and fourth in the Dewhurst, though disappointed back at 6f in the Gimcrack in between.

Bolshoi Ballet (Ire)

4 b c Galileo - Alta Anna (Anabaa)

Aidan O'Brien (Ire) | Magnier, Tabor, Smith & Weste

PLACINGS: 315/11714469- | RPR **117+**

Starts	1st	2nd	3rd	4th	Win & Pl
11	4	-	1	2	£620,115

7/21	Belm	1m2f Gd1 3yo good	£390,511
5/21	Leop	1m2f Gp3 3yo good	£36,875
4/21	Leop	1m2f Gp3 3yo good	£26,339
10/20	Leop	1m Mdn 2yo yld-sft	£8,250

Ultimately disappointing last season having gone off a warm Derby favourite in June; did manage a Grade 1 win in the US after managing only fourth at Epsom but well beaten in four more top international races; could travel again given preference for quick ground.

Boundless Ocean (Ire)

3 b c Teofilo - Novel Approach (New Approach)

Jim Bolger (Ir) | Mrs J S Bolger

PLACINGS: 245- | RPR **103+**

Starts	1st	2nd	3rd	4th	Win & Pl
3	-	1	-	1	£5,477

Showed promise despite failing to win in three

runs last season; beaten a neck on debut and pitched into Group company twice subsequently, finishing a close fourth behind Glounthaune before a below-par fifth when favourite for the Eyrefield; should relish middle distances.

Broome (Ire)

6 b h Australia - Sweepstake (Acclamation)

Aidan O'Brien (Ire) — Matsushima, Magnier, Tabor & Smith

PLACINGS: 1146/40/11122142020- — RPR **121**

Starts	1st	2nd	3rd	4th	Win & Pl
22	7	6	-	3	£1,265,993

7/21	StCl	1m4f Gp1 soft	£204,071
5/21	Curr	1m2f Gp2 yield	£52,679
4/21	Curr	1m2f Gp3 good	£26,339
3/21	Naas	1m2f List soft	£19,754
5/19	Leop	1m2f Gp3 3yo gd-yld	£53,153
4/19	Leop	1m2f Gp3 3yo soft	£31,892
8/18	Gway	1m½f Mdn 2yo yld-sft	£9,812

Ran consistently well during a busy campaign last season, with an overdue Group 1 victory in the Grand Prix de Saint-Cloud among four victories; beaten no more than half a length in four other Group 1 races, including last season's Tattersalls Gold Cup and Breeders' Cup Turf.

Bubble Gift (Fr)

4 ch c Nathaniel - Bubble Back (Grand Lodge)

Mikel Delzangles (Fr) — Zak Bloodstock

PLACINGS: 4/2112618- — RPR **118**

Starts	1st	2nd	3rd	4th	Win & Pl
8	3	2	-	1	£165,583

9/21	Lonc	1m4f Gp2 3yo good	£66,161
5/21	Lonc	1m3f Gp2 3yo soft	£66,161
4/21	Chan	1m4f 3yo good	£12,054

Developed into a high-class middle-distance colt last season; returned from a mid-season break to win the Prix Niel (second Group 2 win at Longchamp) and finish a good eighth in the Arc, staying on well.

Cadamosto (Ire)

3 b/br c No Nay Never - Saucy Spirit (Invincible Spirit)

Aidan O'Brien (Ire) — Tabor, Smith, Magnier & Westerberg

PLACINGS: 147- — RPR **102+**

Starts	1st	2nd	3rd	4th	Win & Pl
3	1	-	-	1	£11,847

4/21	Dund	5f Mdn 2yo stand	£7,375

Looked a potentially high-class colt early last

Broome (second right): big player in Group races over middle distances

season, winning well on debut and going off favourite for the Norfolk at Royal Ascot when beaten less than a length in fourth; only seventh in the Railway Stakes and didn't run again; looks a sprinter on pedigree.

Cairde Go Deo (Fr)

3 b f Camelot - Elusive Galaxy (Elusive City)

Ger Lyons (Ire) — Mark Dobbin

PLACINGS: 216- — RPR **94**

Starts	1st	2nd	3rd	4th	Win & Pl
3	1	1	-	-	£20,227

	Date	Course	Race	Prize
	8/21	Curr	7f 2yo yield	£14,750

Impressive when getting off the mark at the Curragh on second run last season (won by four and a half lengths); sent off favourite for the Moyglare on strength of that run only to finish a disappointing sixth; should prove much better.

Came From The Dark (Ire)

6 gr g Dark Angel - Silver Shoon (Fasliyev)

Ed Walker — P K Siu

PLACINGS: 91267812/02107/3121- — RPR **115**

Starts	1st	2nd	3rd	4th	Win & Pl
19	5	4	2	1	£123,794

	Date	Course	Race	Prize
	7/21	Sand	5f Cls1 Gp3 gd-sft	£45,368
101	4/21	Newb	5f Cls2 94-105 Hcap good	£9,793
95	9/20	Hayd	5f Cls2 80-97 Hcap good	£24,900
80	9/19	Hayd	5f Cls4 70-86 Hcap soft	£6,469
75	6/19	Hayd	6f Cls4 67-82 3yo Hcap heavy	£7,116

Smart and progressive sprinter who won twice last season, most notably when landing a first Group win at Sandown, either side of a near miss in the Palace House Stakes; plagued by injuries later in the year, missing several Group 1 targets over 5f and 6f.

Castle Star (Ire)

3 b c Starspangledbanner - Awohaam (Iffraaj)

Fozzy Stack (Ire) — Craig Bernick & Antony Beck

PLACINGS: 2211242- — RPR **113+**

Starts	1st	2nd	3rd	4th	Win & Pl
7	2	4	-	1	£134,793

	Date	Course	Race	Prize
	5/21	Curr	6f Gp3 2yo sft-hvy	£26,339
	5/21	Curr	5f List 2yo yield	£19,754

Ran a huge race when a half-length second behind Perfect Power in last season's Middle Park Stakes; had begun to look exposed during a busy campaign prior to that, finishing second in the Railway Stakes and fourth in the Phoenix after wins at Group 3 and Listed level.

Caturra (Ire)

3 b c Mehmas - Shoshoni Wind (Sleeping Indian)

Clive Cox — Saeed Bin Mohammed Al Qassimi

PLACINGS: 41717215- — RPR **111**

Starts	1st	2nd	3rd	4th	Win & Pl
8	3	1	-	1	£104,621

	Date	Course	Race	Prize
	9/21	Donc	5f Cls1 Gp2 2yo gd-fm	£63,799
	7/21	Newb	6f Cls1 List 2yo good	£17,013
	5/21	Bath	5f Cls5 2yo gd-sft	£2,862

Progressive two-year-old last season, benefiting from switch to hold-up tactics and producing a fine late burst to win the Flying Childers Stakes; ran equally well in defeat when a close fifth in the Middle Park; held in high regard by a trainer noted for his sprinters.

Chil Chil

6 b m Exceed And Excel - Tiana (Diktat)

Andrew Balding — King Power Racing Co

PLACINGS: 271131/21534/211953- — RPR **115**

Starts	1st	2nd	3rd	4th	Win & Pl
18	6	3	3	2	£161,546

	Date	Course	Race	Prize
	6/21	Newc	6f Cls1 Gp3 stand	£39,697
97	5/21	NmkR	6f Cls2 92-98 Hcap gd-fm	£18,039
85	8/20	Asct	6f Cls2 85-98 Hcap gd-fm	£12,938
78	9/19	NmkR	6f Cls2 72-92 Hcap good	£31,125
69	9/19	Wind	6f Cls5 57-73 Hcap gd-fm	£3,429
63	8/19	Kemp	6f Cls6 56-67 3yo Hcap std-slw	£3,105

Smart and progressive sprinter who graduated from handicap company to Group 1 level last season, winning a 6f Group 3 at Newcastle along the way; got steadily closer in three Group 1 races and beaten less than a length when third in the Sprint Cup at Haydock.

Chindit (Ire)

4 b c Wootton Bassett - Always A Dream (Oasis Dream)

Richard Hannon — Michael Pescod

PLACINGS: 1119/155543- — RPR **115**

Starts	1st	2nd	3rd	4th	Win & Pl
10	4	-	1	1	£147,523

	Date	Course	Race	Prize
	4/21	Newb	7f Cls1 Gp3 3yo good	£31,191
	9/20	Donc	7f Cls1 Gp2 2yo good	£35,520
	7/20	Asct	7f Cls1 List 2yo gd-fm	£11,342
	7/20	Donc	7f Cls5 Mdn 2yo good	£4,140

Won the Craven Stakes first time out last season but unable to build on that subsequently; finished fifth in three Group 1 races and little better when dropped in class, though unsuited by drop to 7f when third in the Challenge Stakes on final run; might appreciate 1m2f.

Feeding Fibre for Health & Performance

Feeding isn't simply a case of supplying energy and nutrients, it's also vital for supporting health and well-being. At Dengie, we have a range of premium quality fibre feeds that promote digestive health, provide energy and supply quality protein for top line and muscle tone.

ALFA-A OIL

Ultimate pure alfalfa, high-fibre feed for fuelling work and promoting condition

PERFORMANCE FIBRE

A tasty blend of alfalfa and grass, to tempt picky performance horses

ALFA-A ORIGINAL

A pure alfalfa fibre feed naturally abundant in calcium for bone development

Dengie

Discover more at **www.dengie.com**

01621 841 188

Claymore (Fr)

3 b c New Bay - Brit Wit (High Chaparral)

Jane Chapple-Hyam — Mrs Mary Slack

PLACINGS: 1- — RPR **93+**

Starts	1st	2nd	3rd	4th	Win & Pl
1	1	-	-	-	£4,860

	Date	Course	Race	Prize
	10/21	NmkR	7f Cls4 2yo soft	£4,860

Hacked up by four lengths on sole start at Newmarket last season, landing a major touch (backed down from big prices overnight) and belying £10,000 breeze-ups price; bred for middle distances (out of a High Chaparral mare who won over 1m4f) and looks exciting.

Commanche Falls

5 br g Lethal Force - Joyeaux (Mark Of Esteem)

Michael Dods — Doug Graham, Ian Davison, Alan Drysdale

PLACINGS: 746/109116/14141170- — RPR **111**

Starts	1st	2nd	3rd	4th	Win & Pl
18	8	-	-	3	£167,218

RPR	Date	Course	Race	Prize
101	7/21	Gdwd	6f Cls2 94-109 Hcap soft	£115,965
95	7/21	Haml	6f Cls2 82-99 Hcap good	£15,462
90	6/21	Ripn	6f Cls3 81-90 Hcap gd-fm	£6,443
84	4/21	Ayr	6f Cls3 78-96 Hcap gd-fm	£6,210
82	9/20	Hayd	6f Cls3 75-90 Hcap good	£9,057
77	9/20	Hayd	6f Cls5 61-77 Hcap soft	£3,429
73	6/20	Thsk	6f Cls5 65-74 3yo Hcap gd-sft	£3,493
	6/19	Thsk	6f Cls5 Mdn Auct 2yo gd-sft	£3,946

Hugely progressive sprint handicapper during the last two seasons and peaked with victory in

Claymore (left) leads the way before scoring on his debut at Newmarket in October

last year's Stewards' Cup at Goodwood (fourth win of 2021 and sixth in last nine starts at the time); twice beaten subsequently, though still a fair seventh in the Ayr Gold Cup.

Concert Hall (Ire)

3 b f Dubawi - Was (Galileo)

Aidan O'Brien (Ire) — Smith, Magnier, Tabor & Westerberg

PLACINGS: 217416- — RPR **106**

Starts	1st	2nd	3rd	4th	Win & Pl
6	2	1	-	1	£54,870
9/21	Curr	7f Gp3 2yo good			£26,339
7/21	Curr	7f Mdn 2yo good			£8,692

Patchy form last season (beaten favourite either side of maiden win) but showed potential by making amends in a Group 3 at the Curragh; did well to win that race over 7f given strong middle-distance pedigree, though only sixth when stepped up in trip for Fillies' Mile.

Contarelli Chapel (Ire)

3 gr f Caravaggio - Chenchikova (Sadler's Wells)

Aidan O'Brien (Ire) — Westerberg, Magnier, Tabor & Smith

PLACINGS: 14- — RPR **93+**

Starts	1st	2nd	3rd	4th	Win & Pl
2	1	-	-	1	£10,593
4/21	Naas	6f Mdn 2yo good			£8,165

Looked a potentially high-class filly when hacking up first time out last season; sent off just 2-7 in a Group 3 at Naas in May but was a well-beaten fourth and didn't run again; set to come back from long layoff and remains a fascinating prospect.

Coroebus (Ire)

3 b c Dubawi - First Victory (Teofilo)

Charlie Appleby **Godolphin**

PLACINGS: 121- RPR **116+**

Starts	1st	2nd	3rd	4th	Win & Pl
3	2	1	-	-	£60,980

10/21	NmkR	1m Cls1 Gp3 2yo good	£34,026
8/21	NmkJ	1m Cls4 2yo gd-fm	£5,454

Hugely promising two-year-old last season when shaping even better than solid race record; nailed close home in the Royal Lodge having tanked clear with a fine turn of foot and easily made amends in the Autumn Stakes when ridden with slightly more restraint; looks a pure miler.

Creative Flair (Ire)

4 b f Dubawi - Hidden Gold (Shamardal)

Charlie Appleby **Godolphin**

PLACINGS: 61/121334-1 RPR **108**

Starts	1st	2nd	3rd	4th	Win & Pl
9	4	1	2	1	£223,149

2/22	Meyd	1m1f Gp2 good	£80,000
6/21	Newb	1m2f Cls1 List 3yo gd-fm	£26,654
4/21	Asct	1m Cls3 3yo gd-fm	£8,370
8/20	Sand	7f Cls5 Mdn 2yo gd-sft	£4,140

Progressive filly last season who won a 1m2f Listed race at Newbury; knocking on the door at Group level subsequently (beaten a head and a nose at Chantilly) before breaking through at Meydan this winter.

Creative Force (Ire)

4 ch g Dubawi - Choose Me (Choisir)

Charlie Appleby — Godolphin

PLACINGS: 10/11115261- — RPR **121+**

Starts	1st	2nd	3rd	4th	Win & Pl
10	6	1	-	-	£445,888

	10/21	Asct	6f Cls1 Gp1 gd-sft	£301,272
	6/21	Asct	7f Cls1 Gp3 3yo soft	£44,400
	5/21	Newb	6f Cls1 List 3yo gd-sft	£22,684
97	5/21	NmkR	6f Cls2 86-97 3yo Hcap gd-fm	£10,800
89	4/21	NmkR	6f Cls2 76-95 3yo Hcap gd-fm	£10,800
	6/20	NmkR	6f Cls5 Mdn 2yo gd-fm	£3,493

Proved himself a Group I horse when winning last season's Champions Sprint on third run at the top level; had made rapid strides early in the season, completing a four-timer in the Jersey Stakes; has won three times on good to firm but gained two big Ascot wins with some cut.

Desert Crown

3 b c Nathaniel - Desert Berry (Green Desert)

Sir Michael Stoute — Saeed Suhail

PLACINGS: 1- — RPR **92+**

Starts	1st	2nd	3rd	4th	Win & Pl
1	1	-	-	-	£5,130

11/21	Nott	1m1½f Cls4 Mdn 2yo soft	£5,130

Well-bred colt who cost 280,000gns as a yearling and became a fifth winner out of five for his dam when storming home by five and a half lengths on sole start at Nottingham last season; looks a nice middle-distance type.

Dhabab (Ire)

3 ch c No Nay Never - Habbat Reeh (Mastercraftsman)

John & Thady Gosden — Poseidon Thoroughbred Racing

PLACINGS: 16345- — RPR **104**

Starts	1st	2nd	3rd	4th	Win & Pl
5	1	-	1	1	£32,359

6/21	Leic	6f Cls4 Mdn 2yo gd-fm	£4,266

Failed to live up to lofty expectations last season when a beaten favourite three times at Group 2 level despite winning only a Leicester maiden and finishing no better than third otherwise; still far from disgraced, including when fifth in the Dewhurst, and could yet do better.

Diligent Harry

4 b c Due Diligence - Harryana To (Compton Place)

Clive Cox — The Dilinquents

PLACINGS: 1121320- — RPR **112**

Starts	1st	2nd	3rd	4th	Win & Pl
7	3	2	1	-	£70,780

4/21	Ling	6f Cls2 3yo stand	£38,655
2/21	Kemp	5f Cls5 std-slw	£3,429
1/21	Wolv	6f Cls5 Mdn stand	£3,946

Sharply progressive on the all-weather early last year and showed he could handle quick turf when a neck second in the Hackwood Stakes at Newbury; disappointed on soft on only subsequent run when well backed for another Group 3 at Ascot; still very lightly raced.

Creative Force (left) makes light work of landing the Listed Carnarvon Stakes at Newbury

Discoveries (Ire)

3 b f Mastercraftsman - Alpha Lupi (Rahy)

Jessica Harrington (Ire) — Niarchos Family

PLACINGS: 4131- RPR **110**

Starts	1st	2nd	3rd	4th	Win & Pl
4	2	-	1	1	£175,352

	9/21	Curr	7f Gp1 2yo good	£158,036
	6/21	Curr	7f Mdn 2yo good	£8,692

Won last season's Moyglare Stud Stakes, joining superstar full-sister Alpha Centauri and half-sister Alpine Star as Group 1 winners; improved past Debutante winner Agartha having finished only fourth in that race, though beaten horses did little for form subsequently.

Dr Zempf

3 gr c Dark Angel - Souvenir Delondres (Siyouni)

Ger Lyons (Ire) — Peter M Brant

PLACINGS: 1428- RPR **111+**

Starts	1st	2nd	3rd	4th	Win & Pl
4	1	1	-	1	£57,571

	6/21	Curr	6f 2yo yield	£11,589

Didn't quite live up to initial promise last season but was very highly tried after debut win and again underlined potential with close second behind Ebro River in the Phoenix Stakes; failed to confirm that form when only eighth in the Middle Park (sent off just 9-2).

Dragon Symbol

4 gr c Cable Bay - Arcamist (Arcano)

Roger Varian — Yoshiro Kubota

PLACINGS: 111121d22340- RPR **119**

Starts	1st	2nd	3rd	4th	Win & Pl
11	4	4	1	1	£351,908

	5/21	Haml	5f Cls2 3yo gd-fm	£18,039
85	4/21	Kemp	6f Cls4 73-85 3yo Hcap std-slw	£4,347
	3/21	Newc	6f Cls5 std-slw	£3,429
	3/21	Wolv	6f Cls5 stand	£3,429

Quickly developed into a top-class sprinter last

Dream Of Dreams lands last season's Diamond Jubilee Stakes

season, winning his first four races and unlucky not to add a Group 1 prize; demoted to second in the Commonwealth Cup and filled that spot in the July Cup before also making the frame in the Nunthorpe and Flying Five; has since joined Roger Varian from Archie Watson.

Dream Of Dreams (Ire)

8 ch g Dream Ahead - Vasilia (Dansili)

Sir Michael Stoute — Saeed Suhail

PLACINGS: 2220/112080/2118/11- RPR **123**

Starts	1st	2nd	3rd	4th	Win & Pl
31	9	9	2	-	£945,802

	Date	Course	Race	Prize
	6/21	Asct	6f Cls1 Gp1 soft	£396,970
	5/21	Wind	6f Cls1 List soft	£22,684
	9/20	Hayd	6f Cls1 Gp1 soft	£133,200
	8/20	Newb	7f Cls1 Gp2 gd-sft	£34,026
	5/19	Wind	6f Cls1 List good	£20,983
	4/19	Chmf	6f Cls2 stand	£16,173
	11/17	Donc	6f Cls1 List soft	£22,684
	9/17	Ling	7f Cls3 gd-sft	£9,767
	5/16	Hayd	6f Cls4 2yo gd-sft	£4,270

Brilliant veteran sprinter who has won Group 1 races in each of the last two seasons; won last year's Diamond Jubilee Stakes to make up for a near miss in 2020, having broken through in the Sprint Cup at Haydock in between, but missed the rest of the year through injury.

Dubai Honour (Ire)

4 b g Pride Of Dubai - Mondelice (Montjeu)

William Haggas — Mohamed Obaida

PLACINGS: 4214/411124- RPR **122+**

Starts	1st	2nd	3rd	4th	Win & Pl
10	4	2	-	4	£789,046

	Date	Course	Race	Prize
	10/21	Lonc	1m2f Gp2 v soft	£101,786
	8/21	Deau	1m2f Gp2 3yo gd-sft	£203,571
93	7/21	NmkJ	1m2f Cls2 85-102 3yo Hcap gd-fm	£38,655
	9/20	Hayd	1m Cls4 2yo good	£5,175

Hugely progressive last season, adding a pair of Group 2 wins in France to handicap success at Newmarket before a close second in the Champion Stakes; ran a fine race when an unlucky fourth in the Hong Kong Vase to fuel further international ambitions for connections.

Dubawi Legend (Ire)

3 b c Dubawi - Lovely Pass (Raven's Pass)

Hugo Palmer — Dr Ali Ridha

PLACINGS: 1320- RPR **115**

Starts	1st	2nd	3rd	4th	Win & Pl
4	1	1	1	-	£135,009

	Date	Course	Race	Prize
	7/21	Donc	7f Cls5 2yo gd-fm	£3,780

Ran a huge race when second behind Native Trail in last season's Dewhurst Stakes, staying on well having raced keenly in front; slightly disappointing in two other Group assignments following a winning debut, though very badly drawn at the Breeders' Cup.

Duke De Sessa (Ire)

3 b c Lope De Vega - Dark Crusader (Cape Cross)

Dermot Weld (Ire) — Newtown Anner Stud Farm

PLACINGS: 3161- RPR **106+**

Starts	1st	2nd	3rd	4th	Win & Pl
4	2	-	1	-	£39,562

	Date	Course	Race	Prize
	10/21	Leop	1m1f Gp3 2yo good	£26,339
	8/21	Curr	1m Mdn 2yo soft	£9,219

Impressive winner of a 1m1f Group 3 at Leopardstown on final run last season; had also won a maiden in good style only to finish an underwhelming sixth in the National Stakes; trainer plans to come back to a mile but should get a lot further (dam won twice over 1m6f).

Ebro River (Ire)

3 ch c Galileo Gold - Soft Power (Balmont)

Hugo Palmer — Al Shaqab Racing

PLACINGS: 611544138- RPR **113**

Starts	1st	2nd	3rd	4th	Win & Pl
9	3	-	1	2	£186,854

	Date	Course	Race	Prize
	8/21	Curr	6f Gp1 2yo yield	£131,696
	5/21	Sand	5f Cls1 List 2yo soft	£14,461
	5/21	Donc	5f Cls4 2yo soft	£3,726

Surprise winner of last season's Phoenix Stakes at the Curragh, benefiting from a front-running ride and prime position on the rail to land sole win from six attempts at Group level; probably flattered by that form but still far from disgraced when third in the National Stakes.

Egot (Ire)

4 b c Invincible Spirit - Entertains (Street Cry)

Andre Fabre (Fr) Godolphin

PLACINGS: 81/21711- RPR **118+**

Starts	1st	2nd	3rd	4th	Win & Pl
7	4	1	-	-	£96,266
10/21	Chan	6f Gp3 v soft			£35,714
10/21	StCl	7f List 3yo soft			£24,554
8/21	Deau	1m List 3yo good			£24,554
12/20	Porn	1m½f 2yo stand			£6,695

Progressive and versatile French colt; won beyond a mile as a two-year-old but gradually dropped back in trip throughout last season and signed off with a 6f Group 3 victory at Chantilly to follow Listed wins over a mile and 7f; smart prospect.

El Bodegon (Ire)

3 b c Kodiac - Al Andalyya (Kingmambo)

James Ferguson Nas Syndicate & A F O'Callaghan

PLACINGS: 21311- RPR **111+**

Starts	1st	2nd	3rd	4th	Win & Pl
5	3	1	1	-	£181,147
10/21	StCl	1m2f Gp1 2yo v soft			£127,545
9/21	Chan	1m1f Gp3 2yo soft			£35,714
7/21	Sand	7f Cls4 2yo heavy			£5,400

Fairytale maiden Group 1 winner for young trainer in last season's Criterium de Saint-Cloud, capping a fine autumn in France having also won at Chantilly; looks a very strong stayer having already won over 1m2f; has gained all three wins on soft ground or worse.

Eldar Eldarov

3 b c Dubawi - All At Sea (Sea The Stars)

Roger Varian KHK Racing

PLACINGS: 1- RPR **94+**

Starts	1st	2nd	3rd	4th	Win & Pl
1	1	-	-	-	£3,780
10/21	Nott	1m½f Cls5 Mdn 2yo gd-sft			£3,780

Cost £480,000 at the breeze-ups and justified the outlay when running to a big Racing Post Rating for a debutant on his sole run at Nottingham last season, winning by five lengths; looks a fine prospect for middle distances.

Emaraaty Ana

6 b g Shamardal - Spirit Of Dubai (Cape Cross)

Kevin Ryan Sheikh Mohammed Obaid Al Maktoum

PLACINGS: /0051/338/233701214- RPR **121**

Starts	1st	2nd	3rd	4th	Win & Pl
20	5	2	5	1	£473,297
9/21	Hayd	6f Cls1 Gp1 gd-fm			£162,800
7/21	Haml	5f Cls3 gd-fm			£8,504
9/19	Sals	6f Cls3 gd-fm			£8,733
8/18	York	6f Cls1 Gp2 2yo gd-fm			£127,598
4/18	Wind	5f Cls4 2yo good			£4,787

Rejuvenated last season after gelding and wind operations and peaked with a narrow victory in the Sprint Cup at Haydock; had looked faster than ever when excelling over 5f previously, finishing a fine second in the Nunthorpe; has gained all five wins on good or firmer ground.

Eshaada (left) leads before winning the Champions Fillies & Mares Stakes

Eshaada

4 b f Muhaarar - Muhawalah (Nayef)

Roger Varian — Shadwell Estate Company

PLACINGS: 1/1271- — RPR **116**

Starts	1st	2nd	3rd	4th	Win & Pl
5	3	1	-	-	£364,603

	10/21	Asct	1m4f Cls1 Gp1 gd-sft	£283,550
	5/21	Newb	1m2f Cls1 List 3yo gd-sft	£39,697
	11/20	Nott	1m½f Cls5 Mdn 2yo soft	£4,075

Very lightly raced filly who twice excelled at Ascot last season, notably when a 16-1 winner of the Champions Fillies & Mares Stakes; had run just once (disappointing in the Yorkshire Oaks) since a fine second in the Ribblesdale Stakes; big, scopey filly with more to come.

Euchen Glen

9 b g Authorized - Jabbara (Kingmambo)

Jim Goldie — W M Johnstone

PLACINGS: 65514110/8715125029- — RPR **119**

Starts	1st	2nd	3rd	4th	Win & Pl
44	12	4	5	1	£460,012

	7/21	Sand	1m2f Cls1 List good	£29,489
	5/21	Sand	1m2f Cls1 Gp3 soft	£34,026
	10/20	Newb	1m4f Cls1 Gp3 heavy	£28,355
	10/20	York	1m4f Cls1 Gp3 soft	£27,221
101	9/20	Hayd	1m6f Cls2 88-104 Hcap soft	£51,752
99	7/18	York	1m2½f Cls2 91-106 Hcap gd-fm	£124,500
94	6/18	Ayr	1m5f Cls2 81-103 Hcap good	£25,876
89	8/17	Asct	2m Cls2 84-97 Hcap gd-sft	£22,131
88	6/17	Ayr	1m5f Cls3 71-90 Hcap good	£9,057
83	5/17	Ayr	1m2f Cls4 71-83 Hcap gd-fm	£5,822
79	6/16	Ayr	1m2f Cls4 72-85 Hcap good	£6,469
74	6/16	Donc	1m4f Cls5 71-75 3yo Hcap gd-fm	£5,175

Evergreen veteran who was better than ever in first half of last season, winning 1m2f Group 3 and Listed races at Sandown by wide margins; finished second in two similar races later in the year, though also overfaced at times; versatile having also won up to 1m6f.

Ever Present (Ire)

6 b/br g Elusive Pimpernel - Persian Memories (Indian Ridge)

Jessica Harrington (Ire) — Anamoine

PLACINGS: 1121- — RPR **112+**

Starts	1st	2nd	3rd	4th	Win & Pl
4	3	1	-	-	£82,843

100	9/21	Leop	1m5f 78-100 Hcap good	£65,848
	7/21	Leop	1m7f good	£7,638
	6/21	Leop	1m7f Mdn gd-fm	£5,795

Progressive stayer who began life in bumpers but went from strength to strength when switched to the Flat last season, winning three out of four; dropped back in trip to win a 1m5f premier handicap at Leopardstown on Irish Champions Weekend under 10st on final run.

Fast Attack (Ire)

3 b f Kodiac - Fort Del Oro (Lope De Vega)

Simon & Ed Crisford — H H Shaikh Nasser Al Khalifa & F Nass

PLACINGS: 1531- — RPR **104**

Starts	1st	2nd	3rd	4th	Win & Pl
4	2	-	1	-	£45,483

	10/21	NmkR	7f Cls1 Gp3 2yo gd-sft	£34,026
	8/21	Kemp	7f Cls4 2yo std-slw	£5,400

All-the-way winner of the Oh So Sharp Stakes at Newmarket last season, belatedly living up to promise of six-length debut win; form only ordinary for the grade and had been beaten twice in between; not certain to get a mile on breeding.

Filistine (Ire)

3 b c Almanzor - Desire To Win (Lawman)

John & Thady Gosden — A Abukhadra

PLACINGS: 21- — RPR **96+**

Starts	1st	2nd	3rd	4th	Win & Pl
2	1	1	-	-	£7,935

	10/21	NmkR	7f Cls4 2yo good	£5,400

Showed promise in two runs over 7f at Newmarket last autumn; went close on debut before narrowly beating a next-time-out winner at the second attempt (pair six lengths clear); should get at least a mile on pedigree.

Flotus (Ire)

3 b f Starspangledbanner - Floriade (Invincible Spirit)

Simon & Ed Crisford — Katsumi Yoshida

PLACINGS: 106612- — RPR **113**

Starts	1st	2nd	3rd	4th	Win & Pl
6	2	1	-	-	£91,587

	8/21	Ripn	6f Cls1 List 2yo good	£24,102
	5/21	Gdwd	6f Cls4 Mdn 2yo soft	£4,860

Took a long time to build on wide-margin debut win last season but got back on track in late summer, winning a Listed race at Ripon and finishing second in the Cheveley Park before being sold for one million guineas.

Forbearance (Ire)

5 b m Galileo - Nechita (Fastnet Rock)

Jessica Harrington (Ire) — Newtown Anner Stud Farm

PLACINGS: 6/14313131- — RPR **110**

Starts	1st	2nd	3rd	4th	Win & Pl
9	4	-	3	1	£119,091

	9/21	NmkR	1m4f Cls1 Gp3 gd-fm	£45,368
	8/21	York	1m4f Cls1 List good	£39,697
76	6/21	DRoy	1m4½f 68-79 Hcap gd-fm	£12,379
	2/21	Dund	1m Mdn stand	£5,795

Progressive mare who flourished when stepped up to 1m4f last season, winning three of her last five races; finished notably strongly when a clearcut winner of a Group 3 at Newmarket (rare winner from off the pace at the meeting) to add to Listed victory at York.

Foxes Tales (Ire)

4 b c Zoffany - Starfish (Galileo)

Andrew Balding — King Power Racing Co

PLACINGS: 2/1512127- — RPR **116**

Starts	1st	2nd	3rd	4th	Win & Pl
8	3	3	-	-	£120,273

	8/21	Hayd	1m2½f Cls1 Gp3 soft	£45,368
93	6/21	Asct	1m2f Cls2 88-101 3yo Hcap soft	£33,501
	4/21	Newb	1m Cls4 Mdn 3yo good	£5,400

Progressed into a smart Group 3 performer last season having landed a 1m2f handicap at Royal Ascot; won the Rose of Lancaster Stakes at Haydock before being touched off under a penalty at Newbury; well beaten when stepped up in class for the Champion Stakes.

Frantastic

3 b c Frankel - Rhadegunda (Pivotal)

John & Thady Gosden — A E Oppenheimer

PLACINGS: 31- — RPR **86+aw**

Starts	1st	2nd	3rd	4th	Win & Pl
2	1	-	1	-	£7,476

	10/21	Newc	1m Cls5 2yo stand	£3,672

Showed promise in two runs last season; didn't quite live up to market expectations when third on debut at Doncaster's St Leger meeting but made amends when hacking up at Newcastle, albeit still looking green; looks a surefire improver.

Free Wind (Ire)

4 b f Galileo - Alive Alive Oh (Duke Of Marmalade)

John & Thady Gosden — George Strawbridge

PLACINGS: 4/11211- — RPR **113**

Starts	1st	2nd	3rd	4th	Win & Pl
6	4	1	-	1	£117,462

	9/21	Donc	1m6½f Cls1 Gp2 gd-fm	£62,381
	8/21	Deau	1m4½f Gp3 3yo good	£35,714
	6/21	Donc	1m2f Cls5 gd-sft	£3,024
	6/21	Gdwd	1m2f Cls4 Mdn good	£4,860

Smart and progressive filly who won four out of five races last season, culminating in a runaway victory in the Park Hill Stakes at Doncaster on quick ground; took a big step forward when stepped up to 1m6f that day but smart turn of foot a potential weapon over 1m4f.

Geocentric (Ire)

3 b f Kodiac - Rajmahal (Indian Ridge)

Ger Lyons (Ire) — SBA Racing

PLACINGS: 21231- — RPR **105+aw**

Starts	1st	2nd	3rd	4th	Win & Pl
5	2	2	1	-	£51,385

	10/21	Dund	5f List 2yo stand	£25,022
	7/21	Navn	5f Mdn 2yo good	£8,165

Impressive winner of a 6f Listed race at Dundalk on final run last season; had hinted at that kind of performance earlier in the season, notably when second behind Sacred Bridge in a Curragh Group 3, but seemingly found good to firm ground too quick when a beaten favourite at Ayr.

Glen Shiel

8 ch g Pivotal - Gonfilia (Big Shuffle)

Archie Watson — Hambleton Racing & Partner

PLACINGS: 13720121121/4260052- — RPR **119**

Starts	1st	2nd	3rd	4th	Win & Pl
34	8	9	1	4	£721,152

	10/20	Asct	6f Cls1 Gp1 soft	£221,884
	8/20	Curr	6f Gp3 gd-yld	£25,000
	8/20	Newc	6f Cls3 stand	£6,728
100	6/20	Newc	6f Cls2 85-103 Hcap stand	£9,704
96	1/20	Newc	7f Cls3 83-96 Hcap std-slw	£12,602
	10/17	Chan	1m1f List 3yo v soft	£23,504
	5/17	Pari	1m 3yo soft	£12,051
	11/16	StCl	7½f 2yo heavy	£9,926

High-class sprinter who enjoyed his finest hour

when winning the 2020 Champions Sprint at Ascot on soft ground; failed to win last season but produced best runs with cut in the ground at Ascot again, finishing second in the Diamond Jubilee and Champions Sprint.

Glorious Journey

7 b g Dubawi - Fallen For You (Dansili)

Charlie Appleby — Sheikha Al Jalila Racing

PLACINGS: 2819/139513/3431031- RPR **116**

Starts	1st	2nd	3rd	4th	Win & Pl
27	8	2	6	3	£562,100
9/21	Donc	7f Cls1 Gp2 gd-sft			£62,381
6/21	NmkJ	7f Cls1 Gp3 gd-fm			£34,026
9/20	Newb	7f Cls1 List good			£15,737
1/20	Meyd	7f Gp2 good			£112,782
8/19	Newb	7f Cls1 Gp2 soft			£56,710
8/18	Deau	1m Gp3 3yo gd-sft			£35,398
9/17	StCl	7f Gp3 2yo good			£34,188
6/17	NmkJ	6f Cls4 2yo good			£4,528

Six-time Group winner who added to haul by landing the Criterion and Park Stakes last season over specialist trip of 7f as well as finishing third in similar races at York and Haydock; has won over a mile but well beaten for a second time in the July Cup when dropped to 6f.

Glounthaune (Ire)

3 b c Kodiac - Khaimah (Nayef)

Aidan O'Brien (Ire) — Mrs E M Stockwell, Coolmore & Westerberg

PLACINGS: 1610- RPR **104+**

Starts	1st	2nd	3rd	4th	Win & Pl
4	2	-	-	-	£42,137
10/21	Leop	7f Gp3 2yo good			£26,339
4/21	Curr	6f Mdn 2yo good			£8,692

Highly tried last season, running in the Dewhurst Stakes on just his second run, but managed only sixth that day and disappointed again at the Breeders' Cup; justified ambitious campaign when winning a 7f Group 3 in between when described as having a "huge future" by rider.

Go Bears Go (Ire)

3 b c Kodi Bear - In Dubai (Giant's Causeway)

David Loughnane — Amo Racing & P Waney

PLACINGS: 1213472- RPR **112+**

Starts	1st	2nd	3rd	4th	Win & Pl
7	2	2	1	1	£234,471
6/21	Curr	6f Gp2 2yo good			£52,679
5/21	Asct	5f Cls3 2yo soft			£5,400

Breakthrough winner for young trainer in last season's Railway Stakes following a near miss at Royal Ascot; continued to run with distinction when beaten no more than a length in three Group 1 races; sole poor run when stepped up to 7f in the National Stakes.

Golden Lyra (Ire)

3 ch f Lope De Vega - Sea The Sun (Sea The Stars)

William Haggas — Sunderland Holding

PLACINGS: 1- RPR **88+**

Starts	1st	2nd	3rd	4th	Win & Pl
1	1	-	-	-	£5,400
10/21	NmkR	7f Cls4 2yo good			£5,400

Hugely impressive winner of sole start at Newmarket last season, scooting clear by five lengths in what looked a warm 7f novice; bred for much further (half-sister to dual 1m4f winner out of unraced half-sister to Sea The Moon) so should thrive over middle distances.

Goldspur (Ire)

3 b c Dubawi - Pomology (Arch)

Charlie Appleby — Godolphin

PLACINGS: 113- RPR **107+**

Starts	1st	2nd	3rd	4th	Win & Pl
3	2	-	1	-	£64,939
10/21	NmkR	1m2f Cls1 Gp3 2yo good			£34,026
9/21	Sand	1m Cls4 2yo soft			£5,400

Narrow winner of last season's Zetland Stakes when stepped up to 1m2f but couldn't quite build on that when third in a Group 1 at Saint-Cloud (sent off favourite); has a strong staying pedigree and should thrive over at least 1m4f.

Great Ambassador

5 ch g Exceed And Excel - Snoqualmie Girl (Montjeu)

Ed Walker — Ebury Racing

PLACINGS: 22301/772/133112- RPR **116+**

	Starts	1st	2nd	3rd	4th	Win & Pl
	14	4	4	3	-	£139,066
	9/21	York	6f Cls1 List gd-fm			£29,489
97	8/21	NmkJ	6f Cls2 87-103 Hcap gd-fm			£13,500
90	3/21	Kemp	6f Cls2 89-103 Hcap std-slw			£9,793
	11/19	Chmf	7f Cls3 2yo stand			£10,350

Smart and progressive sprinter who was desperately unlucky not to win a big handicap last season, doing best of those on his side when second in the Ayr Gold Cup and third in the Stewards' Cup; still won three times, including a Listed race at York; best on quick ground.

Grocer Jack (Ger)

5 b h Oasis Dream - Good Donna (Doyen)

William Haggas — Prince Faisal Bin Khaled

PLACINGS: 42/223d534/412221-5 RPR **113**

Starts	1st	2nd	3rd	4th	Win & Pl
15	2	6	1	3	£181,650
10/21	Hopp	1m2f Gp3 good			£26,786
5/21	Siro	1m2f Gp3 good			£26,116

Smart German middle-distance performer (dual

Group 3 winner and Group 1 runner-up) who was bought for 700,000gns last autumn and moved to William Haggas; finished fifth in Saudi Arabia on first run for new yard this year.

Gustavus Weston (Ire)

6 br g Equiano - Chrissycross (Cape Cross)

Joseph Murphy (Ire) — Alfred Sweetnam

PLACINGS: /82014/553/56612160- — RPR **115+**

Starts	1st	2nd	3rd	4th	Win & Pl
19	4	2	1	2	£162,430

	8/21	Curr	6f Gp3 yield	£26,339
	5/21	Curr	6f Gp2 sft-hvy	£52,679
	8/19	Curr	6f Gp3 soft	£31,892
	9/18	Fair	6f Mdn Auct 2yo gd-yld	£10,903

Bounced back to form last season when winning two 6f Group races at the Curragh, making all impressively in the Phoenix Sprint; also dropped to 5f for the first time and finished a good second in a Group 2, although only sixth in the Flying Five.

Hafit (Ire)

3 b c Dubawi - Cushion (Galileo)

Charlie Appleby — Godolphin

PLACINGS: 123- — RPR **106**

Starts	1st	2nd	3rd	4th	Win & Pl
3	1	1	1	-	£20,617

	8/21	NmkJ	7f Cls4 Mdn 2yo good	£5,454

Promising two-year-old last season; narrow debut winner at Newmarket and stepped up on a Listed second at Haydock (hung left on good to firm ground) with a neck third in the Zetland Stakes when stepped up to 1m2f; useful prospect for middle distances.

Hamish

6 b g Motivator - Tweed (Sakhee)

William Haggas — B Haggas

PLACINGS: 213112/4/147- — RPR **115**aw

Starts	1st	2nd	3rd	4th	Win & Pl
10	4	2	1	2	£234,132

	9/21	Kemp	1m4f Cls1 Gp3 std-slw	£45,368
98	10/19	York	1m6f Cls2 77-98 3yo Hcap soft	£62,250
92	8/19	York	1m6f Cls2 80-96 3yo Hcap gd-fm	£77,813
	6/19	Wind	1m2f Cls5 gd-sft	£3,752

Returned from a long layoff last season with a surprise Group 3 win over Hukum over 1m4f at Kempton; had been seen as more of a stayer (won twice over 1m6f as a three-year-old) but didn't appear to last over 2m when fourth in the Long Distance Cup.

Hannibal Barca (Ire)

3 b c Zoffany - Innocent Air (Galileo)

Joseph O'Brien (Ire) — Ecurie Ama Zingteam

PLACINGS: 314- — RPR **111**

Starts	1st	2nd	3rd	4th	Win & Pl
3	1	-	1	1	£17,860

	9/21	Sals	7f Cls4 2yo soft	£5,400

Sharply progressive in three runs for Brian Meehan last season, getting off the mark on his second run in a Salisbury novice before taking a huge leap forward to finish fourth in the Vertem Futurity Trophy; a Group 1 colt according to Meehan but has since moved to Joseph O'Brien following 500,000gns purchase.

Happy Power (Ire)

6 gr h Dark Angel - Tamarisk (Selkirk)

Andrew Balding — King Power Racing Co

PLACINGS: 56/3241119/3549368-6 — RPR **115**

Starts	1st	2nd	3rd	4th	Win & Pl
27	7	1	6	4	£352,726

	10/20	NmkR	7f Cls1 Gp2 soft	£61,814
	8/20	Gdwd	7f Cls1 Gp3 gd-sft	£25,520
	8/20	Sals	7f Cls2 gd-fm	£9,704
	6/19	York	1m Cls1 List soft	£28,355
93	4/19	Newb	7f Cls2 80-96 3yo Hcap soft	£12,450
83	10/18	Donc	7f Cls3 74-95 2yo Hcap gd-sft	£7,116
	8/18	Haml	6f Cls4 Mdn 2yo good	£5,434

Progressed as a 7f specialist in 2020, winning two Group races, but struggled to make the same impact last season when mixing up trips; finished a half-length third in the Lennox Stakes on sole run over 7f and fourth in the Diamond Jubilee; disappointed in all four runs over a mile.

Happy Romance (Ire)

4 b f Dandy Man - Rugged Up (Marju)

Richard Hannon — The McMurray Family

PLACINGS: 6151114/01503140-3 — RPR **114**

Starts	1st	2nd	3rd	4th	Win & Pl
16	6	-	2	2	£400,163

	7/21	Newb	6f Cls1 Gp3 gd-fm	£39,697
	4/21	Chmf	6f Cls1 List 3yo stand	£17,013
	9/20	Sals	6f Cls1 Gp3 2yo good	£17,864
	8/20	York	6f Cls2 2yo gd-sft	£88,524
	7/20	Newb	5f Cls2 2yo good	£84,966
	6/20	Sand	5f Cls5 Mdn 2yo good	£4,140

Won Group 3 and Listed races last season, both over 6f, before confirming progress into a high-class sprinter with a length fourth in the Sprint Cup at Haydock; also effective over 5f and 7f judging by half-length thirds at Group 3 level at Sandown and in Saudi Arabia.

Helvic Dream (right): heading to victory in last season's Tattersalls Gold Cup

Hello You (Ire)

3 b f Invincible Spirit - Lucrece (Pivotal)

David Loughnane — Amo Racing

PLACINGS: 1236415- RPR **108**

Starts	1st	2nd	3rd	4th	Win & Pl
7	2	1	1	1	£105,277

9/21	NmkR	7f Cls1 Gp2 2yo gd-fm	£51,039
5/21	Wolv	6f Cls5 2yo stand	£2,862

Highly tried last season, with six of seven races coming in Group company, and landed sole win at that level in the Rockfel Stakes at Newmarket; beat similarly battle-hardened fillies in a race lacking an obvious star and limitations seemingly exposed again at Breeders' Cup.

Helvic Dream (Ire)

5 b g Power - Rachevie (Danehill Dancer)

Noel Meade (Ire) — Mrs Caroline Hendron & Mrs M Cahill

PLACINGS: 3311/2383318/8421- RPR **114**

Starts	1st	2nd	3rd	4th	Win & Pl
15	4	2	5	1	£247,369

5/21	Curr	1m2½f Gp1 sft-hvy	£158,036
10/20	Curr	1m2f Gp3 soft	£25,000
9/19	Rosc	7½f 2yo heavy	£10,649
8/19	Rosc	7½f 2yo soft	£13,288

Won last season's Tattersalls Gold Cup, making the most of preferred conditions to pip odds-on favourite Broome, but missed the rest of the year; has gained all four wins on ground from soft to heavy, with only other Group win at

the Curragh in 2020 rated 10lb higher than all previous form.

Hermana Estrella (Ire)

3 b f Starspangledbanner - The Last Sister (Lord Shanakill)

Fozzy Stack (Ire) — Paul D Smith, Joe Poulin & J Carthy

PLACINGS: 1- — RPR **103**

Starts	1st	2nd	3rd	4th	Win & Pl
1	1	-	-	-	£35,821
5/21	Naas	6f Gp3 2yo soft			£35,821

Remarkably managed to win a Group 3 at Naas on her only start as a two-year-old, justifying connections' huge faith despite odds of 50-1; missed the rest of the year but form worked out well (runner-up Quick Suzy won the Queen Mary); looks a sprinter on pedigree.

High Definition (Ire)

4 b c Galileo - Palace (Fastnet Rock)

Aidan O'Brien (Ire) — Tabor, Smith, Magnier & Westerberg

PLACINGS: 11/3069- — RPR **110**

Starts	1st	2nd	3rd	4th	Win & Pl
6	2	-	1	-	£68,029
9/20	Curr	1m Gp2 2yo gd-yld			£40,000
8/20	Curr	1m Mdn 2yo soft			£8,250

Winter favourite for last season's Derby but proved a big disappointment, missing Epsom after finishing only third in the Dante and regressing from there; sixth when favourite for the Great Voltigeur and ninth in the St Leger having been supplemented; surely capable of better.

Highest Ground (Ire)

5 b g Frankel - Celestial Lagoon (Sunday Silence)

Sir Michael Stoute — Niarchos Family

PLACINGS: 1/120/6195- RPR **105**

Starts	1st	2nd	3rd	4th	Win & Pl
8	3	1	-	-	£31,698

	Date	Course	Race	Prize
	6/21	Leic	1m4f Cls3 gd-fm	£6,210
	6/20	Hayd	1m2½f Cls5 good	£3,493
	9/19	Leic	7f Cls3 2yo gd-fm	£6,469

Looked a top middle-distance prospect at one stage and finished a neck second when odds-on for the Dante Stakes in 2020; hasn't gone on from there, winning only a modest conditions race at Leicester at odds-on; has been gelded since last run.

History (Ire)

3 b f Galileo - Prize Exhibit (Showcasing)

Aidan O'Brien (Ire) — Tabor, Smith, Magnier & Westerberg

PLACINGS: 221- RPR **93+**

Starts	1st	2nd	3rd	4th	Win & Pl
3	1	2	-	-	£15,290

	Date	Course	Race	Prize
	9/21	Gowr	1m Mdn 2yo yield	£8,165

Cost 2.8 million guineas as a yearling and made steady progress in three runs as a two-year-old last season; bumped into smart sorts when second on first two runs before appreciating the step up to a mile when easily off the mark at Gowran Park; should stay 1m2f.

Homeless Songs (Ire)

3 b f Frankel - Joailliere (Dubawi)

Dermot Weld (Ire) — Moyglare Stud Farm

PLACINGS: 156- RPR **99**

Starts	1st	2nd	3rd	4th	Win & Pl
3	1	-	-	-	£14,495

	Date	Course	Race	Prize
	7/21	Leop	7f Mdn 2yo good	£8,692

Looked a very exciting filly (and talked up by trainer) when making a winning debut at Leopardstown last season; failed to live up to market expectations in two subsequent runs, finishing fifth when 9-4 for the Moyglare and sixth when 6-4 favourite back at Group 3 level.

Hoo Ya Mal

3 b c Territories - Sensationally (Montjeu)

Andrew Balding — Ahmad Al Shaikh

PLACINGS: 312- RPR **105**

Starts	1st	2nd	3rd	4th	Win & Pl
3	1	1	1	-	£45,946

	Date	Course	Race	Prize
	8/21	York	7f Cls2 Mdn 2yo gd-fm	£36,078

Impressive winner of the valuable Convivial Maiden at York last season and very nearly followed up in a Listed race at Doncaster on only subsequent run (winner finished second in a Group 1 next time); should stay beyond a mile.

Hukum (Ire)

5 b h Sea The Stars - Aghareed (Kingmambo)

Owen Burrows — Shadwell Estate Company

PLACINGS: 31/115/4131121- RPR **121+**

Starts	1st	2nd	3rd	4th	Win & Pl
12	7	1	2	1	£270,281

	Date	Course	Race	Prize
	10/21	Asct	1m4f Cls1 Gp3 soft	£45,368
	8/21	Newb	1m5½f Cls1 Gp3 good	£39,697
	7/21	York	1m6f Cls1 Gp3 good	£45,368
	5/21	Gdwd	1m4f Cls1 List soft	£22,684
	8/20	Newb	1m5½f Cls1 Gp3 gd-sft	£20,983
90	6/20	Asct	1m4f Cls2 79-100 3yo Hcap good	£38,814
	11/19	Kemp	1m Cls4 2yo std-slw	£10,350

Progressive middle-distance performer who won four times last season, the last three at Group 3 level; most impressive when storming to a wide-margin win in the Cumberland Lodge Stakes at Ascot on soft ground, though has also proved effective on good.

Hurricane Ivor (Ire)

5 b g Ivawood - Quickstep Queen (Royal Applause)

William Haggas — Ms Fiona Carmichael

PLACINGS: 17/17541d5/01203118- RPR **114**

Starts	1st	2nd	3rd	4th	Win & Pl
16	5	1	1	1	£143,390

	Date	Course	Race	Prize
	9/21	Newb	5f Cls1 Gp3 good	£39,697
102	9/21	Donc	5½f Cls2 87-102 Hcap gd-sft	£38,655
94	7/21	Sand	5f Cls3 77-94 Hcap gd-sft	£9,464
	5/20	Chan	6f 3yo gd-sft	£10,508
	5/19	Chan	5f 2yo gd-sft	£12,162

Smart and progressive sprinter who did well in handicaps last season, finally nailing a big one in the Portland, before making a successful step up to Group company at Newbury; found soft ground against him when a disappointing favourite in a Listed race at Ascot on final run.

Hurricane Lane (Ire)

4 ch c Frankel - Gale Force (Shirocco)

Charlie Appleby — Godolphin

PLACINGS: 1/1131113- RPR **125+**

Starts	1st	2nd	3rd	4th	Win & Pl
8	6	-	2	-	£1,980,000

	Date	Course	Race	Prize
	9/21	Donc	1m6½f Cls1 Gp1 3yo gd-sft	£421,355
	7/21	Lonc	1m4f Gp1 3yo v soft	£306,107
	6/21	Curr	1m4f Gp1 3yo good	£508,929
	5/21	York	1m2½f Cls1 Gp2 3yo good	£93,572
	4/21	Newb	1m2f Cls3 3yo good	£8,370
	10/20	NmkR	1m Cls2 2yo heavy	£10,350

Three-time Group 1 winner last season in between third-place finishes in the Derby and the Arc; arguably peaked with a six-length demolition job in the Grand Prix de Paris before adding the St Leger; just run out of Arc victory late on when sent off favourite at Longchamp.

Ilaraab (Ire)

5 b h Wootton Bassett - Belova (Soviet Star)

William Haggas — Sheikh Ahmed Al Maktoum

PLACINGS: 711111/180331- — RPR **115+**

Starts	1st	2nd	3rd	4th	Win & Pl
12	7	-	2	-	£131,675

	10/21	Newb	1m4f Cls1 Gp3 soft	£39,697
102	5/21	York	1m4f Cls2 83-103 Hcap gd-sft	£18,039
95	10/20	York	1m2½f Cls2 85-104 Hcap soft	£15,563
90	9/20	Newb	1m2f Cls2 82-101 Hcap good	£24,900
84	8/20	Bevl	1m2f Cls2 83-90 3yo Hcap soft	£9,704
	8/20	Wolv	1m1½f Cls5 std-slw	£3,493
	7/20	Thsk	1m Cls5 good	£4,140

Formerly prolific middle-distance performer who got back on track when winning a 1m4f Group 3 on final run last season at Newbury; had won six in a row when landing a York handicap first time out but progress stalled up in class and might have found a weak race for the grade.

Imperial Fighter (Ire)

3 b c The Gurkha - Endure (Green Desert)

Andrew Balding — Michael Blencowe

PLACINGS: 1225- — RPR **110**

Starts	1st	2nd	3rd	4th	Win & Pl
4	1	2	-	-	£47,485

	7/21	Gdwd	7f Cls2 Mdn 2yo soft	£13,085

Acquitted himself well in Group races last season following debut win; finished second behind subsequent Royal Lodge winner Royal Patronage in the Acomb Stakes and top-class prospect Coroebus in the Autumn Stakes before a fair fifth in the Vertem Futurity Trophy.

Inspiral

3 b f Frankel - Starscope (Selkirk)

John & Thady Gosden — Cheveley Park Stud

PLACINGS: 1111- — RPR **114+**

Starts	1st	2nd	3rd	4th	Win & Pl
4	4	-	-	-	£375,514

	10/21	NmkR	1m Cls1 Gp1 2yo gd-sft	£283,550
	9/21	Donc	1m Cls1 Gp2 2yo gd-fm	£63,799
	7/21	Sand	7f Cls1 List 2yo gd-fm	£24,385
	6/21	NmkJ	7f Cls4 Mdn 2yo gd-fm	£3,780

Favourite for the 1,000 Guineas and Oaks after a brilliant unbeaten two-year-old season; hacked up in the May Hill Stakes before easily beating a much stronger field at odds-on in the Fillies' Mile; a strong stayer at a mile and should come into her own over middle distances.

Invite (Ire)

4 b f The Gurkha - Katiyra (Peintre Celebre)

Andrew Balding — Team Valor

PLACINGS: 1/221515- — RPR **106+**

Starts	1st	2nd	3rd	4th	Win & Pl
7	3	2	-	-	£60,345

	9/21	Ches	1m4½f Cls1 List gd-sft	£28,355
80	5/21	Donc	1m2f Cls3 78-90 Hcap soft	£11,081
	10/20	Ling	7f Cls5 Auct 2yo stand	£4,399

Showed rich promise at times last season, notably when an impressive winner of a Listed race at Chester; disappointed when favourite for the Italian Oaks and again in the Champions Fillies & Mares Stakes at Ascot (too keen both times).

Hurricane Ivor edges the verdict in the Portland Handicap at Doncaster

Israr

3 b c Muhaarar - Taghrooda (Sea The Stars)

John & Thady Gosden — Shadwell Estate Company

PLACINGS: 12- — RPR **86**

Starts	1st	2nd	3rd	4th	Win & Pl
2	1	1	-	-	£18,735

9/21	Donc	1m Cls2 Mdn 2yo gd-fm	£16,200

Beautifully bred colt (second foal of Oaks winner Taghrooda) who won a strong mile maiden at Doncaster's St Leger meeting on debut last season; well below that level when a beaten favourite on soft ground at Salisbury; should bounce back on a quicker surface.

John Leeper (Ire)

4 b c Frankel - Snow Fairy (Intikhab)

Ed Dunlop — Anamoine

PLACINGS: 4/1193738- — RPR **108**

Starts	1st	2nd	3rd	4th	Win & Pl
8	2	-	2	1	£35,678

5/21	NmkR	1m2f Cls1 List 3yo good	£20,983
4/21	Newc	1m2f Cls5 3yo std-slw	£3,024

Promised much early last season and was even sent off just 8-1 for the Derby after landing the Feilden Stakes at Newmarket; finished only ninth at Epsom and did little better in four subsequent races at a lower level, twice finishing third in Listed races; has a bit to prove.

Jumbly

3 b f Gleneagles - Thistle Bird (Selkirk)

Roger Charlton — Emmy Rothschild And Partner

PLACINGS: 1141- — RPR **106+**

Starts	1st	2nd	3rd	4th	Win & Pl
4	3	-	-	1	£36,052

10/21	Newb	7f Cls1 List 2yo soft	£17,013
9/21	Kemp	7f Cls3 2yo std-slw	£8,762
7/21	Leic	6f Cls4 Mdn 2yo good	£5,454

Hugely impressive winner of a 7f Listed race at Newbury on soft ground final run last season having also won by a similarly wide margin at Kempton; had finished only fourth in the Rockfel Stakes in between, with quicker ground possibly to blame (also ridden further back than ideal).

Jumby (Ire)

4 b c New Bay - Sound Of Guns (Acclamation)

Eve Johnson Houghton — Anthony Pye-Jeary & David Ian

PLACINGS: 143/3100311- — RPR **113+**

Starts	1st	2nd	3rd	4th	Win & Pl
10	4	-	3	1	£52,346

104	9/21	NmkR	7f Cls2 86-104 Hcap gd-fm	£13,500
	8/21	Sals	6f Cls3 good	£8,370
95	5/21	NmkR	6f Cls2 80-98 3yo Hcap good	£18,900
	7/20	Asct	7f Cls5 Auct 2yo good	£3,493

Progressive handicapper last season; won over 6f at Newmarket early in the season and came good again in the autumn after a mixed summer, winning twice more including back at Newmarket when stepped up to 7f for the first time since 2020; still on a feasible mark.

King's Lynn (noseband): smart sprinter with give in the ground

Just Beautiful

4 br f Pride Of Dubai - Astrelle (Makfi)

Paddy Twomey (Ire) — Gary White & The Giggle Factor

PLACINGS: 11/11621- — RPR **111**

Starts	1st	2nd	3rd	4th	Win & Pl
7	5	1	-	-	£92,617

	9/21	Donc	7f Cls1 Gp3 gd-fm	£45,368
	6/21	Muss	7f Cls1 List good	£20,983
	4/21	Chmf	7f Cls5 Auct 3-5yo stand	£2,862
	11/20	Kemp	7f Cls6 Auct 2yo std-slw	£2,782
	10/20	Kemp	7f Cls5 Auct 2yo std-slw	£3,429

Progressive filly who won Group 3 and Listed races last season, both over 7f; also showed good form over a mile, finishing a half-length second in a Group 3 at Deauville and sixth in the Falmouth Stakes; bought out of Ivan Furtado's yard for 625,000gns.

Kawida

3 b f Sir Percy - Kandahari (Archipenko)

Ed Walker — Miss K Rausing

PLACINGS: 2211- — RPR **98+**

Starts	1st	2nd	3rd	4th	Win & Pl
4	2	2	-	-	£34,069

	10/21	NmkR	1m Cls1 List 2yo good	£24,385
	8/21	Hayd	7f Cls4 Mdn 2yo soft	£5,400

Signed off with victory in a Listed race at Newmarket last season, staying on strongly over a mile; had twice been pulled out of Group 2 races owing to good to firm ground since maiden win on soft; should prove best over middle distances.

King Of Bavaria (Ire)

3 bl c No Nay Never - Enharmonic (E Dubai)

Aidan O'Brien (Ire) — Tabor, Smith, Magnier & Westerberg

PLACINGS: 11- — RPR **104+**

Starts	1st	2nd	3rd	4th	Win & Pl
2	2	-	-	-	£28,446

95	10/21	Naas	6f 77-95 2yo Hcap heavy	£21,071
	5/21	Naas	5f Mdn 2yo yld-sft	£7,375

Made light of a long absence to win a premier nursery at Naas under top weight having missed much of last season after debut win in May (had been considered a Royal Ascot horse at that time); unproven on good ground; likely to step up to Group level.

King's Lynn

5 b g Cable Bay - Kinematic (Kyllachy)

Andrew Balding — The Queen

PLACINGS: 21/202/321736521- — RPR **114+**

Starts	1st	2nd	3rd	4th	Win & Pl
14	3	5	2	-	£238,950

	11/21	Donc	6f Cls1 List soft	£24,385
	5/21	Hayd	5f Cls1 List gd-sft	£20,983
	9/19	Donc	6½f Cls2 2yo gd-fm	£147,540

Improved after a gelding operation last season and won Listed races over 5f and 6f at Haydock and Doncaster; gained both victories with cut in the ground but also ran a big race on good to firm when seventh in the King's Stand.

Kinross

5 b g Kingman - Ceilidh House (Selkirk)

Ralph Beckett — Marc Chan

PLACINGS: 15/68491/6611549- **RPR 117+**

Starts	1st	2nd	3rd	4th	Win & Pl
14	4	-	-	2	£207,726

7/21	Gdwd	7f Cls1 Gp2 soft	£102,078
5/21	Hayd	7f Cls1 Gp3 gd-sft	£34,026
11/20	Kemp	1m Cls1 List std-slw	£22,684
10/19	NmkR	7f Cls4 2yo gd-sft	£5,175

Won a pair of 7f Group races last season, most notably the valuable Lennox Stakes at Glorious Goodwood; appeared to just lack the pace for Group I sprints either side of a strong-finishing fourth in the Prix de la Foret.

Kyprios (Ire)

4 ch c Galileo - Polished Gem (Danehill)

Aidan O'Brien (Ire) — Moyglare Stud Farm, Sue Magnier & Michael Ta

PLACINGS: 16/14- **RPR 101+**

Starts	1st	2nd	3rd	4th	Win & Pl
4	2	-	-	1	£19,266

4/21	Cork	1m2f 3yo good	£7,112
9/20	Gway	1m½f Mdn 2yo heavy	£8,250

Lightly raced colt who began last season as a Derby prospect but didn't run again after disappointing when 7-2 for the Listed trial at Lingfield; had been set to run over 1m6f at Royal Ascot before being withdrawn.

La Barrosa (Ire)

4 b g Lope De Vega - Bikini Babe (Montjeu)

Charlie Appleby — Godolphin

PLACINGS: 115/260-30 **RPR 110**

Starts	1st	2nd	3rd	4th	Win & Pl
8	2	1	1	-	£54,316

9/20	NmkR	7f Cls1 Gp3 2yo good	£22,684
9/20	Asct	7f Cls3 Mdn 2yo good	£11,644

Won a Group 3 as a two-year-old in 2020 and began last season brightly when second in the Craven Stakes; disappointed in two subsequent runs but slightly more promise on return at Meydan this winter before bleeding next time.

La Petite Coco (Ire)

4 b f Ruler Of The World - La Petite Virginia (Konigstiger)

Paddy Twomey (Ire) — Team Valor International

PLACINGS: 6/412111- **RPR 114**

Starts	1st	2nd	3rd	4th	Win & Pl
7	4	1	-	1	£155,794

9/21	Curr	1m2f Gp2 good	£92,188
8/21	Cork	1m4f Gp3 soft	£34,241
7/21	Klny	1m3f yield	£11,063
5/21	Klny	1m 3yo soft	£9,746

Hugely progressive filly who won four times last season, the last two in Group company; hacked up in a 1m4f Group 3 before dropping back in trip to upset Love in a 1m2f Group 2 on Irish Champions Weekend; could be a Group 1 filly.

Laneqash

4 b g Cable Bay - Bonhomie (Shamardal)

Roger Varian — Shadwell Estate Company

PLACINGS: 120/234- **RPR 115**

Starts	1st	2nd	3rd	4th	Win & Pl
6	1	2	1	1	£48,756

8/20	Asct	7f Cls5 Mdn 2yo gd-fm	£3,881

Missed much of last season but ran a mighty race on belated return when second in the Hungerford Stakes at Newbury; failed to run to that level in two subsequent races, including when stepped up to a mile for the first time; has since been gelded.

Lavender's Blue (Ire)

6 b m Sea The Stars - Beatrice Aurore (Danehill Dancer)

Amanda Perrett — Benny Andersson

PLACINGS: 12014/763302/135810- **RPR 113**

Starts	1st	2nd	3rd	4th	Win & Pl
17	4	2	3	1	£190,886

8/21	Gdwd	1m Cls1 Gp2 gd-fm	£70,888
4/21	Kemp	1m Cls1 List std-slw	£15,879
8/19	Sand	1m Cls1 Gp3 gd-fm	£39,697
4/19	NmkR	1m Cls4 Mdn 3yo gd-fm	£6,469

Claimed biggest victory in last season's Celebration Mile at Goodwood when beating Benbatl by a short head; has largely struggled otherwise in the last two seasons, including four defeats at Group I level (no better than sixth) in that time.

Lazuli (Ire)

5 b g Dubawi - Floristry (Fasliyev)

Charlie Appleby — Godolphin

PLACINGS: 118/21541/3167-21 **RPR 117**

Starts	1st	2nd	3rd	4th	Win & Pl
14	6	2	1	1	£201,409

2/22	Meyd	5f Gp2 good	£80,000
5/21	NmkR	5f Cls1 Gp3 gd-fm	£34,026
9/20	Newb	5f Cls1 Gp3 good	£25,520
6/20	Sand	5f Cls1 List 3yo good	£14,461
9/19	Donc	6f Cls2 2yo gd-fm	£11,205
8/19	NmkJ	6f Cls4 2yo gd-fm	£5,175

Very useful sprinter who has won 5f Group 3 races in each of the last two seasons, most recently in the Palace House Stakes at Newmarket; below par in two subsequent runs last term but bounced back to winning ways at Meydan earlier this year.

Light Infantry (Fr)

3 ch c Fast Company - Lights On Me (Kyllachy)

David Simcock — Never Say Die Partnership

PLACINGS: 11- **RPR 107+**

Starts	1st	2nd	3rd	4th	Win & Pl
2	2	-	-	-	£35,105

10/21	Newb	7f Cls1 Gp3 2yo soft	£28,355
9/21	Yarm	6f Cls4 2yo good	£6,750

Unbeaten in two runs as a two-year-old last season, following up wide-margin debut success

by landing the Horris Hill at Newbury on soft ground despite greenness; trainer expects better back on a quicker surface and sees him as a 2,000 Guineas prospect.

Lights On

5 ch m Siyouni - In The Light (Inchinor)

Sir Michael Stoute — Cheveley Park Stud

PLACINGS: 2123/118127- RPR **113**

Starts	1st	2nd	3rd	4th	Win & Pl
10	4	3	1	-	£90,873

	7/21	Pont	1m Cls1 List soft	£29,489
92	5/21	Asct	1m Cls2 72-97 Hcap soft	£23,193
85	4/21	Nott	1m½f Cls3 76-88 Hcap gd-fm	£11,610
	9/20	Newc	1m Cls5 stand	£3,429

Sharply progressive early last season and ran away with a Listed race at Pontefract by ten lengths having been beaten by the draw when on a hat-trick at Royal Ascot; twice came up short at Group level but had excuses (got no run) when stepped up to 1m2f at Newmarket.

Limiti Di Greccio (Ire)

3 b f Elzaam - Grotta Del Fauno (Galileo)

Paddy Twomey (Ire) — Martin Schwartz

PLACINGS: 62121- RPR **107+**

Starts	1st	2nd	3rd	4th	Win & Pl
5	2	2	-	-	£49,799

10/21	Curr	1m List 2yo yield	£19,754
8/21	Leop	7f Mdn 2yo gd-yld	£8,692

Progressive two-year-old last season; signed off with a career-best Listed win at the Curragh when stepped up to a mile having been narrowly denied at that level previously; unlikely to get further but should hold her own in Group races.

Logo Hunter (Ire)

4 b g Brazen Beau - Jadanna (Mujadil)

Michael Browne (Ire) — Patrick Moyles

PLACINGS: 23/1212115- RPR **116+**

Starts	1st	2nd	3rd	4th	Win & Pl
9	4	3	1	-	£68,448

	6/21	Cork	5f List yield	£19,754
	5/21	Naas	5f List soft	£19,754
89	4/21	Cork	5f 73-93 3yo Hcap yield	£8,165
	3/21	Dund	6f Mdn stand	£5,795

Remarkable success story last season, winning four times after being bought for a bargain 5,000gns; most impressive when a wide-margin winner of a 5f Listed race at Naas and followed up under a penalty at that level at Cork; injured when only fifth in a Group 2 at the Curragh.

Lone Eagle (Ire)

4 b c Galileo - Modernstone (Duke Of Marmalade)

Martyn Meade — Ballylinch Stud & Aquis Farm

PLACINGS: 2111/4125- RPR **120**

Starts	1st	2nd	3rd	4th	Win & Pl
8	4	2	-	1	£267,756

	5/21	Gdwd	1m3f Cls1 List 3yo soft	£26,654
	10/20	NmkR	1m2f Cls1 Gp3 2yo soft	£26,654
84	9/20	Donc	1m Cls2 75-89 2yo Hcap good	£12,450
	8/20	Gdwd	1m Cls4 2yo soft	£5,175

Developed into a high-class middle-distance performer last season, thrashing subsequent Breeders' Cup hero Yibir in a Listed race at Goodwood and running Hurricane Lane to a neck in the Irish Derby; injured when last of five in the King George and missed the rest of the season.

Lord Glitters (Fr)

9 gr g Whipper - Lady Glitters (Homme De Loi)

David O'Meara — Geoff & Sandra Turnbull

PLACINGS: 433265/1316442401-41 RPR **119**

Starts	1st	2nd	3rd	4th	Win & Pl
44	11	10	5	6	£2,209,849

	2/22	Meyd	1m1f Gp2 good	£80,000
	11/21	Sakh	1m2f Gp3 good	£262,500
	3/21	Meyd	1m1f Gp1 good	£113,869
	1/21	Meyd	1m1f Gp2 good	£71,387
	6/19	Asct	1m Cls1 Gp1 good	£340,260
	8/18	York	1m1f Cls1 Gp3 gd-fm	£56,710
102	10/17	Asct	1m Cls2 98-110 Hcap soft	£155,625
	5/17	StCl	1m soft	£11,966
	4/17	Chan	1m stand	£11,966
	6/16	Le L	1m2f 3yo heavy	£9,926
	5/16	Chat	1m2f 3yo soft	£5,882

Evergreen veteran who hasn't won in Europe since the 2019 Queen Anne Stakes but has thrived on the international stage, including victories in Bahrain and Dubai this winter; best known for exploits over a mile but recent form suggests he might now be best at around 1m2f.

Lord North (Ire)

6 b g Dubawi - Najoum (Giant's Causeway)

John & Thady Gosden — Sheikh Zayed Bin Mohammed Racing

PLACINGS: 1/182121/11304/1-2 RPR **122+**

Starts	1st	2nd	3rd	4th	Win & Pl
14	7	3	1	1	£2,308,066

	3/21	Meyd	1m1f Gp1 good	£1,751,825
	6/20	Asct	1m2f Cls1 Gp1 good	£148,000
	6/20	Hayd	1m2f Cls1 Gp3 gd-sft	£20,983
	11/19	NmkR	1m2f Cls1 List heavy	£20,983
98	9/19	NmkR	1m1f Cls2 83-107 Hcap good	£99,600
	4/19	Newc	1m Cls5 stand	£3,752
	10/18	Rdcr	1m Cls4 2yo soft	£7,116

Second in this year's Winter Derby having gained a second Group 1 win on only run last

Lord Glitters: tough and durable performer who has done particularly well at Meydan in recent times

Lusail lands the Group 2 Gimcrack Stakes at York

year, adding the Dubai Turf at Meydan to the 2020 Prince of Wales's Stakes; had failed to land a blow in three stronger Group 1 races in between, including when stepped up to 1m4f.

Lusail (Ire)

3 b c Mehmas - Diaminda (Diamond Green)

Richard Hannon — Al Shaqab Racing

PLACINGS: 131114- — RPR **112**

Starts	1st	2nd	3rd	4th	Win & Pl
6	4	-	1	1	£157,532

	Date	Course	Race	Prize
	8/21	York	6f Cls1 Gp2 2yo gd-fm	£85,065
	7/21	NmkJ	6f Cls1 Gp2 2yo gd-fm	£51,039
	6/21	NmkJ	7f Cls4 2yo gd-sft	£4,320
	5/21	York	6f Cls2 Mdn 2yo good	£8,100

Landed a Group 2 double over 6f last season, beating subsequent Richmond winner Asymmetric in the July Stakes and defying a penalty to follow up in the Gimcrack; tame fourth in the Champagne Stakes on softer ground but had won over 7f previously and should get a mile.

Lust (Ire)

4 b g Fastnet Rock - Desire Moi (Galileo)

Ger Lyons (Ire) — Newtown Anner Stud Farm

PLACINGS: 736/15101- — RPR **111**

Starts	1st	2nd	3rd	4th	Win & Pl
8	3	-	1	-	£27,076

	Date	Course	Race	Prize
90	10/21	Gowr	1m 71-90 3yo Hcap soft	£8,165
84	5/21	Curr	7f 73-93 3yo Hcap sft-hvy	£11,063
	4/21	Gowr	7f Mdn 3yo soft	£6,321

Sharply progressive handicapper last season, signing off with a six-length win at Gowran; ran just twice after May owing to need for soft ground and disappointed when connections took a chance on good in the Irish Cambridgeshire; raised 10lb for latest win.

Luxembourg (Ire)

3 b c Camelot - Attire (Danehill Dancer)

Aidan O'Brien (Ire) — Westerberg, Magnier, Tabor & Smith

PLACINGS: 111- — RPR **116+**

Starts	1st	2nd	3rd	4th	Win & Pl
3	3	-	-	-	£186,882

	Date	Course	Race	Prize
	10/21	Donc	1m Cls1 Gp1 2yo soft	£118,400
	9/21	Curr	1m Gp2 2yo good	£52,679
	7/21	Klny	1m 2yo good	£15,804

Emerged as a much-needed star two-year-old colt for Ballydoyle last season when winning the Beresford Stakes and Vertem Futurity Trophy in impressive fashion; clear winter favourite for the Derby but looks to have sufficient pace to take in the 2,000 Guineas first.

Mac Swiney (Ire)

4 ch c New Approach - Halla Na Saoire (Teofilo)

Jim Bolger (Ir) — Mrs J S Bolger

PLACINGS: 519181/41465030- — RPR **119**

Starts	1st	2nd	3rd	4th	Win & Pl
14	4	-	1	2	£621,335

	Date	Course	Race	Prize
	5/21	Curr	1m Gp1 3yo sft-hvy	£203,571
	10/20	Donc	1m Cls1 Gp1 2yo heavy	£127,280
	8/20	Curr	7f Gp2 2yo soft	£47,500
	7/20	Curr	7f Mdn 2yo yield	£8,500

Won last season's Irish 2,000 Guineas, relishing soft/heavy ground having also won the 2020 Vertem Futurity Trophy on heavy; largely below par otherwise but bounced back in third when getting some cut again in the Champion Stakes.

Magisterial (Ire)

3 b c Frankel - Hoity Toity (Darshaan)

John & Thady Gosden — B E Nielsen

PLACINGS: 41- — RPR **87+**

Starts	1st	2nd	3rd	4th	Win & Pl
2	1	-	-	1	£6,034

	Date	Course	Race	Prize
	10/21	Hayd	1m Cls4 2yo soft	£5,400

Good winner of a mile novice at Haydock last season, building on an encouraging debut fourth behind Subastar at Newmarket; full sister Flaunt won over just shy of 1m4f last season and should be coming into his own over similar trips.

Magny Cours (USA)

7 b g Medaglia D'Oro - Indy Five Hundred (A.P. Indy)

Andre Fabre (Fr) — Godolphin

PLACINGS: 5/122/11/136221213-0 — RPR **118+**

Starts	1st	2nd	3rd	4th	Win & Pl
17	7	5	2	-	£1,303,456

	Date	Course	Race	Prize
	10/21	StCl	1m Gp3 v soft	£35,714
	8/21	Claf	1m1f List soft	£23,214
	3/21	Chan	1m1½f stand	£13,393
	7/20	Sand	1m2f Cls1 List gd-fm	£14,461
	6/20	Chan	1m List gd-sft	£17,161
	2/19	Chan	1m1½f 4yo stand	£8,108
	11/17	Chan	1m 2yo stand	£11,538

Gained biggest win in a Group 3 at Saint-Cloud last autumn, improving on two seconds in that grade and adding to three wins in Listed races; beaten on all four runs at a higher level, doing best when second in last season's Prix Dollar.

Majestic Dawn (Ire)

6 ch h Dawn Approach - Jolie Chanson (Mount Nelson)

Paul & Oliver Cole — Green & Norman

PLACINGS: 221773513/01/35312- — RPR **116**

Starts	1st	2nd	3rd	4th	Win & Pl
16	4	3	4	-	£143,697

	Date	Course	Race	Prize
104	9/21	Sals	1m2f Cls2 85-104 Hcap soft	£10,260
94	9/20	NmkR	1m1f Cls2 86-112 Hcap good	£74,700
89	10/19	Nott	1m2f Cls3 77-89 Hcap heavy	£9,338
	4/19	Newb	1m3f Cls3 Mdn 3yo gd-sft	£9,704

Wide-margin winner of the Cambridgeshire in 2020 and struck in similar fashion in another handicap at Salisbury last autumn; had looked hard to place prior to that, with further 7lb rise no help, but did well when a close second in a Listed race at Newmarket on final run.

Majestic Glory

3 b f Frankel - Bella Nouf (Dansili)

Andrew Balding — Mrs Doreen Tabor

PLACINGS: 621169- — RPR **100+**

Starts	1st	2nd	3rd	4th	Win & Pl
6	2	1	-	-	£43,176

	Date	Course	Race	Prize
	8/21	NmkJ	7f Cls1 Gp3 2yo good	£34,026
	7/21	NmkJ	6f Cls4 2yo good	£5,400

Good winner of last season's Sweet Solera Stakes at Newmarket, beating subsequent Grade I scorer Wild Beauty; had looked progressive to that point but regressed in the autumn when disappointing in the Rockfel Stakes and Fillies' Mile.

Man Of Promise (USA)

5 b g Into Mischief - Involved (Speightstown)

Charlie Appleby — Godolphin

PLACINGS: 3/12/188-1 — RPR **116**

Starts	1st	2nd	3rd	4th	Win & Pl
7	3	1	1	-	£90,343

	Date	Course	Race	Prize
	1/22	Meyd	6f List good	£44,444
96	2/21	Meyd	6f List 93-110 Hcap good	£38,540
	6/20	Yarm	7f Cls5 Mdn good	£3,493

Hasn't run in Europe since winning a 6f handicap at Newmarket in June 2020 but has since developed into a smart sprinter in Dubai; most impressive when easily beating Lazuli and Khaadem first time out this year.

Mandoob

4 b g Farhh - Fingertips (Royal Applause)

Brian Meehan — Shadwell Estate Company

PLACINGS: 1123- — RPR **107**

Starts	1st	2nd	3rd	4th	Win & Pl
4	2	1	1	-	£51,187

	Date	Course	Race	Prize
	6/21	Hayd	1m3½f Cls4 3yo gd-fm	£4,347
	4/21	Ling	1m4f Cls5 3yo stand	£3,024

Lightly raced gelding who won two novice races

last season before a solid second behind Yibir in the Bahrain Trophy; well-beaten third in a Listed race at Ascot when stepped up to 1m6f but remains a useful staying prospect.

Mangoustine (Fr)

3 b f Dark Angel - Zotilla (Zamindar)

Mikel Delzangles (Fr) Infinity Nine Horses, Ecurie Des Monceaux et al

PLACINGS: 111- RPR **104**

Starts	1st	2nd	3rd	4th	Win & Pl
3	3	-	-	-	£74,553

10/21	Chan	7f Gp3 2yo v soft	£35,714
9/21	Pari	1m List 2yo soft	£26,786
8/21	Deau	1m 2yo gd-sft	£12,054

Subject of much hype last season, being owned by NBA star Tony Parker, and justified the publicity by winning all three starts, including a Group 3 at Chantilly on final run; seen as a Classic filly by former trainer Frederic Rossi, though unlikely to stay beyond a mile.

Manobo (Ire)

4 b g Sea The Stars - Tasaday (Nayef)

Charlie Appleby Godolphin

PLACINGS: 1111-1 RPR **115+**

Starts	1st	2nd	3rd	4th	Win & Pl
5	5	-	-	-	£222,977

2/22	Meyd	1m6f Gp3 good	£88,889
10/21	Lonc	1m7f Gp2 3yo v soft	£101,786
9/21	StCl	1m4f List 3yo good	£24,554
6/21	Kemp	1m4f Cls5 std-slw	£2,862
5/21	Newb	1m2f Cls4 Mdn 3yo gd-sft	£4,887

Quickly developed into a smart stayer last season, completing a four-timer when stepped up in trip for the Prix Chaudenay at Chantilly; maintained unbeaten record when hacking up on first run in Dubai this year and looks set to be a contender for top staying prizes.

Mare Australis (Ire)

5 ch h Australia - Miramare (Rainbow Quest)

Andre Fabre (Fr) Gestut Schlenderhan

PLACINGS: 1/412/21- RPR **120**

Starts	1st	2nd	3rd	4th	Win & Pl
6	3	2	-	1	£220,430

5/21	Lonc	1m2½f Gp1 gd-sft	£153,054
6/20	Chan	1m4f List 3yo gd-sft	£18,136
11/19	Muni	1m 2yo soft	£2,703

Progressive middle-distance performer who claimed Group 1 honours at the first attempt in last season's Prix Ganay (moderate race for the grade) only to miss the rest of the year through injury; could prove ideally suited by 1m4f and already seen by trainer as an Arc horse.

Marianafoot (Fr)

7 ch h Footstepsinthesand - Marianabaa (Anabaa)

Jerome Reynier (Fr) Jean-Claude Seroul

PLACINGS: /152401/21/1111111-3 RPR **119+**

Starts	1st	2nd	3rd	4th	Win & Pl
24	15	2	2	2	£581,498

8/21	Deau	6½f Gp1 soft	£193,868
7/21	Lonc	7f Gp3 v soft	£35,714
5/21	Lonc	7f Gp3 gd-sft	£35,714
4/21	Chan	6f List good	£23,214
3/21	Chan	6½f stand	£12,500
2/21	Cagn	6½f stand	£12,500
1/21	Ponv	7½f stand	£6,250
12/20	Deau	6½f stand	£8,602
12/19	Deau	7½f List stand	£23,423
2/19	Doh	1m good	£89,764
12/18	Deau	7½f List stand	£23,009
10/18	Toul	7f 3yo good	£13,274
6/18	Toul	7f 3yo v soft	£13,274
9/17	Cagn	1m 2yo stand	£10,256
7/17	Vich	7f 2yo gd-sft	£7,692

Remarkable improver who rocketed through the ranks with eight successive wins, culminating in victory in the Group 1 Prix Maurice de Gheest having begun on the all-weather through the winter; hasn't won above Group 3 level otherwise, though has run well up to a mile.

Masekela (Ire)

3 b c El Kabeir - Lady's Purse (Doyen)

Andrew Balding Mick & Janice Mariscotti

PLACINGS: 15214- RPR **108**

Starts	1st	2nd	3rd	4th	Win & Pl
5	2	1	-	1	£56,507

8/21	Newb	7f Cls1 List 2yo good	£26,937
5/21	Gdwd	6f Cls4 2yo soft	£4,860

Showed smart form against top two-year-olds last season, running champion juvenile Native

Mighty Ulysses (left): created a good impression when scoring on his only start at two

Trail to a head in the Superlative Stakes before edging out Champagne winner Bayside Boy in a Listed race at Newbury; only fourth when favourite for the Royal Lodge.

Master Of Reality (Ire)

7 b g Frankel - L'Ancresse (Darshaan)

Joseph O'Brien (Ire) — Lloyd J Williams Syndicate

PLACINGS: /143352d/62210/25105- RPR **112**

Starts	1st	2nd	3rd	4th	Win & Pl
23	5	4	2	2	£424,132

7/21	DRoy	1m5½f List gd-fm	£19,754
9/20	DRoy	1m6f List soft	£18,750
4/19	Navn	1m6f Gp3 yield	£33,514
5/18	StCl	1m4f 3yo good	£15,487
5/18	StCl	1m4f 3yo soft	£13,274

Useful stayer who has won the same Listed race at Down Royal in each of the last two seasons; hasn't won a Group race since 2019 (also went close in the Gold Cup and Melbourne Cup that year) but was a half-length second in last season's Vintage Crop Stakes.

Master Of The Seas (Ire)

4 b g Dubawi - Firth Of Lorne (Danehill)

Charlie Appleby — Godolphin

PLACINGS: 114/21237- RPR **119**

Starts	1st	2nd	3rd	4th	Win & Pl
8	3	2	1	1	£172,503

4/21	NmkR	1m Cls1 Gp3 3yo gd-fm	£25,520
7/20	NmkJ	7f Cls1 Gp2 2yo good	£23,081
6/20	NmkR	7f Cls5 2yo soft	£4,140

Finished a short-head second in last season's 2,000 Guineas behind Poetic Flare having impressed when winning the Craven; absent for four months subsequently and twice not quite at his best in the autumn; has since been gelded.

Megallan

4 b c Kingman - Eastern Belle (Champs Elysees)

John & Thady Gosden — A E Oppenheimer

PLACINGS: 12247/212015- RPR **115**

Starts	1st	2nd	3rd	4th	Win & Pl
11	3	4	-	1	£125,290

8/21	Sals	1m Cls1 Gp3 good	£38,279
4/21	Newc	1m Cls1 List 3yo std-slw	£28,355
8/20	NmkJ	1m Cls5 2yo gd-fm	£4,140

Won Group 3 and Listed races over a mile last season and proved himself over further when second behind Hurricane Lane in the Dante; twice disappointed in France but badly hampered in the Prix du Jockey Club and possibly unsuited by very soft ground in the Prix Dollar.

Mighty Ulysses

3 b c Ulysses - Token Of Love (Cape Cross)

John & Thady Gosden — Saeed Suhail

PLACINGS: 1- RPR **84+**

Starts	1st	2nd	3rd	4th	Win & Pl
1	1	-	-	-	£5,400

9/21	Yarm	1m Cls4 Mdn 2yo good	£5,400

Easy winner of sole start at Yarmouth last season, producing a strong late burst over a mile; precocity bodes well given sire's progeny very much ought to progress with time; out of a mile Listed winner and might well get further, at least 1m2f.

Migration (Ire)

6 b g Alhebayeb - Caribbean Ace (Red Clubs)

David Menuisier — Gail Brown Racing

PLACINGS: 85/22177125/4117- — RPR **112+**

Starts	1st	2nd	3rd	4th	Win & Pl
14	4	3	-	1	£109,362

103	8/21	York	1m2½f Cls2 88-107 Hcap good	£36,078
95	7/21	Gdwd	1m2f Cls2 92-105 Hcap heavy	£38,655
88	8/19	Sand	1m2f Cls3 77-88 3yo Hcap good	£9,338
86	5/19	NmkR	1m Cls4 69-86 3yo Hcap gd-fm	£7,763

Flourished on return from more than 18 months off the track last season, winning 1m2f handicaps at Glorious Goodwood and York's Ebor meeting; disappointed on final run when favourite for a Listed race back at Goodwood; still on a feasible mark.

Minzaal (Ire)

4 b c Mehmas - Pardoven (Clodovil)

Owen Burrows — Shadwell Estate Company

PLACINGS: 4113/23- — RPR **114**

Starts	1st	2nd	3rd	4th	Win & Pl
6	2	1	2	1	£153,364

8/20	York	6f Cls1 Gp2 2yo good	£56,710
8/20	Sals	6f Cls5 2yo gd-fm	£4,140

Missed nearly all of last season but returned with two fine runs at Ascot in October, finishing third in the Champions Sprint after a close second in a 5f Listed race; had been a high-class two-year-old, winning the Gimcrack; still fairly unexposed.

Mishriff (right): top-class performer over middle distances

Mise En Scene

3 b f Siyouni - Gadfly (Galileo)

James Ferguson — Qatar Racing

PLACINGS: 1140- — RPR **106**

Starts	1st	2nd	3rd	4th	Win & Pl
4	2	-	-	1	£71,905

8/21	Gdwd	7f Cls1 Gp3 2yo good	£34,026
7/21	Hayd	7f Cls5 2yo good	£3,780

Did well to win a Group 3 at Goodwood on just her second run last season; couldn't build on that in two subsequent runs, though stayed on fairly well having been tapped for toe when fourth in the Fillies' Mile; should come into her own over middle distances.

Mishriff (Ire)

5 b h Make Believe - Contradict (Raven's Pass)

John & Thady Gosden — Prince A A Faisal

PLACINGS: 431/21118/113214-0 — RPR **128**

Starts	1st	2nd	3rd	4th	Win & Pl
15	7	2	2	2	£11,158,059

8/21	York	1m2½f Cls1 Gp1 good	£567,100
3/21	Meyd	1m4f Gp1 good	£2,189,781
2/21	Jana	1m1f fast	£7,299,270
8/20	Deau	1m2f Gp2 3yo heavy	£152,064
7/20	Chan	1m2½f Gp1 3yo gd-sft	£489,854
6/20	NmkR	1m2f Cls1 List 3yo gd-fm	£14,461
11/19	Nott	1m½f Cls5 Mdn 2yo heavy	£3,881

Three-time Group 1 winner who landed last season's Juddmonte International by six lengths;

possibly unsuited by slower ground when fourth in the Champion Stakes; best over 1m2f, though did win the Sheema Classic and finish second in the King George over 1m4f.

Modern Games (Ire)

3 ch c Dubawi - Modern Ideals (New Approach)

Charlie Appleby — Godolphin

PLACINGS: 512111- — RPR **114+**

Starts	1st	2nd	3rd	4th	Win & Pl
6	4	1	-	-	£434,633

	11/21	Delm	1m Gd1 2yo firm	£379,562
	9/21	NmkR	7f Cls1 Gp3 2yo good	£34,026
90	9/21	Donc	7f Cls2 71-92 2yo Hcap gd-fm	£13,085
	7/21	NmkJ	7f Cls4 Mdn 2yo gd-fm	£5,400

Progressive two-year-old last season, winning his last three races including the Breeders' Cup Juvenile Turf (controversially deemed a non-runner for betting purposes); had previously landed the Tattersalls Stakes impressively at Newmarket and could be back for 2,000 Guineas.

Mohaafeth (Ire)

4 ch c Frankel - French Dressing (Sea The Stars)

William Haggas — Shadwell Estate Company

PLACINGS: 73/111134- — RPR **116+**

Starts	1st	2nd	3rd	4th	Win & Pl
8	4	-	2	1	£143,996

	6/21	Asct	1m2f Cls1 Gp3 3yo gd-fm	£44,400
	5/21	NmkR	1m2f Cls1 List 3yo gd-fm	£22,684
85	4/21	NmkR	1m2f Cls3 79-92 3yo Hcap good	£6,750
	3/21	Ling	1m Cls5 stand	£3,429

Quickly developed into a smart middle-distance colt last season, running away with the Feilden Stakes at Newmarket and adding the Hampton Court at Royal Ascot; only third in the York Stakes before a well-beaten fourth in the Juddmonte International; could drop back to a mile.

Mojo Star (Ire)

4 b c Sea The Stars - Galley (Zamindar)

Richard Hannon — Amo Racing

PLACINGS: 2/225120- — RPR **118**

Starts	1st	2nd	3rd	4th	Win & Pl
7	1	4	-	-	£431,739

8/21	Newb	1m4f Cls3 Mdn 3yo good	£8,640

Remarkable second at 50-1 in last season's Derby when still a maiden and proved that was no fluke when filling the same spot in the St Leger; only tenth in the Arc and connections could explore staying trips this year.

Mooneista (Ire)

4 b f Dandy Man - Moon Unit (Intikhab)

Jack Davison (Ire) — Mrs Paula Davison

PLACINGS: 5225231/3212d610- — RPR **113**

Starts	1st	2nd	3rd	4th	Win & Pl
14	3	4	3	-	£128,364

7/21	Curr	5f Gp2 good	£52,679
4/21	Naas	5f List good	£19,754
9/20	DRoy	5f Mdn 2yo yield	£7,000

Speedy filly who produced a career-best when winning a Group 2 at the Curragh last July; failed to build on that when well beaten on only subsequent run in the Flying Five; yet to win in five runs beyond 5f, though was beaten just a neck by A Case Of You in a Group 3 at Naas.

Mostahdaf (Ire)

4 br c Frankel - Handassa (Dubawi)

John & Thady Gosden — Shadwell Estate Company

PLACINGS: 111011- — RPR **119+**

Starts	1st	2nd	3rd	4th	Win & Pl
6	5	-	-	-	£109,061

10/21	NmkR	1m1f Cls1 Gp3 good	£45,368
9/21	Sand	1m Cls1 List soft	£29,489
5/21	Sand	1m Cls1 List 3yo soft	£20,983
4/21	Kemp	1m Cls2 3yo std-slw	£9,793
3/21	Newc	7f Cls5 std-slw	£3,429

Has won five out of six races, with sole defeat coming in last season's St James's Palace Stakes (badly hampered); bounced back with a second Listed win at Sandown before impressing in the Darley Stakes at Newmarket; expected to prove best at 1m2f.

Mother Earth (Ire)

4 b f Zoffany - Many Colours (Green Desert)

Aidan O'Brien (Ire) — Smith, Magnier & Tabor

PLACINGS: 23133032/1232132504- — RPR **116**

Starts	1st	2nd	3rd	4th	Win & Pl
18	3	5	6	1	£1,046,617

8/21	Deau	1m Gp1 soft	£153,054
5/21	NmkR	1m Cls1 Gp1 3yo gd-fm	£212,663
7/20	Naas	6f Gp3 2yo yld-sft	£34,000

Tough and consistent filly who mixed it at Group 1 level throughout last season and won twice in the 1,000 Guineas and Prix Rothschild; finished second or third five times more but came up short against colts later in the year, including when fifth in the Queen Elizabeth II Stakes.

Mujtaba

4 b g Dubawi - Majmu (Redoute's Choice)

William Haggas — Shadwell Estate Company

PLACINGS: 111- — RPR **103+**

Starts	1st	2nd	3rd	4th	Win & Pl
3	3	-	-	-	£16,826

90	10/21	Rdcr	1m Cls3 77-93 Hcap soft	£6,480
	9/21	Ches	7½f Cls4 good	£6,674
	8/21	Chep	1m Cls5 gd-sft	£3,672

Unbeaten in three races having only made debut

GOOD FRIDAY RACE MEETING

FRIDAY 15TH APRIL

Chelmsford City Racecourse

as a three-year-old last August; looked a long way ahead of opening mark of 90 when easily completing the hat-trick on handicap debut over a mile at Redcar; up 8lb and could well end up in Group races.

Mutasaabeq

4 br c Invincible Spirit - Ghanaati (Giant's Causeway)

Charlie Hills — Shadwell Estate Company

PLACINGS: 1/17018- — RPR **109**

Starts	1st	2nd	3rd	4th	Win & Pl
6	3	-	-	-	£19,313

7/21	Hayd	7f Cls3 good	£6,750
4/21	NmkR	7f Cls3 3yo good	£8,100
10/20	NmkR	7f Cls4 2yo heavy	£4,464

Lightly raced colt who promised much at times last season, even going off just 6-1 for the 2,000 Guineas after a six-length win at Newmarket in April; blew more cold than hot subsequently and yet to finish better than seventh in three runs above Class 3 level.

My Astra (Ire)

4 b f Lope De Vega - My Titania (Sea The Stars)

William Haggas — Sunderland Holding

PLACINGS: 112- — RPR **103**

Starts	1st	2nd	3rd	4th	Win & Pl
3	2	1	-	-	£18,893

7/21	NmkJ	1m Cls4 good	£5,400
7/21	Yarm	1m Cls5 Mdn gd-fm	£3,672

Very lightly raced filly who did well in just three races last season; won her first two last July in minor company at Yarmouth and Newmarket, both over a mile, before a narrow defeat in Listed company at Saint-Cloud when stepped up to Listed grade on much softer ground.

My Oberon (Ire)

5 b g Dubawi - My Titania (Sea The Stars)

William Haggas — Sunderland Holding

PLACINGS: 51225/173453-1 — RPR **116**

Starts	1st	2nd	3rd	4th	Win & Pl
12	3	2	2	1	£137,133

	Date	Course	Race	Prize
	2/22	Sthl	1m Cls2 std-slw	£10,800
	4/21	NmkR	1m1f Cls1 Gp3 good	£25,520
	7/20	York	1m Cls5 good	£3,881

Won the Earl of Sefton Stakes last season having finished second in two other Group 3 races in 2020; later finished a neck third in the Prix d'Ispahan and fourth in the Prince of Wales's Stakes before form tailed off; subsequently gelded before a winning return down in class at Southwell.

Nagano

4 b g Fastnet Rock - Nazym (Galileo)

Roger Varian — Nurlan Bizakov

PLACINGS: 311612- — RPR **108**

Starts	1st	2nd	3rd	4th	Win & Pl
6	3	1	1	-	£54,839

	Date	Course	Race	Prize
94	7/21	Gdwd	1m4f Cls2 79-98 3yo Hcap soft	£25,770
	5/21	Newc	1m2f Cls5 stand	£3,024
	5/21	Nott	1m2f Cls5 3yo gd-sft	£3,024

Lightly raced gelding who won three times last season, most notably a strong 1m4f handicap at Glorious Goodwood; sent off odds-on when stepped up in class and trip on only subsequent run in a Group 3 back at Goodwood and finished a head second; likely improver.

Nagano (nearest): winner of three races should be capable of adding further success this season

Nahaarr (Ire)

6 b h Dark Angel - Charlotte Rua (Redback)

William Haggas — Sheikh Ahmed Al Maktoum

PLACINGS: 11113/43191/427- — RPR **119**

Starts	1st	2nd	3rd	4th	Win & Pl
13	6	1	2	2	£103,965

100	9/20	Ayr	6f Cls2 94-105 Hcap gd-sft	£46,688
94	7/20	Newb	6f Cls2 90-104 Hcap good	£9,704
81	7/19	Chmf	7f Cls5 64-81 3yo Hcap stand	£5,175
75	6/19	NmkJ	7f Cls4 70-80 3yo Hcap good	£6,469
	6/19	Ling	6f Cls5 gd-fm	£3,752
	5/19	Donc	6f Cls5 good	£3,752

Restricted to just two runs on turf last season but showed he had graduated from handicaps (won the Ayr Gold Cup in 2020) to Group sprints when running Starman to a neck in the Duke of York Stakes; missed the rest of the year after finishing seventh in the Diamond Jubilee.

Natasha

3 ch f Frankel - Darkova (Maria's Mon)

John & Thady Gosden — George Strawbridge

PLACINGS: 2118- — RPR **90+**

Starts	1st	2nd	3rd	4th	Win & Pl
4	2	1	-	-	£11,445

9/21	Sand	1m Cls4 2yo good	£5,400
8/21	Kemp	1m Cls5 2yo std-slw	£3,510

Easily won mile novices at Kempton and Sandown last season only to disappoint in the Prix Marcel Boussac; should get 1m4f (half-sister to Almanzor and by a stronger stamina influence in Frankel) and looks a fine middle-distance prospect.

Native Trail

3 b c Oasis Dream - Needleleaf (Observatory)

Charlie Appleby — Godolphin

PLACINGS: 1111- — RPR **122+**

Starts	1st	2nd	3rd	4th	Win & Pl
4	4	-	-	-	£511,847

10/21	NmkR	7f Cls1 Gp1 2yo good	£298,507
9/21	Curr	7f Gp1 2yo good	£158,036
7/21	NmkJ	7f Cls1 Gp2 2yo gd-fm	£51,039
6/21	Sand	7f Cls4 Mdn 2yo good	£4,266

Favourite for the 2,000 Guineas after a brilliant unbeaten two-year-old campaign; particularly impressive when running away with the National Stakes and comfortably followed up in the Dewhurst; unlikely to stay beyond a mile according to his trainer.

Naval Crown

4 b c Dubawi - Come Alive (Dansili)

Charlie Appleby — Godolphin

PLACINGS: 33133/312428-10 — RPR **113**

Starts	1st	2nd	3rd	4th	Win & Pl
13	3	2	5	1	£211,244

1/22	Meyd	7f Gp2 good	£80,000
2/21	Meyd	1m List 3yo good	£38,540
8/20	York	7f Cls2 Mdn 2yo good	£18,675

Good fourth in last season's 2,000 Guineas at Newmarket and backed up that run when second in the Jersey Stakes at Royal Ascot; returned from a break with a Group 2 win in Dubai earlier this year but well beaten when favourite for a hugely valuable contest in Saudi Arabia.

Native Trail: the high-class colt streaks into favouritism for the 2,000 Guineas by winning the Group 1 Dewhurst Stakes

Nayef Road (Ire)

6 ch h Galileo - Rose Bonheur (Danehill Dancer)

Charlie & Mark Johnston — Mohamed Obaida

PLACINGS: 1537/1223/3556531-40 — RPR **115**

Starts	1st	2nd	3rd	4th	Win & Pl
28	6	4	6	1	£495,360

	9/21	NmkR	2m Cls1 List good	£29,489
	6/20	Newc	2m½f Cls1 Gp3 stand	£20,983
	8/19	Gdwd	1m4f Cls1 Gp3 3yo good	£99,243
96	5/19	NmkR	1m2f Cls3 83-96 3yo Hcap good	£12,938
85	8/18	NmkJ	7f Cls3 80-92 2yo Hcap gd-fm	£9,704
	8/18	Hayd	7f Cls4 2yo gd-fm	£7,116

Smart stayer who was out of sorts for much of last season but did land a six-length Listed win at Newmarket on final run; had won the Sagaro Stakes and finished second in the Gold Cup and Goodwood Cup in 2020.

Nazanin (USA)

3 b/br f Declaration Of War - Woodland Scene (Act One)

Archie Watson — Imad Alsagar

PLACINGS: 1481- — RPR **100**

Starts	1st	2nd	3rd	4th	Win & Pl
4	2	-	-	1	£29,626

9/21	Ayr	6f Cls1 Gp3 2yo good	£22,684
6/21	Newb	6f Cls4 2yo soft	£3,726

Highly tried in four runs last season and finally came good when winning a 6f Group 3 at Ayr on final run (runner-up won a Listed race next time); reportedly benefited from rain-softened ground having twice struggled on a quicker surface in Group races after debut win.

Nobel (Ire)

3 ch c Lope De Vega - Starlet (Sea The Stars)

Andrew Balding — Qatar Racing

PLACINGS: 1- — RPR **81+aw**

Starts	1st	2nd	3rd	4th	Win & Pl
1	1	-	-	-	£3,510

12/21	Kemp	1m Cls5 2yo std-slw	£3,510

Cost 825,000gns as a yearling and made the first dent in that investment when winning by three lengths on debut in a mile novice at Kempton in December; bred to get further (out of a 1m4f winner) and looks a smart middle-distance prospect.

Noble Truth (Fr)

3 b c Kingman - Speralita (Frankel)

Charlie Appleby — Godolphin

PLACINGS: 314124-0 — RPR **111**

Starts	1st	2nd	3rd	4th	Win & Pl
7	2	1	1	2	£119,861

9/21	Donc	7f Cls1 List 2yo gd-fm	£22,684
7/21	NmkJ	7f Cls3 Mdn 2yo gd-fm	£6,480

Headstrong but talented two-year-old last season; made amends for a disappointing run in the Acomb Stakes with a narrow Listed win at Doncaster and a fine second in the Prix Jean-Luc Lagardere; flopped when favourite for the Horris Hill, pulling much too hard, and again in Saudi Arabia this year.

Noon Star (USA)

4 b f Galileo - Midday (Oasis Dream)

Sir Michael Stoute — Juddmonte

PLACINGS: 31/126- — RPR **104+**

	Starts	1st	2nd	3rd	4th	Win & Pl
	5	2	1	1	-	£27,640
	4/21	Weth	1m2f Cls5 good			£2,862
	10/20	Nott	1m½f Cls5 Mdn 2yo soft			£4,075

Blue-blooded Galileo filly (out of multiple Group 1 winner Midday) who didn't quite live up to massive expectations last season when a beaten favourite in the Musidora and Ribblesdale Stakes; far from disgraced both times and could yet benefit from being given more time.

Ocean Wind

6 b h Teofilo - Chan Tong (Hampstead)

Roger Teal — Rockingham Reins

PLACINGS: 3111/2223- — RPR **116+**

	Starts	1st	2nd	3rd	4th	Win & Pl
	8	3	3	2	-	£70,653
96	10/20	Donc	1m6½f Cls2 82-96 Hcap soft			£11,972
89	9/20	NmkR	2m2f Cls2 74-98 Hcap gd-fm			£23,655
	8/20	Ling	1m3½f Cls5 Mdn gd-sft			£3,493

Progressive stayer who has made giant strides in less than 12 months of racing on the Flat, starting in 2020 and peaking last spring with a length second behind Stradivarius in the Sagaro Stakes; missed the rest of the season after a tame third at odds-on for a Group 3 at Sandown.

Order Of Australia (Ire)

5 b h Australia - Senta's Dream (Danehill)

Aidan O'Brien (Ire) — Smith, Magnier, Tabor & Mrs A M O'Brien

PLACINGS: 5/34711916/815320- — RPR **119**

	Starts	1st	2nd	3rd	4th	Win & Pl
	15	4	1	2	1	£1,147,484
	7/21	Curr	7f Gp2 good			£52,679
	11/20	Keen	1m Gd1 firm			£781,955
	9/20	Curr	1m4f gd-yld			£8,500
	9/20	Dund	1m2½f stand			£6,750

Shock winner of the Breeders' Cup Mile in 2020, finding his niche dropped in trip after struggling over middle distances; added a Group 2 at the Curragh last season but came up short back at Group 1 level, though still placed in the Prix Jacques le Marois and Prix du Moulin.

Ottoman Emperor (Ire)

4 ch c Excelebration - Ibiza Empress (Tertullian)

Johnny Murtagh (Ire) — OTI Racing

PLACINGS: 611110- — RPR **113**

	Starts	1st	2nd	3rd	4th	Win & Pl
	6	4	-	-	-	£127,269
	7/21	Gdwd	1m4f Cls1 Gp3 3yo gd-sft			£99,243
	7/21	Navn	1m2f 3yo good			£9,746
90	6/21	Gowr	1m1½f 73-90 Hcap good			£8,165
	4/21	Cork	1m2f Mdn Auct good			£10,009

Progressive, lightly raced colt who rose from maiden to Group company during a four-race

winning streak last season; peaked with a half-length win in the Gordon Stakes on first run over 1m4f but failed to stay when stepped up in trip again for the St Leger.

Oxted

6 b g Mayson - Charlotte Rosina (Choisir)

Roger Teal — S Piper, T Hirschfeld, D Fish & J Collins

PLACINGS: 5/126421/115/72313- — RPR **121**

	Starts	1st	2nd	3rd	4th	Win & Pl
	15	5	3	2	1	£514,740
	6/21	Asct	5f Cls1 Gp1 gd-fm			£198,485
	7/20	NmkJ	6f Cls1 Gp1 good			£141,775
	6/20	NmkR	6f Cls1 Gp3 gd-fm			£20,983
105	9/19	Donc	5½f Cls2 90-106 Hcap gd-fm			£37,350
	4/19	Sals	7f Cls5 3yo gd-fm			£5,111

Top-class sprinter who won last season's King's Stand Stakes on first run over 5f, landing a second Group 1 to go with the 2020 July Cup; good third when attempting to defend Newmarket crown but missed the rest of the season with a leg injury.

Panama Red (Ire)

3 ch f Showcasing - Allegation (Lawman)

Ger Lyons (Ire) — Against All Odds Partnership

PLACINGS: 4411- — RPR **102**

	Starts	1st	2nd	3rd	4th	Win & Pl
	4	2	-	-	2	£61,071
	9/21	Leop	7f List 2yo good			£52,679
	8/21	Tipp	7½f Mdn 2yo gd-yld			£7,375

Progressive two-year-old last season; won her maiden at the third attempt at Tipperary before

Ottoman Emperor (5): excelled through the ranks last season

taking a big step forward to win a Listed race at Leopardstown (runner-up won at that level next time); should make a useful miler.

Pearls Galore (Fr)

5 b m Invincible Spirit - Pearl Banks (Pivotal)

Paddy Twomey (Ire) — Scea Haras De Saint Pair

PLACINGS: 66/1125/311226- — RPR **115**

Starts	1st	2nd	3rd	4th	Win & Pl
12	4	3	1	-	£244,170

	8/21	Tipp	7½f Gp3 gd-yld	£28,973
	7/21	Fair	7f Gp3 good	£34,241
87	8/20	Cork	7f 73-89 Hcap good	£10,250
	7/20	Limk	7f Mdn good	£5,500

Progressed into a very smart filly last season; won two Group 3 races, doing particularly well to defy a penalty at Tipperary, and showed she belonged at Group 1 level when second in the Matron Stakes and Prix de la Foret; effective from 7f-1m and acts on any ground.

Perfect Power (Ire)

3 b c Ardad - Sagely (Frozen Power)

Richard Fahey — Sheikh Rashid Dalmook Al Maktoum

PLACINGS: 311511- — RPR **115+**

Starts	1st	2nd	3rd	4th	Win & Pl
6	4	-	1	-	£385,943

9/21	NmkR	6f Cls1 Gp1 2yo gd-fm	£151,345
8/21	Deau	6f Gp1 2yo gd-sft	£178,563
6/21	Asct	5f Cls1 Gp2 2yo gd-fm	£47,360
6/21	Haml	5f Cls5 Mdn 2yo gd-fm	£3,132

Dual Group 1 winner last season, confirming himself the best two-year-old sprinter with victory in the Middle Park Stakes to follow up a win in the Prix Morny; seems versatile regarding ground; breeding and patient running style give hope of staying a mile.

Piz Badile (Ire)

3 b/br c Ulysses - That Which Is Not (Elusive Quality)

Donnacha O'Brien (Ire) — Flaxman Stables Ireland

PLACINGS: 12- — RPR **105**

Starts	1st	2nd	3rd	4th	Win & Pl
2	1	1	-	-	£15,857

7/21	Klny	1m Mdn 2yo yield	£7,375

Killarney maiden winner who ran a big race for just his second run when a half-length second behind Duke De Sessa in a 1m1f Group 3 at Leopardstown on final outing; looks a good middle-distance prospect.

Point Lonsdale (Ire)

3 b c Australia - Sweepstake (Acclamation)

Aidan O'Brien (Ire) — Smith, Magnier, Tabor & Westerberg

PLACINGS: 11112- — RPR **113**

Starts	1st	2nd	3rd	4th	Win & Pl
5	4	1	-	-	£177,082

8/21	Curr	7f Gp2 2yo soft	£52,679
7/21	Leop	7f Gp3 2yo good	£26,339
6/21	Asct	7f Cls1 List 2yo soft	£38,480
6/21	Curr	7f Mdn 2yo yield	£8,692

Looked a future star when winning first four races last season, including twice at Group level, though bare form of those 1-6 and 1-8 wins not up to much; comprehensively beaten into second by Native Trail when again odds-on to follow up in the National Stakes.

Power Under Me (Ire)

4 b g Mehmas - Oonagh (Arakan)

Ger Lyons (Ire) Vincent Gaul

PLACINGS: 1/423261- RPR **116**

Starts	1st	2nd	3rd	4th	Win & Pl
7	2	2	1	1	£53,504
	10/21	Curr	6f List yld-sft		£19,754
	10/20	Naas	6f Mdn 2yo soft		£7,750

Lightly raced sprinter who produced a career-best when signing off last season with a runaway Listed win at the Curragh; had twice finished second in 6f Group 3 races earlier in the season and third in a 7f Group 2, though seemingly best at the shorter trip.

Princess Zoe (Ger)

7 gr m Jukebox Jury - Palace Princess (Tiger Hill)

Anthony Mullins (Ire) Patrick F Kehoe & Mrs P Crampton

PLACINGS: 3722/2111114/94225-0 RPR **115**

Starts	1st	2nd	3rd	4th	Win & Pl
28	7	8	3	2	£334,060
	10/20	Lonc	2m4f Gp1 heavy		£98,009
	9/20	Gway	1m4f List heavy		£18,750
90	8/20	Gway	1m4f 77-98 Hcap soft		£37,500
83	7/20	Gway	2m1f 82-100 Hcap soft		£37,500
70	7/20	Curr	1m4f 58-84 Hcap gd-yld		£10,500
	11/18	Muni	1m3f Hcap soft		£3,451
	9/18	Muni	1m2f 3yo soft		£2,655

Fairytale mare who enjoyed an incredible rise in 2020, starting on a mark of 64 and ending with victory in the Prix du Cadran; hasn't won since then but confirmed herself a top-class stayer given a sufficient stamina test when second on ground quicker than ideal in the Gold Cup at Ascot.

Prosperous Voyage (Ire)

3 b f Zoffany - Seatone (Mizzen Mast)

Ralph Beckett M Chan & A Rosen

PLACINGS: 412322- RPR **107**

Starts	1st	2nd	3rd	4th	Win & Pl
6	1	3	1	1	£146,328
	7/21	Epsm	7f Cls4 Mdn 2yo good		£5,400

Won only an Epsom maiden from six races last season but was placed three times in Group company, including when twice chasing home Inspiral; did best when rallying strongly for second in the Fillies' Mile and should be well suited by middle distances.

Pyledriver

5 b h Harbour Watch - La Pyle (Le Havre)

William Muir & Chris Grassick La Pyle Partnership

PLACINGS: 1417/210137/2112-0 RPR **122**

Starts	1st	2nd	3rd	4th	Win & Pl
15	6	3	1	1	£821,412
	11/21	Ling	1m2f Cls1 List stand		£24,385
	6/21	Epsm	1m4f Cls1 Gp1 gd-sft		£187,143
	8/20	York	1m4f Cls1 Gp2 3yo good		£42,533
	6/20	Asct	1m4f Cls1 Gp2 3yo gd-sft		£65,120
	9/19	Hayd	1m Cls1 List 2yo soft		£14,461
	7/19	Sals	7f Cls4 2yo firm		£5,175

Has developed into a top-class middle-distance performer during the last two seasons and won the Coronation Cup last May when outbattling Al Aasy; missed domestic summer targets

Prosperous Voyage (second left): could be smart over middle distances

through injury but has the King George as first aim this time after an international campaign.

Quickthorn

5 b g Nathaniel - Daffydowndilly (Oasis Dream)

Hughie Morrison — Lady Blyth

PLACINGS: 96/13/1182149- RPR **115+**

Starts	1st	2nd	3rd	4th	Win & Pl
11	4	1	1	1	£150,066

	9/21	Sals	1m6f Cls2 good	£10,308
97	6/21	Asct	1m4f Cls2 94-104 Hcap heavy	£35,100
84	5/21	Hayd	1m4f Cls3 80-92 Hcap gd-sft	£5,927
	6/20	Kemp	1m3f Cls5 Auct Mdn 3-5yo std-slw	£3,493

Twice disappointed in the autumn but had looked a progressive stayer up to that point; won 1m4f handicaps at Haydock and Ascot early last season before stepping up again with a head second in the Ebor at York and a career-best win in a 1m6f conditions race at Salisbury.

Raclette

3 b f Frankel - Emollient (Empire Maker)

Andre Fabre (Fr) — Juddmonte

PLACINGS: 11- RPR **100+**

Starts	1st	2nd	3rd	4th	Win & Pl
2	2	-	-	-	£27,232

9/21	Chan	1m 2yo soft	£15,179
8/21	Deau	7½f 2yo soft	£12,054

Unbeaten in two runs last season and had been set to go off a warm favourite for the Prix Marcel Boussac until withdrawn (trainer concerned about heavy ground); had won previous race at Chantilly by four lengths and looks an exciting filly over a mile and beyond.

Rainbow Fire (Ire)

4 b c Kodiac - Heroine Chic (Big Bad Bob)

John & Thady Gosden — Saeed Suhail

PLACINGS: 81/ RPR **92**

Starts	1st	2nd	3rd	4th	Win & Pl
2	1	-	-	-	£5,175

9/20	NmkR	7f Cls4 Mdn 2yo good	£5,175

Missed last season through injury but had looked a potential Group horse when winning a 7f maiden at Newmarket in September 2020, staying on well; unlikely to stay much further (full brother Dhahmaan never raced beyond 7f) but should have more to offer at around a mile.

Reach For The Moon

3 b c Sea The Stars - Golden Stream (Sadler's Wells)

John & Thady Gosden — The Queen

PLACINGS: 22112- RPR **111**

Starts	1st	2nd	3rd	4th	Win & Pl
5	2	3	-	-	£82,429

8/21	Sand	7f Cls1 Gp3 2yo good	£34,026
7/21	Newb	7f Cls4 2yo good	£5,400

Made a big impression when hacking up by four lengths in last season's Solario Stakes; softer ground reportedly to blame when just beaten at odds-on by Bayside Boy in the Champagne Stakes on only subsequent run; should stay middle distances.

Real Appeal (Ger)

5 b g Sidestep - Runaway Sparkle (Green Desert)

Jessica Harrington (Ire) — Zhang Yuesheng

PLACINGS: 10745/058353/131319- RPR **114**

Starts	1st	2nd	3rd	4th	Win & Pl
20	6	1	4	1	£211,739

	9/21	Leop	1m Gp2 good	£79,018
	6/21	Leop	7f Gp3 good	£26,339
90	4/21	Leop	7f 83-100 Hcap good	£11,063
	5/19	MsnL	5f List 2yo good	£27,027
	5/19	Mars	6f 2yo good	£12,162
	4/19	Chan	5½f 2yo gd-sft	£12,162

Big improver last season and gained biggest win in the Group 2 Boomerang Mile at Leopardstown on Irish Champions Weekend; particularly effective at that track and also won twice over 7f there last season; needs good ground or quicker.

Real World (Ire)

5 b h Dark Angel - Nafura (Dubawi)

Saeed bin Suroor — Godolphin

PLACINGS: 12/3341111-10 RPR **122+**

Starts	1st	2nd	3rd	4th	Win & Pl
11	6	1	2	1	£347,444

	1/22	Meyd	1m Gp2 good	£80,000
	10/21	Lonc	1m Gp2 v soft	£101,786
	8/21	York	1m1f Cls1 Gp3 good	£56,710
	7/21	Newb	1m2f Cls1 List gd-fm	£25,520
94	6/21	Asct	1m Cls2 93-109 Hcap gd-fm	£64,800
	10/20	Chmf	1m2f Cls5 stand	£3,752

Proved a revelation when facing turf for the first time last season, running away with the Royal Hunt Cup and going on to complete a four-timer in a Group 2 at Longchamp; had struggled on dirt at Meydan and again failed to take to the surface in the Saudi Cup.

Revolver (Ire)

5 b g Slade Power - Swizzle Stick (Sadler's Wells)

Sir Mark Prescott — Ne'Er Do Wells

PLACINGS: 606/1111114/ RPR **107**

Starts	1st	2nd	3rd	4th	Win & Pl
10	6	-	-	1	£30,649

91	8/20	Pont	2m1f Cls4 73-91 Hcap gd-fm	£5,175
85	8/20	Sand	1m6f Cls3 80-88 3yo Hcap gd-fm	£6,728
78	7/20	Hayd	1m6f Cls4 77-82 3yo Hcap gd-sft	£4,690
71	6/20	Donc	1m6½f Cls5 52-71 3yo Hcap gd-fm	£3,493
63	6/20	Rdcr	1m6f Cls6 45-63 3yo Hcap good	£2,782
57	6/20	Pont	1m4f Cls5 51-71 3yo Hcap good	£3,493

Missed last season through injury but had been a typical Sir Mark Prescott improver when stepped up in trip in 2020, rattling off a six-timer; found big step up in class beyond him when only fourth in the Doncaster Cup on final run; still on feasible mark for top staying handicaps.

Ribhi (Ire)

3 gr c Dark Angel - Rihaam (Dansili)

Marcus Tregoning — Shadwell Estate Company

PLACINGS: 151- RPR **99+**

Starts	1st	2nd	3rd	4th	Win & Pl
3	2	-	-	-	£16,736

	9/21	Sals	6f Cls2 2yo soft	£10,260
	8/21	Sals	6f Cls4 2yo good	£5,400

Won two out of three last season and unlucky not to go close when suffering sole defeat in a Listed race at Doncaster; bounced back with a narrow win at Salisbury when reverting to 6f, proving versatility regarding ground.

Rohaan (Ire)

4 b g Mayson - Vive Les Rouges (Acclamation)

David Evans — Chris Kiely Racing & J Tomkins

PLACINGS: 7111/252151110950-87 RPR **120**

Starts	1st	2nd	3rd	4th	Win & Pl
20	7	2	-	-	£184,377

112	6/21	Asct	6f Cls2 96-112 Hcap soft	£64,800
	5/21	Hayd	6f Cls1 Gp2 3yo heavy	£51,039
	4/21	Asct	6f Cls1 Gp3 3yo gd-fm	£39,697
91	3/21	Ling	6f Cls3 79-94 3yo Hcap stand	£7,246
73	12/20	Ling	6f Cls4 73-83 2yo Hcap stand	£5,822
61	12/20	Kemp	7f Cls5 61-74 2yo Hcap std-slw	£3,429
55	12/20	Newc	6f Cls6 45-59 2yo Hcap stand	£2,782

Progressive in late 2020 and early 2021, starting on a mark of 55 and winning seven times, including two 6f Group races and the Wokingham off 112; couldn't land a blow in four Group 1 sprints subsequently.

Romantic Proposal (Ire)

6 b m Raven's Pass - Playwithmyheart (Diktat)

Edward Lynam (Ire) — Clipper Logistics Group

PLACINGS: 22411/614647/321310- RPR **116+**

Starts	1st	2nd	3rd	4th	Win & Pl
18	5	3	3	3	£281,991

	9/21	Curr	5f Gp1 good	£158,036
	6/21	Curr	6f List good	£39,509
83	7/20	Curr	6½f 83-105 Hcap yield	£37,500
71	10/19	Cork	7f 71-91 Hcap yld-sft	£9,584
	9/19	Cork	7f Mdn good	£6,655

Surprise winner of last season's Flying Five at the Curragh, relishing a burn-up over 5f with best form previously coming over 6f; had been a big improver earlier in the season, albeit at a lower level, winning a Listed race and finishing second in a Group 3.

Royal Patronage (Fr)

3 b c Wootton Bassett - Shaloushka (Dalakhani)

Charlie & Mark Johnston — Highclere T'Bred Racing - Woodland Walk

PLACINGS: 521118- RPR **112**

Starts	1st	2nd	3rd	4th	Win & Pl
6	3	1	-	-	£120,822

	9/21	NmkR	1m Cls1 Gp2 2yo gd-fm	£56,710
	8/21	York	7f Cls1 Gp3 2yo good	£56,710
	7/21	Epsm	7f Cls4 2yo gd-sft	£5,400

Remarkable winner of last season's Royal Lodge Stakes, showing terrific stamina to run down Coroebus from a seemingly hopeless position; had also won the Acomb Stakes but was struck into when last in the Vertem Futurity Trophy; seems sure to get a mile and a half.

Sacred

4 b f Exceed And Excel - Sacre Caroline (Blame)

William Haggas — Cheveley Park Stud

PLACINGS: 12228/171- RPR **115+**

Starts	1st	2nd	3rd	4th	Win & Pl
8	3	3	-	-	£126,589

	8/21	Newb	7f Cls1 Gp2 good	£56,710
	4/21	NmkR	7f Cls1 Gp3 3yo good	£25,520
	6/20	NmkR	5f Cls5 Mdn 2yo gd-fm	£4,140

Won the Hungerford Stakes and Nell Gwyn last season to atone for three near misses at Group level last season; otherwise held up by need for quick ground, running just once more when seventh in the 1,000 Guineas (didn't stay a mile); could thrive at 6f or 7f.

Sacred Bridge

3 b f Bated Breath - Sacred Shield (Beat Hollow)

Ger Lyons (Ire) — Juddmonte

PLACINGS: 11118- RPR **110+**

Starts	1st	2nd	3rd	4th	Win & Pl
5	4	-	-	-	£188,165

	8/21	Curr	6f Gp3 2yo good	£26,339
	8/21	Naas	6f 2yo good	£132,589
	6/21	Tipp	5f List 2yo gd-fm	£21,071
	6/21	Naas	6f Mdn 2yo good	£8,165

Looked a hugely exciting filly when completing a four-timer with a wide-margin win in a Group 3 at the Curragh last season; duly sent off a warm 13-8 favourite for the Cheveley Park but blotted her copybook when well beaten in eighth; looks an out-and-out sprinter.

Saffron Beach (Ire)

4 ch f New Bay - Falling Petals (Raven's Pass)

Jane Chapple-Hyam — Mrs B V Sangster, J Wigan & O Sangster

PLACINGS: 11/228011- RPR **118**

Starts	1st	2nd	3rd	4th	Win & Pl
8	4	2	-	-	£309,271

	10/21	NmkR	1m Cls1 Gp1 good	£141,775
	8/21	Sand	1m Cls1 Gp3 good	£45,368
	10/20	NmkR	7f Cls1 Gp3 2yo soft	£26,654
	9/20	NmkR	7f Cls4 Mdn 2yo good	£5,175

Clearcut winner of the Sun Chariot Stakes last autumn to arguably stamp herself as the leading three-year-old filly over a mile, comprehensively turning the tables on 1,000 Guineas winner Mother Earth after finishing second in the Classic; hadn't stayed 1m4f in the Oaks.

Sandrine: very smart at two and promises to stay a mile this term

Sandrine

3 b f Bobby's Kitten - Seychelloise (Pivotal)

Andrew Balding — Miss K Rausing

PLACINGS: 11123- — RPR **108**

Starts	1st	2nd	3rd	4th	Win & Pl
5	3	1	1	-	£155,432

7/21	NmkJ	6f Cls1 Gp2 2yo gd-fm	£51,039
6/21	Asct	6f Cls1 Gp3 2yo heavy	£38,480
5/21	Kemp	6f Cls5 2yo std-slw	£3,132

Not far off last season's top two-year-old fillies; won the Albany and Duchess of Cambridge Stakes before a good second under a penalty in the Lowther and a solid third in the Cheveley Park (best of those drawn low); could well stay a mile.

Scope (Ire)

4 ch c Teofilo - Look So (Efisio)

Ralph Beckett — J H Richmond-Watson

PLACINGS: 1/235611- — RPR **118**

Starts	1st	2nd	3rd	4th	Win & Pl
7	3	1	1	-	£267,135

10/21	Lonc	1m7½f Gp1 v soft	£178,563
10/21	Asct	1m6f Cls1 List 3yo gd-sft	£60,963
10/20	Newb	1m Cls4 2yo heavy	£4,464

Unexposed stayer who won last season's Prix Royal-Oak on very soft ground at Longchamp; hadn't looked up to that level over middle distances and when well beaten in the St Leger, though hinted at potential as a stayer with a wide-margin Listed win at Ascot.

Sealiway (Fr)

4 ch c Galiway - Kensea (Kendargent)

Francis Graffard (Fr) — Le Haras De La Gousserie & Guy Pariente

PLACINGS: 1131215/28251-0 — RPR **124**

Starts	1st	2nd	3rd	4th	Win & Pl
13	5	3	1	-	£1,375,996

10/21	Asct	1m2f Cls1 Gp1 gd-sft	£714,546
10/20	Lonc	7f Gp1 2yo heavy	£130,647
8/20	Vich	7f List 2yo gd-sft	£20,042
6/20	Chan	6f 2yo gd-sft	£12,881
5/20	StCl	6f 2yo soft	£10,508

Proved a top-class colt when stepped up to middle distances last season and signed off by winning the Champion Stakes at Ascot; had finished second in the Prix du Jockey Club and fifth in the Arc (given too much to do); didn't seem to take to dirt in Saudi Arabia this year.

Search For A Song (Ire)

6 ch m Galileo - Polished Gem (Danehill)

Dermot Weld (Ire) — Moyglare Stud Farm

PLACINGS: 12411/6P312/25614- — RPR **116**

Starts	1st	2nd	3rd	4th	Win & Pl
15	5	3	1	2	£719,718

9/21	Curr	2m Gp3 good	£26,339
9/20	Curr	1m6f Gp1 good	£193,220
9/19	Curr	1m6f Gp1 gd-fm	£308,108
8/19	York	1m4f Cls1 List good	£39,697
5/19	Fair	1m2f Mdn gd-fm	£6,659

Top-class stayer who won the Irish St Leger in 2019 and 2020; largely out of sorts last season, including a disappointing sixth in the Irish St

Leger when coming off a much longer absence than usual, but did manage a wide-margin Group 3 win at the Curragh.

Silent Escape (Ire)

5 ch m New Approach - Rosewater (Pivotal)

Saeed bin Suroor — Godolphin

PLACINGS: 1/1211- — RPR **115**

Starts	1st	2nd	3rd	4th	Win & Pl
5	4	1	-	-	£39,098

	9/21	Newb	7f Cls1 List gd-sft	£22,684
91	8/21	Sand	7f Cls3 82-92 Hcap good	£7,731
	6/21	Newc	7f Cls5 stand	£3,024
	11/20	Wolv	7f Cls5 stand	£3,429

Has won four out of five races and progressed into a very smart filly last season; made up for a narrow defeat on handicap debut by hacking up at Sandown and then stepped up in class to win a Listed race at Newbury; yet to race beyond 7f.

Sir Busker (Ire)

6 b g Sir Prancealot - Street Kitty (Tiger Hill)

William Knight — Kennet Valley Thoroughbreds

PLACINGS: /11292204/34372430-8 — RPR **116**

Starts	1st	2nd	3rd	4th	Win & Pl
31	5	8	3	5	£221,004

96	6/20	Asct	1m Cls2 88-96 Hcap good	£22,642
92	6/20	Newc	1m Cls2 90-99 Hcap std-slw	£9,704
89	9/19	Kemp	1m Cls3 83-90 Hcap std-slw	£9,338
77	6/19	Gdwd	7f Cls5 59-77 3yo Hcap gd-sft	£6,404
	9/18	Newb	6f Cls4 Mdn 2yo gd-sft	£6,469

Progressed out of handicaps in 2020 and slightly struggled in stronger company last season, though ran some big races in defeat; finished third in the Queen Anne Stakes behind Palace Pier and came closest to winning when a length second in a Group 3 at Salisbury.

Sir Busker leads before scoring at Ascot in the 2020 Silver Royal Hunt Cup

Sisfahan (Fr)

4 ch c Isfahan - Kendalee (Kendargent)

Henk Grewe (Ger) — Darius Racing

PLACINGS: 1/21237- — RPR **117**

	Starts	1st	2nd	3rd	4th	Win & Pl
	6	2	2	1	-	£429,642
	7/21	Hamb	1m4f Gp1 3yo gd-sft			£348,214
	11/20	Pari	1m2f 2yo v soft			£6,695

High-class German colt who was a brilliant winner of last season's German Derby and pushed Torquator Tasso close in what proved a red-hot Grosser Preis von Baden; only third behind Alpinista at Cologne (reportedly unsuited by slow pace) and seventh in the Breeders' Cup Turf.

Siskany

4 b g Dubawi - Halay (Dansili)

Charlie Appleby — Godolphin

PLACINGS: 51/1142142-13 — RPR **121**

	Starts	1st	2nd	3rd	4th	Win & Pl
	11	5	2	1	2	£335,480
	1/22	Meyd	1m6f List good			£44,444
103	10/21	NmkR	1m4f Cls2 82-103 3yo Hcap gd-sft			£61,848
86	5/21	Sand	1m2f Cls3 77-90 3yo Hcap soft			£5,927
	4/21	Wind	1m2f Cls5 3yo gd-fm			£2,862
	9/20	Kemp	1m Cls5 2yo std-slw			£4,075

Progressive middle-distance handicapper last season and produced a particularly big run on first run since being gelded when landing a valuable 1m4f contest at Newmarket; twice beaten at odds-on in Group/Listed company before easily back to winning ways in a Listed race in Dubai.

Sissoko (Ire)

3 b c Australia - Love Excelling (Polish Precedent)

Donnacha O'Brien (Ire) — J Carthy

PLACINGS: 612- — RPR **112**

Starts	1st	2nd	3rd	4th	Win & Pl
3	1	1	-	-	£53,695

	10/21	Curr	1m1f Mdn 2yo yield	£8,692

Quickly developed into a high-class two-year-old last autumn; put a disappointing debut behind him to win a Curragh maiden by six lengths and then pushed Luxembourg closest when second in the Vertem Futurity Trophy; bred for middle distances and should stay well.

Skalleti (Fr)

7 gr g Kendargent - Skallet (Muhaymin)

Jerome Reynier (Fr) — Jean-Claude Seroul

PLACINGS: 11111/331127/111141- — RPR **121+**

Starts	1st	2nd	3rd	4th	Win & Pl
23	17	1	2	1	£1,000,336

	11/21	Capa	1m2f Gp2 heavy	£93,973
	7/21	Muni	1m2f Gp1 gd-sft	£53,571
	5/21	Lonc	1m1f Gp1 gd-sft	£127,545
	4/21	Lonc	1m2f Gp2 v soft	£66,161
	3/21	StCl	1m2f Gp3 heavy	£35,714
	10/20	Lonc	1m2f Gp2 heavy	£76,032
	8/20	Deau	1m2f Gp3 heavy	£26,695
	11/19	Capa	1m2f Gp2 heavy	£105,405
	10/19	Lonc	1m2f Gp2 v soft	£102,703
	8/19	Deau	1m Gp3 good	£36,036
	7/19	Vich	1m List soft	£23,423
	6/19	Ponv	1m2f slow	£22,523
	5/19	Lonc	1m soft	£12,613
	3/19	Chan	1m stand	£12,613
	1/19	Ponv	1m2f 4yo stand	£7,658
	11/18	Ponv	1m2f 3yo stand	£6,195
	10/18	Nime	1m1½f 3yo soft	£5,089

Dual Group 1 winner last season, edging home in the Prix Ganay before readily justifying short odds in a much weaker race in Germany; second in the Champion Stakes in 2020 but missed the race last season (ground quicker than ideal), instead landing a Group 2 in Italy on final run.

Skazino (Fr)

6 ch g Kendargent - Skallet (Muhaymin)

Richard Chotard (Fr) — Le Haras De La Gousserie

PLACINGS: /115413/545112142-57 — RPR **117**

Starts	1st	2nd	3rd	4th	Win & Pl
27	10	2	2	5	£414,226

	8/21	Deau	1m7f Gp2 gd-sft	£66,161
	5/21	Lonc	1m7½f Gp2 v soft	£66,161
	5/21	Lonc	1m7½f Gp3 gd-sft	£35,714
	11/20	Mars	1m2f List gd-sft	£20,042
	8/20	Vich	1m4f gd-sft	£9,068
	7/20	Comp	1m4f gd-sft	£10,508
0	11/19	StCl	1m4f 3yo Hcap heavy	£18,018
	6/19	Mars	1m2½f 3yo good	£13,514
	5/19	Saln	1m4f 3yo gd-sft	£9,910
	5/19	Mars	1m2f 3yo Hcap gd-fm	£7,658

Smart and progressive stayer who won a pair of Group 2 races last season; finished a fair fourth in a red-hot Prix du Cadran before a length second behind Scope when favourite for the Prix Royal-Oak.

Solid Stone (Ire)

6 br g Shamardal - Landmark (Arch)

Sir Michael Stoute — Saeed Suhail

PLACINGS: 223/103123/5133411-0 — RPR **117**

Starts	1st	2nd	3rd	4th	Win & Pl
23	7	4	5	2	£187,937

	9/21	Newb	1m3f Cls1 Gp3 good	£39,697
	8/21	Wind	1m2f Cls1 Gp3 gd-fm	£34,026
	5/21	Wind	1m Cls1 List gd-sft	£22,684
101	9/20	Chmf	1m2f Cls2 88-103 Hcap stand	£11,828
94	6/20	Sand	1m Cls2 87-95 Hcap good	£9,704
85	4/19	NmkR	1m2f Cls3 83-95 3yo Hcap gd-fm	£12,938
	11/18	Newc	7f Cls4 2yo stand	£4,787

Progressive gelding who signed off last season with successive Group 3 wins having moved out of handicaps only at the start of the year to win a first Listed race; looked a strong stayer when stepped up to 1m3f for the first time for final win at Newbury and could get 1m4f.

Sonnyboyliston (Ire)

5 ch g Power - Miss Macnamara (Dylan Thomas)

Johnny Murtagh (Ire) — Kildare Racing Club

PLACINGS: 600/13114/331611-2 — RPR **121**

Starts	1st	2nd	3rd	4th	Win & Pl
15	6	1	3	1	£1,037,459

	9/21	Curr	1m6f Gp1 good	£254,464
108	8/21	York	1m6f Cls2 101-116 Hcap good	£300,000
	6/21	Limk	1m4½f List good	£19,754
99	9/20	Curr	1m2f 83-105 Hcap good	£62,500
86	7/20	Curr	1m2f 68-88 3yo Hcap gd-yld	£7,750
68	6/20	Gowr	1m 62-75 3yo Hcap yield	£5,000

Hugely progressive when stepped up in trip last season and won the Irish St Leger after an even bigger payday when landing the Ebor at York; second in Saudi Arabia first time out this year; has run just four times over 1m6f (outpaced in slowly run race the first time) and still unexposed as a stayer.

Star Of India (Ire)

3 b c Galileo - Shermeen (Desert Style)

Aidan O'Brien (Ire) — Tabor, Smith, Magnier & Westerberg

PLACINGS: 1- — RPR **93+**

Starts	1st	2nd	3rd	4th	Win & Pl
1	1	-	-	-	£8,691

	10/21	Leop	7f Mdn 2yo good	£8,692

Fascinating winner of a 7f Leopardstown maiden first time out last season, finishing really strongly having been off the bridle for much of the race; should come on in leaps and bounds for the experience and looks a proper middle-distance type.

State Of Rest (Ire)

4 b c Starspangledbanner - Repose (Quiet American)

Joseph O'Brien (Ire) — Teme Valley Racing

PLACINGS: 125435/311- — RPR **121**

Starts	1st	2nd	3rd	4th	Win & Pl
9	3	1	2	1	£2,146,955

Date	Course	Race	Prize
10/21	Moon	1m2f Gp1 gd-sft	£1,713,483
8/21	Sara	1m1½f Gd1 3yo firm	£390,511
6/20	Fair	6f Mdn 2yo gd-fm	£12,508

Proved a major money-spinner abroad last season, winning the Saratoga Derby in the US and followed up in the Cox Plate in Australia; has won no more than a maiden in Europe (best run when a length third in 2020 Champagne Stakes) but has clearly improved since.

Storm Damage

4 b g Night Of Thunder - Sundrop (Sunday Silence)

Saeed bin Suroor — Godolphin

PLACINGS: 1911-41 — RPR **113**

Starts	1st	2nd	3rd	4th	Win & Pl
6	4	-	-	1	£71,658

	Date	Course	Race	Prize
	2/22	Meyd	7f List good	£44,444
97	8/21	NmkJ	1m Cls2 86-97 3yo Hcap good	£10,800
	7/21	NmkJ	1m Cls4 gd-fm	£5,400
	6/21	Kemp	7f Cls4 std-slw	£4,347

Progressive miler last season, winning two novice events before hacking up on handicap debut at Newmarket; looked to have improved again when successful at Meydan this winter; could make a mark in Group company back in Europe.

Stradivarius (Ire)

8 ch h Sea The Stars - Private Life (Bering)

John & Thady Gosden — B E Nielsen

PLACINGS: 11112/311270/141123- — RPR **119**

Starts	1st	2nd	3rd	4th	Win & Pl
32	19	4	4	2	£3,198,425

	Date	Course	Race	Prize
	9/21	Donc	2m2f Cls1 Gp2 gd-fm	£62,381
	8/21	York	2m½f Cls1 Gp2 gd-fm	£85,065
	4/21	Asct	2m Cls1 Gp3 gd-fm	£39,697
	7/20	Gdwd	2m Cls1 Gp1 good	£141,775
	6/20	Asct	2m4f Cls1 Gp1 soft	£148,000
	9/19	Donc	2m2f Cls1 Gp2 gd-fm	£56,710
	8/19	York	2m½f Cls1 Gp2 gd-fm	£127,598
	7/19	Gdwd	2m Cls1 Gp1 good	£283,550
	6/19	Asct	2m4f Cls1 Gp1 soft	£283,550
	5/19	York	1m6f Cls1 Gp2 gd-fm	£93,572
	10/18	Asct	2m Cls1 Gp2 soft	£300,563
	8/18	York	2m½f Cls1 Gp2 gd-fm	£127,598
	7/18	Gdwd	2m Cls1 Gp1 good	£283,550
	6/18	Asct	2m4f Cls1 Gp1 gd-fm	£283,550
	5/18	York	1m6f Cls1 Gp2 gd-fm	£93,572
	8/17	Gdwd	2m Cls1 Gp1 good	£296,593
	6/17	Asct	1m6f Cls1 Gp2 3yo gd-fm	£91,445
78	4/17	Bevl	1m2f Cls4 64-80 3yo Hcap gd-fm	£5,041
	11/16	Newc	1m Cls5 Mdn 2yo stand	£3,235

Legendary stayer who has won three Gold Cups at Ascot and four Goodwood Cups; not quite at his best last season but did win the Lonsdale Cup and Doncaster Cup to take Group haul to 17 – 19 wins in all – and had excuses when placed behind Trueshan in the Prix du Cadran and Long Distance Cup.

Straight Answer

3 b c Kodiac - Straight Thinking (Mizzen Mast)

Ger Lyons (Ire) — Juddmonte

PLACINGS: 118- — RPR **112+**

Starts	1st	2nd	3rd	4th	Win & Pl
3	2	-	-	-	£29,763

Date	Course	Race	Prize
9/21	Fair	6f List 2yo gd-fm	£21,071
8/21	Curr	6f Mdn 2yo soft	£8,692

Hugely impressive winner of a Listed race at Fairyhouse last season, storming clear by five and a half lengths; sent off just 7-1 when supplemented for the Dewhurst but trailed home last of eight; will surely prove better than that, possibly when dropped back to sprint trips.

Subastar (Ire)

3 b c Sea The Stars - Suba (Seeking The Gold)

Roger Varian — Sheikh Mohammed Obaid Al Maktoum

PLACINGS: 1- — RPR **90+**

Starts	1st	2nd	3rd	4th	Win & Pl
1	1	-	-	-	£5,400

Date	Course	Race	Prize
9/21	NmkR	1m Cls4 Mdn 2yo good	£5,400

Belied odds of 14-1 to win what looked a really strong mile maiden on sole run last season at Newmarket (runner-up had been second in Convivial Maiden, third and fourth won three times between them before end of year); fascinating prospect over a mile and beyond.

Suesa (Ire)

4 b f Night Of Thunder - Sally Is The Boss (Orpen)

Francois Rohaut (Fr) — George Strawbridge

PLACINGS: 11/118145- — RPR **122**

Starts	1st	2nd	3rd	4th	Win & Pl
8	5	-	-	1	£302,486

Date	Course	Race	Prize
7/21	Gdwd	5f Cls1 Gp2 gd-sft	£170,130
5/21	Chan	6f Gp3 3yo soft	£35,714
4/21	Chan	5½f Gp3 3yo gd-sft	£35,714
11/20	Chan	5½f List 2yo heavy	£20,042
10/20	Chan	6f 2yo heavy	£10,508

Lightly raced sprinter who won three Group races last season, most notably the King George Stakes at Glorious Goodwood; sent off favourite three times at Group 1 level but finished no better than fourth (two biggest defeats on heavy ground, though does handle some cut).

Sunray Major

5 b h Dubawi - Zenda (Zamindar)

John & Thady Gosden — Juddmonte

PLACINGS: 14/110- — RPR **111+**

Starts	1st	2nd	3rd	4th	Win & Pl
5	3	-	-	1	£14,389

	Date	Course	Race	Prize
95	10/21	Asct	7f Cls3 83-95 Hcap gd-sft	£6,480
	9/21	Chmf	7f Cls5 stand	£3,510
	6/20	NmkR	1m Cls5 3yo good	£4,140

Very lightly raced and had missed more than a year before returning last autumn but quickly made a big impression in easily winning at Chelmsford and Ascot; sent off just 2-1 when disappointing in the Balmoral Handicap on Champions Day; seems sure to bounce back.

Symbolize (Ire)

5 ch g Starspangledbanner - French Flirt (Peintre Celebre)

Andrew Balding — Sheikh Juma Dalmook Al Maktoum

PLACINGS: 145/343288/20701722- RPR **110**

Starts	1st	2nd	3rd	4th	Win & Pl
17	2	4	2	2	£125,177

	8/21	Thsk	7f Cls3 soft	£8,640
	5/19	Sals	5f Cls4 2yo gd-fm	£5,111

Did really well in second half of last season, winning at Thirsk and running two big races at Ascot when second in the Balmoral Handicap behind Aldaary having also chased home that horse previously; seemingly well suited by plenty of cut; one for top 7f-1m handicaps.

Tashkhan (Ire)

4 b g Born To Sea - Tarziyna (Raven's Pass)

Brian Ellison — P Boyle

PLACINGS: 087/121912552- RPR **118**

Starts	1st	2nd	3rd	4th	Win & Pl
12	3	3	-	-	£184,885

86	7/21	Hayd	1m6f Cls2 73-94 3yo Hcap soft	£51,540
75	5/21	Hayd	1m2f Cls4 64-79 3yo Hcap soft	£4,347
57	3/21	Navn	1m2f 49-69 3yo Hcap heavy	£5,531

Thorough stayer who proved a revelation when getting a decent test over 2m in the Long Distance Cup at Ascot, finishing second behind Trueshan at 50-1; had won a 1m6f handicap at Haydock before just coming up short in stronger races at around that trip.

Team Of Firsts

4 b g Zoffany - Mount Crystal (Montjeu)

Ger Lyons (Ire) — David Spratt, Sean Jones & Mrs Lynne Lyons

PLACINGS: 42/1541- RPR **108+**

Starts	1st	2nd	3rd	4th	Win & Pl
6	2	1	-	2	£21,855

86	10/21	Naas	1m2f 71-86 Hcap heavy	£8,165
	3/21	Navn	1m2f Mdn Auct 3yo heavy	£10,009

Remarkably easy seven-length winner of a handicap at Naas in October on second run after being gelded, having also won at Navan earlier in the year; gained both wins on heavy ground and yet to fire on a quicker surface, though still lightly raced.

Tenebrism (USA)

3 b/br f Caravaggio - Immortal Verse (Pivotal)

Aidan O'Brien (Ire) — Westerberg, Coolmore & Merribelle Stables

PLACINGS: 11- RPR **116+**

Starts	1st	2nd	3rd	4th	Win & Pl
2	2	-	-	-	£168,289

	9/21	NmkR	6f Cls1 Gp1 2yo gd-fm	£160,915
	3/21	Naas	5f Mdn 2yo soft	£7,375

Remarkable winner of last season's Cheveley Park Stakes, overcoming a six-month layoff since March debut and an unpromising track position to produce a stunning turn of foot, though bare form questionable; likely to start in the 1,000 Guineas, though could yet end up a sprinter.

Thunderous (left): talented performer is on something of a recovery mission this season

Teona (Ire)

4 b f Sea The Stars - Ambivalent (Authorized)

Roger Varian — Ali Saeed

PLACINGS: 21/30113- — RPR **118+**

Starts	1st	2nd	3rd	4th	Win & Pl
7	3	1	2	-	£604,064

9/21	Lonc	1m4f Gp1 good	£306,107
8/21	Wind	1m3½f Cls1 List gd-fm	£20,983
11/20	Newc	1m2f Cls4 Mdn 2yo std-slw	£5,111

Lightly raced filly who disappointed in last season's Oaks but proved much better after a subsequent break and made her Group I breakthrough when surprising Snowfall in the Prix Vermeille; good third in the Breeders' Cup Turf having missed the Arc because of soft ground.

The Revenant

7 ch g Dubawi - Hazel Lavery (Excellent Art)

Francis Graffard (Fr) — Al Asayl France

PLACINGS: /1211/11112/11/3424- — RPR **121**

Starts	1st	2nd	3rd	4th	Win & Pl
17	10	3	2	2	£1,036,955

10/20	Asct	1m Cls1 Gp1 soft	£368,615
10/20	Lonc	1m Gp2 heavy	£76,032
10/19	Lonc	1m Gp2 v soft	£102,703
5/19	Badn	1m Gp2 good	£36,036
3/19	StCl	1m Gp3 good	£36,036
3/19	StCl	1m List heavy	£23,423
11/18	StCl	1m 3yo v soft	£15,487
10/18	Mars	1m 3yo soft	£9,735
9/18	Rcpp	1m½f 3-4yo gd-sft	£4,204
9/17	Hayd	1m Cls4 2yo gd-sft	£4,528

Top French miler at his best on heavy ground, enjoying his finest hour when winning the Queen Elizabeth II Stakes on Champions Day in 2020; not quite at that level last season, though came within a short neck of winning a third Prix Dollar when pipped by Real World.

Third Realm

4 b c Sea The Stars - Reem Three (Mark Of Esteem)

Roger Varian — Sheikh Mohammed Obaid Al Maktoum

PLACINGS: 5/115374- — RPR **113**

Starts	1st	2nd	3rd	4th	Win & Pl
7	2	-	1	1	£98,942

5/21	Ling	1m3½f Cls1 List 3yo soft	£34,488
4/21	Nott	1m2f Cls5 Mdn 3yo gd-fm	£2,862

Beat Adayar when winning last season's Lingfield Derby Trial but failed to match that one's subsequent progress; fair fifth at Epsom but managed only third when favourite for the Gordon Stakes, with best run coming when a close fourth in the Prix Dollar.

Thunderous (Ire)

5 b g Night Of Thunder - Souviens Toi (Dalakhani)

Charlie & Mark Johnston — Highclere T'Bred Racing - George Stubbs

PLACINGS: 111/21/7324- — RPR **113**

Starts	1st	2nd	3rd	4th	Win & Pl
9	4	2	1	1	£107,785

7/20	York	1m2½f Cls1 Gp2 3yo gd-sft	£31,191
8/19	Newb	7f Cls1 List 2yo soft	£22,684
7/19	Rdcr	7f Cls5 2yo gd-fm	£3,881
6/19	Donc	7f Cls4 2yo good	£4,787

Impressive winner of the Dante Stakes in 2020, making it four wins out of five at the time; missed the rest of that year through injury and slightly disappointing in four runs last season, albeit

facing stiff tasks in good middle-distances races; has since been gelded.

Tis Marvellous

8 b g Harbour Watch - Mythicism (Oasis Dream)

Clive Cox — Miss J Deadman & S Barrow

PLACINGS: 544/447128/94431131- RPR **117**

Starts	1st	2nd	3rd	4th	Win & Pl
39	8	3	2	10	£344,170

	10/21	Asct	5f Cls1 List soft	£29,489
	8/21	Bevl	5f Cls1 List gd-fm	£26,654
102	8/21	Asct	5f Cls2 92-103 Hcap gd-sft	£20,656
	9/20	Leic	5f Cls3 gd-sft	£9,767
103	7/19	Asct	5f Cls2 86-107 Hcap gd-fm	£62,250
100	8/18	Asct	5f Cls2 85-101 Hcap good	£22,131
	7/16	MsnL	5½f Gp2 2yo good	£54,485
	7/16	Wind	6f Cls5 Mdn 2yo gd-fm	£3,235

Smart sprinter who was better than ever last season, winning three of his last four races; took advantage of a reduced mark to land an Ascot handicap before winning his first Listed races at Beverley and Ascot; likely to be forced into stronger company now.

Title (Ire)

4 b g Camelot - Danehill's Dream (Danehill)

Roger Varian — Highclere Tbred Racing-Charles Church

PLACINGS: 2/213215- RPR **115+**

Starts	1st	2nd	3rd	4th	Win & Pl
7	2	3	1	-	£67,936

103	9/21	Donc	1m4f Cls2 86-103 Hcap gd-sft	£25,770
	5/21	Yarm	1m3½f Cls4 Mdn 3yo good	£4,347

Promising middle-distance performer who bolted up on handicap debut at Doncaster last autumn only to flop when back in Group company at Ascot; had finished third in the Hampton Court but was gelded after coming up short in a Listed race at Hamilton next time.

Torquator Tasso (Ger)

5 ch h Adlerflug - Tijuana (Toylsome)

Marcel Weiss (Ger) — Gestut Auenquelle

PLACINGS: 412312/61211- RPR **126**

Starts	1st	2nd	3rd	4th	Win & Pl
11	5	3	1	1	£2,889,963

10/21	Lonc	1m4f Gp1 heavy	£2,550,893
9/21	Badn	1m4f Gp1 gd-sft	£89,286
7/21	Hamb	1m4f Gp2 gd-sft	£22,321
10/20	Hopp	1m4f Gp1 gd-sft	£50,847
6/20	Colo	1m3f 3yo good	£1,271

Shock winner of the Arc last season, staying on best on heavy ground to run down Tarnawa and Hurricane Lane close home; hadn't run within 8lb of that level previously according to Racing Post Ratings, though had won two more 1m4f Group 1 races in his native Germany.

Triple Time (Ire)

3 b c Frankel - Reem Three (Mark Of Esteem)

Kevin Ryan — Sheikh Mohammed Obaid Al Maktoum

PLACINGS: 3211- RPR **104+**

Starts	1st	2nd	3rd	4th	Win & Pl
4	2	1	1	-	£31,904

9/21	Hayd	1m Cls1 List 2yo gd-fm	£22,968
8/21	Hayd	1m Cls4 2yo soft	£5,400

Progressed into a smart two-year-old last season, winning a strong Listed race at Haydock on his final run; assuaged trainer's fears by proving versatility on good to firm ground that day, with previous runaway novice victory having come on soft.

Leading stayer: Trueshan sure to continue proving a force on soft going

Trueshan (Fr)

6 b g Planteur - Shao Line (General Holme)

Alan King — Singula Partnership

PLACINGS: 6/11211/41811/26111- — RPR **122+**

Starts	1st	2nd	3rd	4th	Win & Pl
16	10	2	-	1	£1,080,777

	10/21	Asct	2m Cls1 Gp2 gd-sft	£283,550
	10/21	Lonc	2m4f Gp1 v soft	£153,054
	7/21	Gdwd	2m Cls1 Gp1 soft	£294,183
	10/20	Asct	2m Cls1 Gp2 soft	£170,130
	9/20	Sals	1m6f Cls2 good	£12,291
	7/20	Hayd	1m4f Cls1 List gd-sft	£14,461
	10/19	Newb	1m5½f Cls2 3yo heavy	£32,345
93	10/19	NmkR	1m4f Cls2 79-100 3yo Hcap gd-sft	£74,700
	8/19	Ffos	1m4f Cls5 good	£3,429
	8/19	Wolv	1m4f Cls5 stand	£3,429

Emerged as last season's dominant stayer in Gold Cup winner Subjectivist's absence, winning the Goodwood Cup, Prix du Cadran and Long Distance Cup; non-runner three times owing to good to firm ground but has won five out of seven races on good or good to soft.

Tuesday (Ire)

3 b f Galileo - Lillie Langtry (Danehill Dancer)

Aidan O'Brien (Ire) — Magnier, Tabor, Smith & Weste

PLACINGS: 2- — RPR **91+**

Starts	1st	2nd	3rd	4th	Win & Pl
1	-	1	-	-	£2,799

Beautifully bred filly (half-sister to Minding out of dual Group 1 winner Lillie Langtry) who made a hugely promising start last season when running subsequent Moyglare heroine Discoveries to a short head on sole start; could well make up into a Classic candidate.

Twilight Jet (Ire)

3 b c Twilight Son - My Lucky Liz (Exceed And Excel)

Michael O'Callaghan (Ire) — Iavarone & O'Callaghan

PLACINGS: 35175633510- — RPR **112+**

Starts	1st	2nd	3rd	4th	Win & Pl
11	2	-	3	-	£100,067

10/21	NmkR	5f Cls1 Gp3 2yo gd-sft	£34,026
6/21	Tipp	5f 2yo yield	£15,804

Put up arguably the best 5f performance by a two-year-old last season when winning the Cornwallis Stakes; had spent much of a busy campaign just coming up short over further, going six races without a win since previous run over 5f but running several good races in defeat.

LAST SEASON'S TOP HORSES ON RACING POST RATINGS AND TOPSPEED PAGES 184-187

Twilight Spinner

4 b f Twilight Son - Spinatrix (Diktat)

Joseph O'Brien (Ire) — Scott C Heider

PLACINGS: 3112- — RPR **108+**

Starts	1st	2nd	3rd	4th	Win & Pl
4	2	1	1	-	£39,073

5/21	Hayd	6f Cls1 List heavy	£26,654
5/21	Ripn	6f Cls5 Mdn 3yo gd-sft	£3,240

Speedy filly who made a big impression when winning a 6f Listed race at Haydock by six and a half lengths, prompting big-money move to Joseph O'Brien; did that on heavy ground and only a fair second on good on only subsequent run but could do better back on softer or up in trip.

Umm Kulthum (Ire)

4 b f Kodiac - Queen's Code (Shamardal)

Richard Fahey — Saeed Bin Mohammed Al Qassimi

PLACINGS: 1313/83- — RPR **109**

Starts	1st	2nd	3rd	4th	Win & Pl
6	2	-	3	-	£62,579

9/20	Ayr	6f Cls1 Gp3 2yo gd-sft	£17,013
7/20	Thsk	5f Cls5 Mdn 2yo good	£4,140

High-class two-year-old in 2020 when winning a Group 3 at Ayr and beaten less than a length in the Cheveley Park; missed the rest of last season having run just twice in the spring, doing best back at 6f when a length third behind Rohaan in a Group 2 at Haydock.

Vadream

4 b f Brazen Beau - Her Honour (Shamardal)

Charlie Fellowes — D R J King

PLACINGS: 1/36327415- — RPR **109**

Starts	1st	2nd	3rd	4th	Win & Pl
9	2	1	2	1	£105,727

10/21	Asct	6f Cls1 Gp3 soft	£45,368
11/20	Newc	6f Cls5 Mdn 2yo std-slw	£3,429

Ran consistently well in Group races during a busy campaign last season and broke through when winning a 6f Group 3 at Ascot in October; also placed three times at that level, most notably in the Jersey Stakes again on soft ground, and fifth in the Champions Sprint.

Valley Forge

4 b g Dansili - Lixirova (Slickly)

Andrew Balding — George Strawbridge

PLACINGS: 5321136- — RPR **95**

Starts	1st	2nd	3rd	4th	Win & Pl
7	2	1	2	-	£85,941

83	8/21	York	1m6f Cls2 75-96 3yo Hcap good	£64,425
	7/21	Ffos	1m4f Cls5 Mdn gd-fm	£3,672

Thorough stayer who won last season's Melrose Handicap at York; fair third when unsuited by a slower pace in another valuable 1m6f handicap at Haydock but ran no race when stepped up to Listed level at Ascot; should appreciate going up to 2m.

Velocidad

3 ch f Gleneagles - Astrantia (Dansili)

Joseph O'Brien (Ire) — Smith, Magnier, Tabor &Westerberg

PLACINGS: 110- — RPR **100+**

Starts	1st	2nd	3rd	4th	Win & Pl
3	2	-	-	-	£63,214

	6/21	Curr	6f Gp2 2yo gd-fm	£52,679
	5/21	Fair	6f Mdn 2yo sft-hvy	£10,536

Did well early last season and won an admittedly soft Group 2 at the Curragh; disappointed on only subsequent run in the Prix Morny, though had been declared for the Cheveley Park before ruled out because of the good to firm ground.

Vertiginous (Ire)

3 b f Oasis Dream - Precipitous (Indian Ridge)

Brian Meehan — G P M Morland & Partners

PLACINGS: 2524217- — RPR **103**

Starts	1st	2nd	3rd	4th	Win & Pl
7	1	3	-	1	£47,718

	9/21	Ayr	5f Cls1 List 2yo gd-fm	£24,385

Won just once in seven races last season but found a good moment to break her duck, winning a 5f Listed race at Ayr in September; beaten favourite three times previously (twice at odds-on) but nice physical sort who looks the type to fulfil potential at three.

Ville De Grace

4 b f Le Havre - Archangel Gabriel (Arch)

Sir Michael Stoute — Hunscote Stud & Chris Humber

PLACINGS: 12/57311- — RPR **110**

Starts	1st	2nd	3rd	4th	Win & Pl
7	3	1	1	-	£92,865

	10/21	NmkR	1m2f Cls1 Gp3 gd-sft	£45,368
	9/21	Yarm	1m2f Cls1 List gd-sft	£32,327
	6/20	Kemp	6f Cls5 2yo std-slw	£4,140

Progressive filly who won Group 3 and Listed races last autumn; benefited from stepping up to 1m2f for the first time when winning well at Yarmouth and narrowly followed up in a stronger race at Newmarket, both on good to soft ground.

Waldkonig

5 b h Kingman - Waldlerche (Monsun)

John & Thady Gosden — Gestut Ammerland & Newsells Park Stud

PLACINGS: 1/32/11- — RPR **117+**

Starts	1st	2nd	3rd	4th	Win & Pl
5	3	1	1	-	£42,523

	4/21	Sand	1m2f Cls1 Gp3 good	£25,520
101	4/21	Pont	1m2f Cls2 86-101 Hcap gd-fm	£9,793
	12/19	Wolv	1m½f Cls5 2yo stand	£3,429

Lightly raced middle-distance performer who has long carried big expectations and began to fulfil them last spring, winning twice including a 1m2f Group 3 at Sandown; missed the rest of the season through injury but should be backed with Group 1 aspirations.

Walk Of Stars

3 b c Dubawi - Sound Reflection (Street Cry)

Charlie Appleby — Godolphin

PLACINGS: 31- RPR **88+**

Starts	1st	2nd	3rd	4th	Win & Pl
2	1	-	1	-	£7,158
11/21	Nott	1m½f Cls4 Mdn 2yo soft			£5,130

Showed promise in two runs last season; made late headway into third on debut at Newmarket and stepped up on that form when winning a mile maiden by four lengths at Nottingham; bred to get further (out of a 1m4f winner) and looks a useful middle-distance prospect.

Wembley (Ire)

4 b c Galileo - Inca Princess (Holy Roman Emperor)

Aidan O'Brien (Ire) — Tabor, Smith & Magnier

PLACINGS: 322122/0096- RPR **102+**

Starts	1st	2nd	3rd	4th	Win & Pl
10	1	4	1	-	£145,711
8/20	Rosc	7½f Mdn 2yo sft-hvy			£7,000

No better than sixth in four runs last season (all at Group 1 level) but had been a top-class two-year-old in 2020, finishing second in the Dewhurst; interesting that powerful connections persist and could step up to middle distances (bred to stay but yet to race beyond a mile).

West Coast (Ire)

3 bg f Dark Angel - Wading (Montjeu)

Aidan O'Brien (Ire) — Magnier, Tabor, Smith *Weste

PLACINGS: 731- RPR **92+**

Starts	1st	2nd	3rd	4th	Win & Pl
3	1	-	1	-	£9,816
10/21	Leop	7f Mdn 2yo good			£8,692

Convincing winner of a 7f maiden at Leopardstown last autumn, getting off the mark at the third attempt; seemingly improved on good ground having been only third when favourite on the all-weather and withdrawn on softer ground previously; looks a useful prospect.

Wild Beauty

3 b f Frankel - Tulips (Pivotal)

Charlie Appleby — Godolphin

PLACINGS: 6112215- RPR **108**

Starts	1st	2nd	3rd	4th	Win & Pl
7	3	2	-	-	£182,058
9/21	Wood	1m Gd1 2yo good			£137,931
6/21	Newb	7f Cls4 2yo soft			£4,266
5/21	Hayd	6f Cls4 Mdn 2yo soft			£4,266

Earned biggest win abroad last season when beating subsequent Breeders' Cup heroine Pizza Bianca in a Grade 1 in Canada; just came up short on home soil either side of that win, though still ran well when second in the Sweet Solera Stakes and fifth in the Fillies' Mile.

Ville De Grace (left): smart operator could well find improvement this season

Wings Of War (Ire)

3 gr c Dark Angel - Futoon (Kodiac)

Clive Cox — Isa Salman Al Khalifa

PLACINGS: 21321- RPR **110**

Starts	1st	2nd	3rd	4th	Win & Pl
5	2	2	1	-	£83,333

	9/21	Newb	6f Cls1 Gp2 2yo good	£44,971
	7/21	Nott	6f Cls5 Mdn 2yo gd-fm	£3,780

Narrow winner of last season's Mill Reef Stakes at Newbury but strong suspicion he made the most of a weak race for the grade (field a combined 1-23 at Group level); had also shown fair form when second in a Group 3 at Kempton and third in a sales race at York previously.

Winter Power (Ire)

4 b f Bungle Inthejungle - Titian Saga (Titus Livius)

Tim Easterby — King Power Racing Co

PLACINGS: 331461011/191108- RPR **119**

Starts	1st	2nd	3rd	4th	Win & Pl
15	7	-	2	1	£336,055

	8/21	York	5f Cls1 Gp1 gd-fm	£226,840
	7/21	York	5f Cls1 List good	£29,489
	5/21	York	5f Cls1 List 3yo good	£26,654
	10/20	NmkR	5f Cls1 Gp3 2yo soft	£26,654
	9/20	Ayr	5f Cls1 List 2yo gd-sft	£16,517
	9/20	Ripn	5f Cls5 2yo gd-sft	£4,075
76	7/20	Rdcr	5f Cls5 53-76 2yo Hcap gd-fm	£3,493

Lightning-quick sprinter who found her niche on quick ground at York last season, with three wins highlighted by the Nunthorpe Stakes; well beaten on all three other runs at Group 1 level last season when unable to maintain early speed.

Wordsworth (Ire)

4 ch c Galileo - Chelsea Rose (Desert King)

Aidan O'Brien (Ire) — Smith Magnier & Tabor

PLACINGS: 2/1223255- RPR **114**

Starts	1st	2nd	3rd	4th	Win & Pl
8	1	4	1	-	£272,666

	4/21	Curr	1m2f Mdn 3yo good	£7,902

Won only a Curragh maiden but went on to run well several times in defeat; finishing second in the Queen's Vase at Royal Ascot before twice placed at Group 1 level behind Hurricane Lane; below-par fifth in the Curragh Cup on final run.

Yibir

4 ch g Dubawi - Rumh (Monsun)

Charlie Appleby — Godolphin

PLACINGS: 3511/34216111- RPR **123**

Starts	1st	2nd	3rd	4th	Win & Pl
12	6	1	2	1	£2,112,885

	11/21	Delm	1m4f Gd1 firm	£1,518,248
	9/21	Belm	1m4f 3yo firm	£390,511
	8/21	York	1m4f Cls1 Gp2 3yo good	£85,065
	7/21	NmkJ	1m5f Cls1 Gp3 3yo gd-fm	£85,065
	9/20	Newb	1m Cls2 2yo good	£8,715
	8/20	Sand	7f Cls5 Mdn 2yo good	£4,140

Narrow winner of last season's Breeders' Cup Turf to cap a terrific second half of the season, winning four out of five after a gelding operation in May; also landed the Great Voltigeur at York on good ground but below par on all five runs on a slower surface.

Zain Claudette (Ire)

3 ch f No Nay Never - Claudette (Speightstown)

Ismail Mohammed — Saeed H Al Tayer

PLACINGS: 21110- RPR **108**

Starts	1st	2nd	3rd	4th	Win & Pl
5	3	1	-	-	£125,451

	8/21	York	6f Cls1 Gp2 2yo good	£85,065
	7/21	Asct	6f Cls1 Gp3 2yo gd-fm	£34,026
	6/21	NmkJ	6f Cls4 Mdn 2yo gd-fm	£4,320

Progressive two-year-old for much of last season, completing a hat-trick when a length winner over Sandrine in the Lowther Stakes; reportedly found the ground too quick when well beaten in the Cheveley Park, though had won twice on good to firm, including the Princess Margaret.

Zakouski

6 b g Shamardal - O'Giselle (Octagonal)

Charlie Appleby — Godolphin

PLACINGS: 1/5/1141/2119-3 RPR **112+**

Starts	1st	2nd	3rd	4th	Win & Pl
11	6	1	1	1	£338,905

	10/21	NmkR	1m Cls1 List good	£29,489
	2/21	Meyd	1m1f Gp2 good	£71,387
	10/20	NmkR	1m Cls1 List heavy	£15,879
	2/20	Meyd	1m Gp2 good	£112,782
100	1/20	Meyd	1m 90-103 Hcap good	£60,902
	11/18	Kemp	7f Cls5 2yo std-slw	£3,881

Very lightly raced in Europe, tending to be given a long break after Dubai, but has a fine strike-rate, including winning the same late-season Listed race at Newmarket for the last two years; didn't see out 1m2f when sent to Bahrain this winter before again moving on to Dubai.

Zellie (Fr)

3 b f Wootton Bassett - Sarai (Nathaniel)

Andre Fabre (Fr) — Al Wasmiyah Farm

PLACINGS: 111221- RPR **113**

Starts	1st	2nd	3rd	4th	Win & Pl
6	4	2	-	-	£286,660

	10/21	Lonc	1m Gp1 2yo heavy	£204,071
	7/21	Deau	7f List 2yo v soft	£26,786
	6/21	StCl	7f 2yo good	£15,179
	5/21	StCl	6f 2yo heavy	£12,054

Won last season's Prix Marcel Boussac, benefiting from heavy ground and coming from nearly last to first off an overly strong gallop; had finished second in both previous runs in Group races and likely to require more at Group 1 level again; unlikely to stay much beyond a mile.

KEY HORSES LISTED BY TRAINER

William Muir & Chris Grassick
Pyledriver

Charlie Appleby
Adayar (Ire)
Al Suhail
Albahr
Coroebus (Ire)
Creative Flair (Ire)
Creative Force (Ire)
Glorious Journey
Goldspur (Ire)
Hafit (Ire)
Hurricane Lane (Ire)
La Barrosa (Ire)
Lazuli (Ire)
Man Of Promise (USA)
Manobo (Ire)
Master Of The Seas (Ire)
Modern Games (Ire)
Native Trail
Naval Crown
Noble Truth (Fr)
Siskany
Walk Of Stars
Wild Beauty
Yibir
Zakouski

Andrew Balding
Alcohol Free (Ire)
Berkshire Rocco (Fr)
Berkshire Shadow
Chil Chil
Foxes Tales (Ire)
Happy Power (Ire)
Hoo Ya Mal
Imperial Fighter (Ire)
Invite (Ire)
King's Lynn
Majestic Glory
Masekela (Ire)
Nobel (Ire)
Sandrine
Symbolize (Ire)
Valley Forge

Ralph Beckett
Albaflora
Angel Bleu (Fr)
Kinross
Prosperous Voyage (Ire)
Scope (Ire)

Edward Bethell
Artistic Rifles (Ire)

Jim Bolger
Boundless Ocean (Ire)
Mac Swiney (Ire)

Michael Browne
Logo Hunter (Ire)

Owen Burrows
Anmaat (Ire)
Hukum (Ire)
Minzaal (Ire)

Jane Chapple-Hyam
Claymore (Fr)
Saffron Beach (Ire)

Harry & Roger Charlton
Jumbly

R Chotard
Skazino (Fr)

Paul & Oliver Cole
Majestic Dawn (Ire)

Robert Cowell
Arecibo (Fr)

Clive Cox
Aratus (Ire)
Caturra (Ire)
Diligent Harry
Tis Marvellous
Wings Of War (Ire)

Simon & Ed Crisford
Fast Attack (Ire)
Flotus (Ire)

Jack Davison
Mooneista (Ire)

Mikel Delzangles
Bubble Gift (Fr)

Michael Dods
Commanche Falls

Ed Dunlop
John Leeper (Ire)

Tim Easterby
Art Power (Ire)
Winter Power (Ire)

Brian Ellison
Tashkhan (Ire)

David Evans
Rohaan (Ire)

Andre Fabre
Ancient Rome (USA)
Egot (Ire)
Magny Cours (USA)
Mare Australis (Ire)
Raclette
Zellie (Fr)

Richard Fahey
Perfect Power (Ire)
Umm Kulthum (Ire)

Charlie Fellowes
Vadream

James Ferguson
El Bodegon (Ire)
Mise En Scene

Ivan Furtado
Just Beautiful

Jim Goldie
Euchen Glen

John & Thady Gosden
Antarah (Ire)
Audience
Dhabab (Ire)
Filistine (Ire)
Frantastic
Free Wind (Ire)
Inspiral
Israr
Lord North (Ire)
Magisterial (Ire)
Megallan
Mighty Ulysses
Mishriff (Ire)
Mostahdaf (Ire)
Natasha
Rainbow Fire (Ire)
Reach For The Moon
Stradivarius (Ire)
Sunray Major
Waldkonig

Francis-Henri Graffard
Sealiway (Fr)
The Revenant

Henk Grewe
Sisfahan (Fr)

William Haggas
Addeybb (Ire)
Al Aasy (Ire)
Aldaary
Alenquer (Fr)
Baaeed
Dubai Honour (Ire)
Golden Lyra (Ire)
Grocer Jack (Ger)
Hamish
Hurricane Ivor (Ire)
Ilaraab (Ire)
Mohaafeth (Ire)
Mujtaba
My Astra (Ire)
My Oberon (Ire)
Nahaarr (Ire)
Sacred

Richard Hannon
Chindit (Ire)
Happy Romance (Ire)
Lusail (Ire)
Mojo Star (Ire)

Jessica Harrington
Discoveries (Ire)
Ever Present (Ire)
Forbearance (Ire)
Real Appeal (Ger)

Charles Hills
Mutasaabeq

Eve Johnson Houghton
Jumby (Ire)

Charlie & Mark Johnston
Nayef Road (Ire)
Royal Patronage (Fr)
Thunderous (Ire)

Alan King
Trueshan (Fr)

William Knight
Sir Busker (Ire)

David Loughnane
Go Bears Go (Ire)
Hello You (Ire)

Edward Lynam
Romantic Proposal (Ire)

Ger Lyons
Atomic Jones (Fr)
Beauty Inspire (Ire)
Cairde Go Deo (Fr)
Dr Zempf
Geocentric (Ire)
Lust (Ire)
Panama Red (Ire)
Power Under Me (Ire)
Sacred Bridge
Straight Answer
Team Of Firsts

Adrian McGuinness
A Case Of You (Ire)

Martyn Meade
Lone Eagle (Ire)

Noel Meade
Helvic Dream (Ire)

Brian Meehan
Mandoob
Vertiginous (Ire)

David Menuisier
Migration (Ire)

Ismail Mohammed
Zain Claudette (Ire)

Hughie Morrison
Quickthorn

Anthony Mullins
Princess Zoe (Ger)

Joseph Murphy
Gustavus Weston (Ire)

Johnny Murtagh
Ottoman Emperor (Ire)
Sonnyboyliston (Ire)

Aidan O'Brien
Bolshoi Ballet (Ire)
Broome (Ire)
Cadamosto (Ire)
Concert Hall (Ire)
Contarelli Chapel (Ire)
Glounthaune (Ire)
High Definition (Ire)
History (Ire)
King Of Bavaria (Ire)
Kyprios (Ire)
Luxembourg (Ire)
Mother Earth (Ire)
Order Of Australia (Ire)
Point Lonsdale (Ire)
Star Of India (Ire)
Tenebrism (USA)
Tuesday (Ire)
Wembley (Ire)
West Coast (Ire)
Wordsworth (Ire)

Donnacha O'Brien
Piz Badile (Ire)
Sissoko (Ire)

Joseph O'Brien
Agartha (Ire)
Baron Samedi
Hannibal Barca (Ire)
Master Of Reality (Ire)
State Of Rest (Ire)
Twilight Spinner
Velocidad

Michael O'Callaghan
Twilight Jet (Ire)

David O'Meara
Lord Glitters (Fr)

Hugo Palmer
Dubawi Legend (Ire)
Ebro River (Ire)

Amanda Perrett
Lavender's Blue (Ire)

Sir Mark Prescott
Alpinista
Revolver (Ire)

Jerome Reynier
Marianafoot (Fr)
Skalleti (Fr)

Francois Rohaut
Suesa (Ire)

F Rossi
Mangoustine (Fr)

Kevin Ryan
Emaraaty Ana
Triple Time (Ire)

David Simcock
Light Infantry (Fr)

Tommy Stack
Castle Star (Ire)
Hermana Estrella (Ire)

Sir Michael Stoute
Bay Bridge
Desert Crown
Dream Of Dreams (Ire)
Highest Ground (Ire)
Lights On
Noon Star (USA)
Solid Stone (Ire)
Ville De Grace

Saeed bin Suroor
Real World (Ire)
Silent Escape (Ire)
Storm Damage

Roger Teal
Ocean Wind
Oxted

Marcus Tregoning
Ribhi (Ire)

Paddy Twomey
La Petite Coco (Ire)
Limiti Di Greccio (Ire)
Pearls Galore (Fr)

Roger Varian
Bayside Boy (Ire)
Believe In Love (Ire)
Dragon Symbol
Eldar Eldarov
Eshaada
Laneqash
Nagano
Subastar (Ire)
Teona (Ire)
Third Realm
Title (Ire)

Ed Walker
Came From The Dark (Ire)
Great Ambassador
Kawida

Archie Watson
Glen Shiel
Nazanin (USA)

Marcel Weiss
Torquator Tasso (Ger)

Dermot Weld
Duke De Sessa (Ire)
Homeless Songs (Ire)
Search For A Song (Ire)

RACING POST RATINGS: LAST SEASON'S LEADING TWO-YEAR-OLDS

KEY: Horse name, best RPR figure, finishing position when earning figure, (details of race where figure was earned)

Native Trail 122[1] (7f, Curr, Gd, Sep 12)
Coroebus (IRE) 116[1] (1m, Newm, Gd, Oct 9)
Luxembourg (IRE) 116[1] (1m, Donc, Sft, Oct 23)
Tenebrism (USA) 116[1] (6f, Newm, GF, Sep 25)
Dubawi Legend (IRE) 115[2] (7f, Newm, Gd, Oct 9)
Perfect Power (IRE) 115[1] (6f, Newm, GF, Sep 25)
Bayside Boy (IRE) 114[3] (7f, Newm, Gd, Oct 9)
Inspiral 114[1] (1m, Newm, GS, Oct 8)
Armor 113[3] (6f, Newm, GF, Sep 25)
Castle Star (IRE) 113[2] (6f, Newm, GF, Sep 25)
Ebro River (IRE) 113[1] (6f, Curr, Yld, Aug 8)
Flotus (IRE) 113[2] (6f, Newm, GF, Sep 25)
Point Lonsdale (IRE) 113[2] (7f, Curr, Gd, Sep 12)
Go Bears Go (IRE) 112[4] (6f, Newm, GF, Sep 25)
Lusail (IRE) 112[1] (6f, York, GF, Aug 20)
Modern Games (IRE) 112[1] (7f, Newm, Gd, Sep 23)
Royal Patronage (Fr) 112[1] (1m, Newm, GF, Sep 25)
Sissoko (IRE) 112[2] (1m, Donc, Sft, Oct 23)
Straight Answer 112[1] (6f, Fair, GF, Sep 20)
Twilight Jet (IRE) 112[1] (5f, Newm, GS, Oct 8)
Caturra (IRE) 111[5] (6f, Newm, GF, Sep 25)
Dr Zempf 111[2] (6f, Curr, Yld, Aug 8)
Hannibal Barca (IRE) 111[4] (1m, Donc, Sft, Oct 23)
Reach For The Moon 111[2] (7f 6y, Donc, GS, Sep 11)
Discoveries (IRE) 110[1] (7f, Curr, Gd, Sep 12)
Imperial Fighter (IRE) 110[5] (1m, Donc, Sft, Oct 23)
Sacred Bridge 110[1] (6f, Curr, Gd, Aug 27)
Wings Of War (IRE) 110[1] (6f, Newb, Gd, Sep 18)
Asymmetric (IRE) 109[7] (6f, Newm, GF, Sep 25)
Berkshire Shadow 109[4] (7f, Newm, Gd, Oct 9)
Flaming Rib (IRE) 109[1] (6f 17y, Ches, Gd, Sep 25)
Hierarchy (IRE) 109[2] (6f, Newb, Gd, Sep 18)
Agartha (IRE) 108[2] (7f, Curr, Gd, Sep 12)
Angel Bleu (Fr) 108[1] (7f, Good, Sft, Jul 27)
Hello You (IRE) 108[1] (7f, Newm, GF, Sep 24)
Masekela (IRE) 108[2] (7f, Newj, GF, Jul 10)
Sandrine 108[2] (6f, York, Gd, Aug 19)
Zain Claudette (IRE) 108[1] (6f, York, Gd, Aug 19)
Goldspur (IRE) 107[1] (1m 2f, Newm, Gd, Oct 9)
Light Infantry (Fr) 107[1] (7f, Newb, Sft, Oct 23)
Limiti Di Greccio (IRE) 107[1] (1m, Curr, Yld, Oct 10)
Prosperous Voyage (IRE) 107[2] (1m, Newm, GS, Oct 8)
Albahr 106[1] (6f 212y, Hayd, GF, Jul 17)
Cachet (IRE) 106[3] (1m, Newm, GS, Oct 8)
Concert Hall (IRE) 106[1] (7f, Curr, Gd, Sep 26)
Duke De Sessa (IRE) 106[1] (1m 1f, Leop, Gd, Oct 23)
Hafit (IRE) 106[3] (1m 2f, Newm, Gd, Oct 9)
Jumbly 106[1] (7f, Newb, Sft, Oct 23)
Khunan 106[2] (6f, Good, GS, Jul 29)
Mise En Scene 106[4] (1m, Newm, GS, Oct 8)
Noble Truth (Fr) 106[1] (7f 6y, Donc, GF, Sep 10)
Quick Suzy (IRE) 106[1] (5f, Asco, GF, Jun 16)
Sam Maximus 106[3] (6f, Newj, GF, Jul 8)
Ultramarine (IRE) 106[4] (7f, Curr, Gd, Sep 12)
Unconquerable (IRE) 106[2] (1m 2f, Newm, Gd, Oct 9)
Absolute Ruler (USA) 105[3] (1m, Leop, Gd, Sep 11)
Atomic Jones (Fr) 105[1] (1m, Leop, Gd, Sep 11)
Dubai Poet 105[3] (1m, Newm, Gd, Oct 9)
El Caballo 105[1] (6f, Ncsw, SD, Feb 23)
Fearby (IRE) 105[3] (6f, Newb, Gd, Sep 18)
Geocentric (IRE) 105[1] (5f, Dunw, SD, Oct 1)
Gis A Sub (IRE) 105[2] (6f, York, GF, Aug 20)
Great Max (IRE) 105[5] (7f, Curr, Gd, Sep 12)
Gubbass (IRE) 105[3] (6f, Good, GS, Jul 29)
Hoo Ya Mal 105[2] (7f 6y, Donc, GF, Sep 10)
New Science 105[1] (7f, Asco, GF, Jul 24)
Piz Badile (IRE) 105[2] (1m 1f, Leop, Gd, Oct 23)
Stone Age (IRE) 105[2] (1m, Leop, Gd, Sep 11)
Tatsumaki 105[1] (6f, Newm, Gd, Oct 2)
Trident (Fr) 105[2] (7f, Newm, Gd, Sep 23)
Wild Beauty 105[5] (1m, Newm, GS, Oct 8)
Aikhal (IRE) 104[4] (1m, Newm, Gd, Oct 9)
Dhabab (IRE) 104[5] (7f, Newm, Gd, Oct 9)
Eldrickjones (IRE) 104[2] (6f, Asco, GF, Jun 15)
Fast Attack (IRE) 104[1] (7f, Newm, GS, Oct 8)
Glounthaune (IRE) 104[6] (7f, Newm, Gd, Oct 9)
King Of Bavaria (IRE) 104[1] (5f 205y, Naas, Hvy, Oct 31)
Project Dante 104[3] (5f, Asco, GF, Jun 17)
Triple Time (IRE) 104[1] (1m 37y, Hayd, GF, Sep 4)
Austrian Theory (IRE) 103[3] (7f, Good, Sft, Jul 27)
Boundless Ocean (IRE) 103[4] (7f, Leop, Gd, Oct 16)
Chipotle 103[1] (5f, Asco, GF, Jun 16)
Cresta (Fr) 103[2] (7f, Newb, Sft, Oct 23)
Desert Dreamer 103[2] (6f, Newj, GF, Jul 9)
Hermana Estrella (IRE) 103[1] (5f 205y, Naas, Sft, May 16)
Howth (IRE) 103[4] (1m, Leop, Gd, Sep 11)
Maglev (IRE) 103[5] (6f, Newb, Gd, Sep 18)
Masseto 103[3] (6f, Curr, Gd, Jun 26)
Oscula (IRE) 103[3] (7f, Newm, GF, Sep 24)
Power Of Beauty (IRE) 103[2] (1m, Sali, Gd, Aug 20)
Snaffles (IRE) 103[1] (7f, Dunw, SD, Oct 1)
Sunset Shiraz (IRE) 103[3] (1m, Curr, Yld, Oct 10)
Tranquil Lady (IRE) 103[2] (1m, Curr, Yld, Oct 10)
Vintage Clarets 103[3] (6f, Asco, GF, Jun 15)
Witch Hunter (Fr) 103[2] (6f, York, GS, Oct 9)
Zechariah (IRE) 103[1] (1m, Newb, GS, Sep 17)
Anchorage (IRE) 102[3] (1m 1f, Leop, Gd, Oct 23)
Beauty Inspire (IRE) 102[1] (6f 63y, Curr, Gd, Jul 17)
Cadamosto (IRE) 102[4] (5f, Asco, GF, Jun 17)
Guilded (IRE) 102[4] (6f, Newm, GF, Sep 25)
Harrow (IRE) 102[3] (7f, Newm, Gd, Sep 23)
Illustrating 102[2] (5f, Newm, GS, Oct 8)
Manaccan 102[4] (5f, Newm, GS, Oct 8)
Manu Et Corde (IRE) 102[5] (1m, Leop, Gd, Sep 11)
Maritime Wings (IRE) 102[2] (7f, Curr, Sft, Aug 21)
Mr Mccann (IRE) 102[4] (7f, Newj, GF, Jul 10)
Panama Red (IRE) 102[1] (7f 37y, Leop, Gd, Sep 11)
Papa Don't Preach (IRE) 102[4] (5f 3y, Donc, GF, Sep 10)
Seisai (IRE) 102[3] (7f, Curr, Gd, Sep 26)
Tacarib Bay 102[3] (7f, Newb, Sft, Oct 23)
Vertiginous (IRE) 102[1] (5f, Ayr, GF, Sep 17)
Alflaila 101[6] (1m, Newm, Gd, Oct 9)
Allayaali (IRE) 101[2] (7f, Newm, GS, Oct 8)
Buckaroo 101[6] (1m, Leop, Gd, Sep 11)
Corazon (IRE) 101[3] (5f 3y, Donc, GF, Sep 10)
Daneh 101[2] (7f, Good, Gd, Aug 28)
Delmona (IRE) 101[3] (6f, Asco, GF, Jul 24)
Eve Lodge 101[1] (6f, Kemw, SS, Sep 4)
Gwan So 101[3] (7f 6y, Donc, GF, Sep 10)
Hellomydarlin (IRE) 101[3] (6f, York, Gd, Aug 18)
Jazz Club (IRE) 101[3] (6f 111y, Donc, GF, Sep 9)
Juncture 101[2] (7f 20y, Leop, Gd, Jul 22)
King X J (IRE) 101[2] (7f, Dunw, SD, Oct 1)
Ladies Church 101[1] (5f, Naas, Gd, Jul 21)
Last Crusader (IRE) 101[2] (5f 217y, Redc, Gd, Oct 2)
Lucci (USA) 101[5] (5f, Asco, GF, Jun 17)
New York City (IRE) 101[9] (6f, Newm, GF, Sep 25)
Prettiest (USA) 101[4] (6f, Asco, Hvy, Jun 18)
Scriptwriter (IRE) 101[5] (1m, Newm, Gd, Oct 9)
Tuwaiq (IRE) 101[3] (1m, Curr, Gd, Sep 25)
Twilight Gleaming (IRE) 101[2] (5f, Asco, GF, Jun 16)
Berkshire Rebel (IRE) 100[5] (1m 2f, Newm, Gd, Oct 9)
Bluegrass (IRE) 100[4] (1m 2f, Newm, Gd, Oct 9)

RACING POST RATINGS: LAST SEASON'S LEADING TWO-YEAR-OLDS

Bosh (IRE) 100[2] (5f 205y, Naas, Gd, Aug 2)
Canonized 100[1] (6f, York, GS, Oct 9)
Deodar 100[2] (6f 2y, Donc, Sft, Oct 23)
Ever Given (IRE) 100[1] (6f, York, Gd, Aug 19)
French Claim (Fr) 100[4] (1m 1f, Leop, Gd, Oct 23)
I Am Magic (IRE) 100[3] (7f, Leop, Gd, Oct 16)
Magical Lagoon (IRE) 100[7] (1m, Newm, GS, Oct 8)
Majestic Glory 100[1] (7f, Newj, Gd, Aug 7)
Markaz Paname (IRE) 100[3] (7f, Dunw, SD, Oct 1)
Mohi 100[3] (6f 2y, Donc, Sft, Oct 23)
Nazanin (USA) 100[1] (6f, Ayr, Gd, Sep 18)
Perfect News 100[1] (7f, Newm, GF, Sep 25)
Rerouting (IRE) 100[3] (7f, Sand, Gd, Aug 21)
Space Cowboy (IRE) 100[1] (6f, Ncsw, SD, Oct 19)
Strapped (IRE) 100[5] (6f, Curr, Yld, Aug 8)
Swan Bay (IRE) 100[4] (1m, Curr, Gd, Sep 25)
United Nations (IRE) 100[7] (1m, Newm, Gd, Oct 9)
Velocidad 100[1] (6f, Curr, GF, Jun 27)
Albion Square 99[6] (5f, Newm, GS, Oct 8)
Homeless Songs (IRE) 99[5] (7f, Curr, Gd, Sep 12)
Leinster House (USA) 99[5] (7f, Dunw, SD, Oct 1)
Ribhi (IRE) 99[5] (7f 6y, Donc, GF, Sep 10)
Robjon 99[3] (7f, Newb, Gd, Aug 14)
Symphony Perfect (IRE) 99[1] (6f, Newm, Gd, Oct 29)
Trevaunance (IRE) 99[4] (7f, Curr, Gd, Sep 26)
Admiral D (IRE) 98[1] (5f 205y, Naas, Yld, Oct 17)
Albula (IRE) 98[2] (1m, Curr, Gd, Aug 27)
Andreas Vesalius (IRE) 98[2] (6f 63y, Curr, Gd, Jul 17)
Attagirl 98[2] (5f 34y, Newb, Gd, Aug 13)
Gisburn (IRE) 98[1] (6f, Newb, Sft, Oct 23)
Grenoble 98[7] (1m 1f, Leop, Gd, Oct 23)
Hala Hala Athmani 98[3] (6f, Ayr, Gd, Sep 18)
Kawida 98[1] (1m, Newm, Gd, Oct 30)
Mitbaahy (IRE) 98[2] (5f, Ayr, GF, Sep 17)
Mr Professor (IRE) 98[1] (1m 6y, Pont, Sft, Oct 18)
Nymphadora 98[5] (6f, York, Gd, Aug 19)
Pennine Hills (IRE) 98[2] (7f, Leop, Gd, Oct 16)
Tardis 98[5] (5f, Newm, GS, Oct 8)
The Acropolis (IRE) 98[5] (7f, Leop, Gd, Oct 16)
The Organiser 98[6] (6f, Newj, GF, Jul 8)
Westover 98[2] (1m, Newb, GS, Sep 17)
Cigamia (USA) 97[5] (7f, Curr, Gd, Sep 26)
Coming Patch (IRE) 97[2] (6f, Newb, Gd, Jul 16)
Confident Star (IRE) 97[7] (7f, Leop, Gd, Oct 16)
Good Heavens (IRE) 97[8] (1m 1f, Leop, Gd, Oct 23)
Head Mistress (IRE) 97[4] (6f, Ayr, Gd, Sep 18)
System (IRE) 97[1] (6f, Newj, GF, Jun 26)
Boonie (IRE) 96[3] (5f, Good, Sft, Jul 28)
Corviglia (USA) 96[3] (7f 37y, Leop, Gd, Sep 11)
Filistine (IRE) 96[1] (7f, Newm, Gd, Oct 29)
Flash Betty 96[2] (1m, Newm, Gd, Oct 30)
Hadman (IRE) 96[3] (6f 63y, Curr, Gd, Jul 17)
Korker (IRE) 96[2] (5f 89y, York, Sft, Oct 8)
Loveday (IRE) 96[2] (5f, Curr, Gd, Aug 13)
Parisiac (IRE) 96[4] (6f 2y, Donc, Sft, Oct 23)
Sweeping 96[4] (7f, Asco, Sft, Jun 19)
The Entertainer (IRE) 96[7] (7f, Dunw, SD, Oct 1)
Tolstoy (IRE) 96[7] (6f, Newj, GF, Jul 8)
Voice Of Angels 96[6] (1m 1f, Leop, Gd, Oct 23)
Cheerupsleepyjean (Fr) 95[3] (5f, Asco, GF, Jun 16)
Cornman (IRE) 95[8] (7f, Dunw, SD, Oct 1)
Dig Two (IRE) 95[2] (5f, Asco, GF, Jun 16)
Doitforandrew 95[1] (7f, Dunw, SD, Dec 1)
Ehraz 95[1] (6f, Asco, GF, Jul 23)
Elliptic (IRE) 95[6] (6f, Asco, Hvy, Jun 18)
Exquisite Acclaim (IRE) 95[4] (5f, Dunw, SD, Oct 1)
Fall Of Rome (IRE) 95[2] (7f, Newj, Gd, Aug 7)
Glengarra (IRE) 95[2] (6f, Fair, GF, Sep 20)
Kaboo (USA) 95[1] (6f, Kemw, SS, Jan 24)
New Energy (IRE) 95[8] (7f, Leop, Gd, Oct 16)
Orazio (IRE) 95[3] (6f, Newb, Gd, Jul 16)
Rishes Baar (IRE) 95[4] (7f, Newm, GS, Oct 8)
Rolling The Dice (IRE) 95[3] (1m, Donc, GF, Sep 9)
Romantic Time 95[1] (6f, Sali, GF, Sep 2)
Sablonne 95[5] (7f 20y, Leop, Gd, Jul 22)
Silent Speech 95[2] (7f, Newm, Gd, Oct 29)
Thunder Eclipse (IRE) 95[2] (6f, Curr, Gd, Sep 25)
Thunder Love 95[5] (5f 3y, Donc, GF, Sep 10)
Warren Beach (IRE) 95 (1m 1f, Leop, Gd, Oct 23)
Artos (IRE) 94[4] (5f, Asco, GF, Jun 16)
Atomic Lady (Fr) 94[2] (6f, York, Gd, Aug 19)
Bouquet 94[8] (1m, Newm, GS, Oct 8)
Cairde Go Deo (Fr) 94[6] (7f, Curr, Gd, Sep 12)
Eldar Eldarov 94[1] (1m 75y, Nott, GS, Oct 13)
Girl On Film (Fr) 94[5] (7f, Newm, GF, Sep 24)
Glory Daze (IRE) 94 (1m 1f, Leop, Gd, Oct 23)
Have A Good Day (IRE) 94[7] (6f, Newm, GF, Sep 25)
Jadhlaan 94[2] (6f, Good, GS, Jul 30)
John The Baptist (IRE) 94[8] (1m, Leop, Gd, Sep 11)
Lady Of Inishfree (IRE) 94[4] (7f 37y, Leop, Gd, Sep 11)
Razzle Dazzle 94[1] (7f, Newj, GF, Aug 27)
Star Girls Aalmal (IRE) 94[1] (7f, Dunw, SD, Nov 17)
Up Above 94[7] (5f 3y, Donc, GF, Sep 10)
Value Theory (IRE) 94[3] (7f, Newj, Gd, Aug 7)
American Star (IRE) 93[1] (7f, Newb, GS, Sep 17)
Antarah (IRE) 93[1] (1m 5y, Ncsw, SD, Oct 25)
Banshee (IRE) 93[4] (1m, Donc, GF, Sep 9)
Bond Chairman 93[4] (5f, Asco, GF, Jun 16)
Breeze Easy 93[2] (7f, Newb, Sft, Oct 23)
Claymore (Fr) 93[1] (7f, Newm, Sft, Oct 20)
Contarelli Chapel (IRE) 93[1] (5f 205y, Naas, Gd, Apr 26)
Dairerin 93[1] (6f, Sali, GS, Jun 23)
Dukebox (IRE) 93[3] (1m 37y, Hayd, GF, Sep 4)
Encountered (IRE) 93[1] (7f 6y, Donc, Gd, Jun 25)
History (IRE) 93[1] (1m, Gowr, Yld, Sep 18)
Honey Sweet (IRE) 93[5] (6f, Newj, GF, Jul 9)
Little Earl (IRE) 93[2] (5f 10y, Sand, Sft, May 27)
Lullaby (IRE) 93[4] (1m, Curr, Gd, Aug 27)
Misty Ayr (IRE) 93[5] (7f, Newm, GS, Oct 8)
Navello 93[1] (5f 15y, Ches, GS, May 5)
Oneforthegutter 93[4] (6f, Newb, Gd, Jul 16)
Saga 93[1] (7f, Asco, Gd, Sep 3)
She's Trouble (IRE) 93[3] (1m, Curr, Gd, Aug 27)
Silk Romance (IRE) 93[2] (7f, Newb, GS, Sep 17)
Star Of India (IRE) 93[1] (7f, Leop, Gd, Oct 23)
With The Moonlight (IRE) 93[3] (1m, Newm, Gd, Oct 30)
Benefit 92[1] (6f, Leic, GS, Oct 12)
Cavalry Charge 92[1] (5f 205y, Naas, Gd, Aug 2)
Chicago Soldier (IRE) 92[5] (1m, Curr, Gd, Sep 25)
Clitheroe 92[5] (7f, Good, Gd, Aug 28)
Crazyland 92[6] (6f, Asco, GF, Jul 24)
Desert Crown 92[1] (1m 75y, Nott, Sft, Nov 3)
Dissociate (IRE) 92[1] (7f, Curr, Sft, Oct 26)
Dynamic Force (IRE) 92[1] (5f 110y, Ayr, GF, Jul 26)
Fearless Angel (IRE) 92[2] (6f 16y, Souw, SS, Jan 11)
Find 92[1] (7f 3y, Yarm, GF, Aug 29)
Green Team (Fr) 92[8] (1m, Newm, Gd, Oct 9)
In Ecstasy (IRE) 92[1] (1m, Dunw, SD, Dec 15)
La Pulga (IRE) 92[2] (1m, Donc, GS, Sep 11)
Millennial Moon 92[1] (7f 3y, Yarm, GS, Sep 15)
Mojomaker (IRE) 92[4] (5f 217y, Redc, Gd, Oct 2)
Mot And The Messer (IRE) 92[1] (6f 17y, Ches, GS, Aug 1)
Nuance 92[1] (7f 6y, Catt, GS, Sep 29)
Orinoco River (USA) 92[3] (5f, Curr, Gd, Aug 13)
Pearl Glory (IRE) 92[2] (6f, Sali, GF, Sep 2)
Princess Shabnam (IRE) 92[8] (5f, Newm, GS, Oct 8)

RACING POST RATINGS: LAST SEASON'S TOP PERFORMERS 3YO+

KEY: Horse name, best RPR figure, finishing position when earning figure, (details of race where figure was earned)

Adayar (IRE) 129[1] (1m 3f 211y, Asco, GF, Jul 24)
Mishriff (IRE) 128[1] (1m 2f 56y, York, Gd, Aug 18)
St Mark's Basilica (Fr) 128[1] (1m 1f 209y, Sand, GS, Jul 3)
Baaeed 127[1] (1m, Asco, GS, Oct 16)
Palace Pier 127[1] (1m, Newb, GS, May 15)
Poetic Flare (IRE) 124[3] (1m 2f, Leop, Gd, Sep 11)
Sealiway (Fr) 124[1] (1m 1f 212y, Asco, GS, Oct 16)
Starman 124[1] (6f, Newj, GF, Jul 10)
Dream Of Dreams (IRE) 123[1] (6f 12y, Wind, Sft, May 17)
Al Aasy (IRE) 122[1] (1m 4f, Newb, GS, May 15)
Dubai Honour (IRE) 122[2] (1m 1f 212y, Asco, GS, Oct 16)
Hurricane Lane (IRE) 122[1] (1m 6f 115y, Donc, GS, Sep 11)
Pyledriver 122[1] (1m 4f 6y, Epso, GS, Jun 4)
Subjectivist 122[1] (2m 3f 210y, Asco, GF, Jun 17)
Suesa (IRE) 122[1] (5f, Good, GS, Jul 30)
Addeybb (IRE) 121[2] (1m 1f 209y, Sand, GS, Jul 3)
Alcohol Free (IRE) 121[1] (1m, Good, Sft, Jul 28)
Creative Force (IRE) 121[1] (6f, Asco, GS, Oct 16)
Emaraaty Ana 121[1] (6f, Hayd, GF, Sep 4)
Hukum (IRE) 121[1] (1m 3f 211y, Asco, Sft, Oct 2)
Motakhayyel 121[1] (7f, Newj, GF, Jul 10)
Oxted 121[1] (5f, Asco, GF, Jun 15)
Siskany 121[1] (1m 4f, Newm, GS, Oct 8)
Snowfall (JPN) 121[1] (1m 3f 188y, York, Gd, Aug 19)
Sonnyboyliston (IRE) 121[1] (1m 6f, Curr, Gd, Sep 12)
Tarnawa (IRE) 121[2] (1m 2f, Leop, Gd, Sep 11)
The Revenant 121[4] (1m, Asco, GS, Oct 16)
Trueshan (Fr) 121[6] (2m 56y, Ncsw, SD, Jun 26)
Art Power (IRE) 120[1] (6f, Curr, Gd, Sep 25)
Lady Bowthorpe 120[3] (1m, Asco, GS, Oct 16)
Lone Eagle (IRE) 120[2] (1m 4f, Curr, Gd, Jun 26)
Masen 120[1] (7f, Leop, Gd, Oct 23)
Real World (IRE) 120[1] (1m 2f, Newb, GF, Jul 17)
Rohaan (IRE) 120[1] (6f, Asco, Sft, Jun 19)
Sir Ron Priestley 120[1] (1m 4f, Newj, GF, Jul 8)
Twilight Payment (IRE) 120[2] (1m 6f, Curr, Gd, Sep 12)
Wonderful Tonight (Fr) 120[1] (1m 3f 211y, Asco, Sft, Jun 19)
Aldaary 119[1] (1m, Asco, GS, Oct 16)
Alenquer (Fr) 119[1] (1m 2f, Linw, SD, Feb 26)
Armory (IRE) 119[3] (1m 1f 212y, Asco, GF, Jun 16)
Audarya (Fr) 119[2] (1m 1f 212y, Asco, GF, Jun 16)
Broome (IRE) 119[2] (1m 3f 211y, Asco, Sft, Jun 19)
Dragon Symbol 119[2] (6f, Newj, GF, Jul 10)
Euchen Glen 119[1] (1m 1f 209y, Sand, Gd, Jul 2)
Glen Shiel 119[2] (6f, Asco, Sft, Jun 19)
Khuzaam (USA) 119[1] (1m 1y, Linw, SD, Apr 2)
Love (IRE) 119[3] (1m 3f 211y, Asco, GF, Jul 24)
Mac Swiney (IRE) 119[3] (1m 1f 212y, Asco, GS, Oct 16)
Master Of The Seas (IRE) 119[2] (1m, Newm, GF, May 1)
Mostahdaf (IRE) 119[1] (1m 1f, Newm, Gd, Oct 9)
Nahaarr (IRE) 119[2] (6f, York, GS, May 12)
Order Of Australia (IRE) 119[1] (7f, Curr, Gd, Jul 18)
Stradivarius (IRE) 119[1] (2m 56y, York, GF, Aug 20)
Winter Power (IRE) 119[1] (5f, York, GF, Aug 20)
Baron Samedi 118[3] (1m 6f, Curr, Gd, Sep 12)
Global Giant 118[1] (1m 1f 219y, Kemw, SS, Mar 27)
Lope Y Fernandez (IRE) 118[2] (1m, Asco, GF, Jun 15)
Lord Glitters (Fr) 118[2] (1m 177y, York, Gd, Aug 21)
Lucky Vega (IRE) 118[3] (1m, Newm, GF, May 1)
Maker Of Kings (IRE) 118[1] (7f 100y, Tipp, Hvy, Oct 4)
Mojo Star (IRE) 118[2] (1m 6f 115y, Donc, GS, Sep 11)
Saffron Beach (IRE) 118[1] (1m, Newm, Gd, Oct 2)
Space Blues (IRE) 118[1] (7f, York, Gd, Aug 21)
Spanish Mission (USA) 118[1] (1m 5f 188y, York, Gd, May 14)
Tashkhan (IRE) 118[2] (1m 7f 209y, Asco, GS, Oct 16)
Tilsit (USA) 118[1] (7f 213y, Asco, GS, Jul 10)
A Case Of You (IRE) 117[1] (6f, Dunw, SD, Feb 11)
Al Suhail 117[1] (7f, Newm, GS, Oct 8)
Bay Bridge 117[1] (1m 2f, Newm, Gd, Oct 30)
Bolshoi Ballet (IRE) 117[1] (1m 2f, Leop, Gd, May 9)
Danyah (IRE) 117[1] (7f, Asco, GF, Jul 24)
King Of The Castle (IRE) 117[4] (1m 6f, Curr, Gd, Sep 12)
Kinross 117[1] (7f, Good, Sft, Jul 27)
Lazuli (IRE) 117[1] (5f, Newm, GF, May 1)
Snow Lantern 117[1] (1m, Newj, GF, Jul 9)
Solid Stone (IRE) 117[1] (1m 3f, Newb, Gd, Sep 18)
Tis Marvellous 117[1] (5f, Asco, Sft, Oct 2)
Waldkonig 117[1] (1m 1f 209y, Sand, Gd, Apr 23)
Yibir 117[1] (1m 3f 188y, York, Gd, Aug 18)
Bangkok (IRE) 116[1] (1m 2f 56y, York, GF, Jul 24)
Benbatl 116[2] (1m, Good, GF, Aug 28)
Campanelle (IRE) 116[2] (6f, Asco, Hvy, Jun 18)
Cape Byron 116[1] (6f, Hayd, Hvy, May 8)
Century Dream (IRE) 116[2] (7f 213y, Asco, GS, Jul 10)
Duhail (IRE) 116[4] (1m, Good, Sft, Jul 28)
Eshaada 116[1] (1m 3f 211y, Asco, GS, Oct 16)
Foxes Tales (IRE) 116[2] (1m 3f, Newb, Gd, Sep 18)
Glorious Journey 116[1] (7f 6y, Donc, GS, Sep 11)
Great Ambassador 116[2] (6f, Ayr, Gd, Sep 18)
Japan 116[1] (1m 1f, Leop, Gd, Jul 15)
Logo Hunter (IRE) 116[1] (5f, Naas, Sft, May 16)
Majestic Dawn (IRE) 116[2] (1m 2f, Newm, Gd, Oct 30)
Mohaafeth (IRE) 116[1] (1m 2f, Newm, GF, May 1)
Mother Earth (IRE) 116[2] (1m, Newj, GF, Jul 9)
My Oberon (IRE) 116[4] (1m 1f 212y, Asco, GF, Jun 16)
Ocean Wind 116[2] (1m 7f 209y, Asco, GF, Apr 28)
Passion And Glory (IRE) 116[1] (1m 3f 218y, Good, GS, Jul 30)
Power Under Me (IRE) 116[1] (6f, Curr, Sft, Oct 10)
Romantic Proposal (IRE) 116[1] (5f, Curr, Gd, Sep 12)
Search For A Song (IRE) 116[1] (2m, Curr, Gd, Sep 26)
Sir Busker (IRE) 116[3] (1m, Asco, GF, Jun 15)
The Highway Rat (IRE) 116[1] (5f, Dunw, SD, Oct 22)
Top Ranked (IRE) 116[2] (1m 31y, Wind, Gd, Jun 26)
Albaflora 115[2] (1m 3f 211y, Asco, GS, Oct 16)
Alounak (Fr) 115[3] (1m 5f 188y, York, Gd, Aug 21)
Arecibo (Fr) 115[2] (5f, Asco, GF, Jun 15)
Away He Goes (IRE) 115[2] (2m, Good, Sft, Jul 27)
Came From The Dark (IRE) 115[1] (5f 10y, Sand, GS, Jul 3)
Chil Chil 115[3] (6f, Hayd, GF, Sep 4)
D'bai (IRE) 115[2] (7f, Newb, GS, Sep 17)
Derab 115[2] (1m 2f, Newb, GF, Jul 17)
El Drama (IRE) 115[4] (1m 1f 209y, Sand, GS, Jul 3)
Gustavus Weston (IRE) 115[1] (6f, Curr, Yld, Aug 8)
Hamish 115[1] (1m 3f 219y, Kemw, SS, Sep 4)
Happy Power (IRE) 115[3] (7f, Good, Sft, Jul 27)
Harry's Bar 115[1] (5f, Dunw, SD, Oct 1)
Ilaraab (IRE) 115[1] (1m 3f 188y, York, GS, May 12)
Indie Angel (IRE) 115[1] (1m, Asco, GF, Jun 16)
Juan Elcano 115[2] (1m 2f 56y, York, GF, Jul 24)
Laneqash 115[2] (7f, Newb, Gd, Aug 14)
Megallan 115[1] (1m, Sali, Gd, Aug 12)
Nayef Road (IRE) 115[3] (1m 7f 209y, Asco, GF, Apr 28)
Princess Zoe (GER) 115[2] (2m 3f 210y, Asco, GF, Jun 17)
Queen Power (IRE) 115[1] (1m 2f 56y, York, Gd, May 13)
Quickthorn 115[1] (1m 6f 44y, Sali, Gd, Sep 10)
Sacred 115[1] (7f, Newb, Gd, Aug 14)
Safe Voyage (IRE) 115[1] (7f 1y, Ches, GS, Jul 10)
Silent Escape (IRE) 115[1] (7f, Newb, GS, Sep 17)
The Mediterranean (IRE) 115[3] (1m 6f 115y, Donc, GS, Sep 11)
Title (IRE) 115[1] (1m 3f 197y, Donc, GS, Sep 11)
Zeyaadah (IRE) 115[2] (1m 1f 197y, Good, GS, Jul 29)
Bedouin's Story 114[2] (1m 1f, Newm, Gd, Oct 9)
Bell Rock 114[1] (1m 1f, Newm, GF, May 1)

RACING POST RATINGS: LAST SEASON'S TOP PERFORMERS 3YO+

Brando 114^{7} (6f, Newj, GF, Jul 10)
Desert Encounter (IRE) 114^{2} (1m 1f 209y, Sand, Gd, Apr 23)
Extravagant Kid (USA) 114^{3} (5f, Asco, GF, Jun 15)
Fox Tal 114^{3} (1m 3f 218y, Good, GS, Jul 30)
Good Effort (IRE) 114^{2} (6f, Ncsw, SD, Jun 26)
Happy Romance (IRE) 114^{4} (6f, Hayd, GF, Sep 4)
Haqeeqy (IRE) 114^{1} (1m, Donc, Gd, Mar 27)
Helvic Dream (IRE) 114^{1} (1m 2f 110y, Curr, Hvy, May 23)
Hurricane Ivor (IRE) 114^{1} (5f 34y, Newb, Gd, Sep 18)
Joan Of Arc (IRE) 114^{3} (1m 1f 197y, Good, GS, Jul 29)
King's Lynn 114^{7} (5f, Asco, GF, Jun 15)
La Petite Coco (IRE) 114^{1} (1m 2f, Curr, Gd, Sep 12)
Lancaster House (IRE) 114^{1} (7f, Curr, Gd, Apr 17)
Lord North (IRE) 114^{2} (1m 2f, Linw, SD, Feb 26)
Mildenberger 114^{5} (2m 56y, Ncsw, SD, Jun 26)
Minzaal (IRE) 114^{3} (6f, Asco, GS, Oct 16)
Njord (IRE) 114^{6} (1m, Asco, GS, Oct 16)
No Speak Alexander (IRE) 114^{1} (1m, Leop, Gd, Sep 11)
Novemba (GER) 114^{4} (7f 213y, Asco, Hvy, Jun 18)
Outbox 114^{2} (1m 5f 188y, York, Gd, Jul 10)
Pearls Galore (Fr) 114^{2} (1m, Leop, Gd, Sep 11)
Real Appeal (GER) 114^{1} (1m, Leop, Gd, Sep 11)
Royal Commando (IRE) 114^{1} (6f 2y, Donc, Gd, Mar 27)
Santa Barbara (IRE) 114^{2} (1m 2f, Curr, GF, Jun 27)
Summerghand (IRE) 114^{1} (6f, Newj, GF, Aug 28)
Thundering Nights (IRE) 114^{1} (1m 2f, Curr, GF, Jun 27)
Toro Strike (USA) 114^{1} (7f, Good, GF, Aug 29)
Accidental Agent 113^{1} (1m, Newj, GF, Jul 17)
Artistic Rifles (IRE) 113^{1} (1m 37y, Hayd, GF, Sep 4)
Battleground (USA) 113^{3} (7f 213y, Asco, GF, Jun 15)
Bopedro (Fr) 113^{3} (7f 37y, Leop, Gd, Sep 11)
Brentford Hope 113^{1} (1m 75y, Nott, Sft, May 23)
Chindit (IRE) 113^{4} (1m, Good, GF, Aug 28)
Circuit Stellar (IRE) 113^{1} (1m, Leop, Gd, Jun 3)
Emperor Of The Sun (IRE) 113^{3} (1m 6f, Curr, Yld, Aug 13)
Escobar (IRE) 113^{2} (1m, Sand, Sft, Sep 15)
Free Wind (IRE) 113^{1} (1m 6f 115y, Donc, GF, Sep 9)
Garrus (IRE) 113^{5} (6f, Asco, Sft, Jun 19)
Highland Dress 113^{2} (7f, Chmf, SD, Mar 4)
Jumby (IRE) 113^{1} (7f, Newm, GF, Sep 25)
Lavender's Blue (IRE) 113^{1} (1m, Good, GF, Aug 28)
Lights On 113^{1} (1m 6y, Pont, Sft, Jul 6)
Line Of Departure (IRE) 113^{1} (6f, Sali, GF, Jun 13)
Lord Of The Lodge (IRE) 113^{1} (7f 1y, Linw, SD, Apr 2)
Maydanny (IRE) 113^{1} (1m, Good, GS, Jul 30)
Mooneista (IRE) 113^{1} (5f, Curr, Gd, Jul 17)
Moss Gill (IRE) 113^{2} (5f, York, Gd, Jul 10)
Naval Crown 113^{4} (1m, Newm, GF, May 1)
Oh This Is Us (IRE) 113^{1} (1m 113y, Epso, GS, Jun 5)
Ottoman Emperor (IRE) 113^{1} (1m 3f 218y, Good, GS, Jul 29)
Perotto 113^{3} (1m, Sali, Gd, Aug 12)
Pogo (IRE) 113^{2} (1m, Newm, GF, Sep 24)
Primo Bacio (IRE) 113^{5} (1m, Newj, GF, Jul 9)
Raise You (IRE) 113^{1} (1m 4f, Curr, Sft, Oct 26)
Sangarius 113^{2} (1m 2f 70y, Ches, GS, May 7)
Scope (IRE) 113^{1} (1m 6f 34y, Asco, GS, Oct 1)
Sinjaari (IRE) 113^{2} (1m 2f 56y, York, Gd, Aug 21)
Snapraeterea (IRE) 113^{1} (7f, Cork, Sft, Aug 7)
Space Traveller 113^{6} (1m, Good, Sft, Jul 28)
Star Safari 113^{3} (1m 4f, Newj, GF, Jul 8)
Storm Damage 113^{1} (1m, Newj, Gd, Aug 7)
Tabdeed 113^{3} (6f, Newb, GF, Jul 17)
Thunderous (IRE) 113^{4} (1m 3f 211y, Asco, Sft, Jun 19)
Victory Chime (IRE) 113^{1} (1m 2f 70y, Ches, GS, Sep 11)
Al Zaraqaan 112^{1} (1m 2f 219y, Kemw, SS, Mar 27)
Battaash (IRE) 112^{4} (5f, Asco, GF, Jun 15)
Champers Elysees (IRE) 112^{4} (1m, Asco, GF, Jun 16)
Diligent Harry 112^{2} (6f, Newb, GF, Jul 17)
Dubai Warrior 112^{1} (1m 2f, Linw, SD, Dec 18)
Duke Of Hazzard (Fr) 112^{3} (7f, Newj, GF, Jun 26)
Epona Plays (IRE) 112^{1} (1m, Curr, Hvy, May 22)
Ever Present (IRE) 112^{1} (1m 4f 180y, Leop, Gd, Sep 11)
Exalted Angel (Fr) 112^{2} (6f 1y, Linw, SD, Apr 2)
Falcon Eight (IRE) 112^{1} (2m 2f 140y, Ches, GS, May 7)
Fancy Man (IRE) 112^{3} (1m 2f, Linw, SD, Feb 26)
Forest Of Dean 112^{1} (1m 2f, Linw, SD, Feb 27)
Georgeville 112^{1} (1m 2f, Leop, Gd, Oct 16)
Glass Slippers 112^{3} (5f, Curr, Gd, Sep 12)
Harrovian 112^{1} (1m 2f 43y, Donc, GF, Sep 9)
Interpretation (IRE) 112^{4} (1m 6f 115y, Donc, GS, Sep 11)
Intuitive (IRE) 112^{2} (1m 1y, Linw, SD, Feb 27)
Magical Morning 112^{3} (1m, Asco, GS, Oct 16)
Make A Challenge (IRE) 112^{2} (6f, Curr, Hvy, May 22)
Master Of Reality (IRE) 112^{2} (1m 6f, Nava, Gd, Apr 25)
Maximal 112^{2} (1m, Newj, GF, Jul 8)
Migration (IRE) 112^{1} (1m 2f 56y, York, Gd, Aug 21)
Misty Grey (IRE) 112^{2} (1m, Kemw, SS, Feb 6)
Montatham 112^{6} (1m, Sand, Gd, Jul 3)
Naamoos (Fr) 112^{1} (1m, Sand, Gd, Apr 23)
Patrick Sarsfield (Fr) 112^{2} (1m 1f 212y, Asco, GF, Jun 15)
Qaader (IRE) 112^{1} (1m 1f 197y, Good, GS, Jul 29)
Santiago (IRE) 112^{4} (1m 6f, Nava, Gd, Apr 25)
Sinawann (IRE) 112^{3} (1m 1f, Leop, Gd, Jul 15)
Sir Lucan (IRE) 112^{4} (1m 3f 188y, York, Gd, Aug 18)
Stormy Antarctic 112^{1} (1m 1f 197y, Good, Sft, May 22)
Urban Beat (IRE) 112^{3} (5f, York, Gd, Jul 10)
Youth Spirit (IRE) 112^{3} (1m 3f 188y, York, Gd, Aug 18)
Zakouski 112^{1} (1m, Newm, Gd, Oct 30)
Amhran Na Bhfiann (IRE) 111^{1} (1m 6f, Curr, GF, Jun 27)
Barney Roy 111^{4} (1m 1f, Newm, Gd, Oct 9)
Camorra (IRE) 111^{1} (1m 4f, Leop, Gd, Sep 11)
Chalk Stream 111^{1} (1m 3f 211y, Asco, GF, Sep 4)
Commanche Falls 111^{1} (6f, Good, Sft, Jul 31)
Create Belief (IRE) 111^{1} (1m, Asco, Hvy, Jun 18)
Current Option (IRE) 111^{1} (7f, Galw, Gd, Aug 1)
Documenting 111^{2} (7f 1y, Linw, SD, Oct 28)
Edraak (IRE) 111^{1} (7f, Kemw, SS, Dec 8)
Felix 111^{2} (1m 2f, Linw, SD, Feb 6)
Finans Bay (IRE) 111^{4} (1m 2f, Curr, Gd, Sep 12)
Finest Sound (IRE) 111^{3} (1m 1f, Newm, Gd, Oct 9)
Fujaira Prince (IRE) 111^{3} (1m 5f 188y, York, Gd, Jul 10)
Garden Paradise (IRE) 111^{1} (1m 3f 219y, Kemw, SS, Dec 1)
Highfield Princess (Fr) 111^{2} (7f, York, Gd, Aug 21)
Horoscope (IRE) 111^{3} (1m, Leop, Gd, Sep 11)
Jason The Militant (IRE) 111^{1} (1m 3f 180y, Naas, Hvy, Oct 31)
Just Beautiful 111^{6} (1m, Newj, GF, Jul 9)
Khaadem (IRE) 111^{1} (5f 3y, Donc, GF, Sep 8)
Laws Of Indices (IRE) 111^{4} (5f 205y, Naas, Sft, May 16)
Light Refrain 111^{1} (6f, York, Gd, Jul 9)
Logician 111^{2} (1m 4f, Newj, GF, Jun 26)
Lust (IRE) 111^{1} (1m, Gowr, Sft, Oct 18)
Modern News 111^{1} (7f 1y, Linw, SD, Oct 28)
Mr Lupton (IRE) 111^{1} (6f, York, GS, May 12)
Mums Tipple (IRE) 111^{2} (7f, Leic, GF, Apr 24)
Palavecino (Fr) 111^{3} (1m 2f 70y, Ches, GS, May 7)
Pondus 111^{2} (1m 6f, Curr, Yld, Jun 2)
Qaysar (Fr) 111^{1} (7f 37y, Hayd, Hvy, May 8)
Red Verdon (USA) 111^{1} (2m 50y, Sand, Gd, Jul 2)
Regal Reality 111^{2} (1m 2f, Linw, SD, Dec 18)
Rhoscolyn 111^{2} (1m, Good, GS, Jul 30)
River Nymph 111^{1} (7f, Asco, Sft, May 8)
Roulston Scar (IRE) 111^{1} (6f, Chmf, SD, Sep 25)
S J Tourbillon (IRE) 111^{2} (1m 1f 212y, Asco, GF, Jun 17)
Shandoz 111^{1} (1m 3f 219y, Kemw, SS, Nov 1)
Soldier's Minute 111^{1} (6f 1y, Linw, SD, Feb 26)
Sunray Major 111^{1} (7f, Asco, GS, Oct 1)

TOPSPEED: LAST SEASON'S LEADING TWO-YEAR-OLDS

KEY: Horse name, best Topspeed figure, finishing position when earning figure, (details of race where figure was earned)

Tenebrism (USA) 107 [1] (6f, Newm, GF, Sep 25)
Armor 105 [1] (5f, Good, Sft, Jul 28)
Flotus (IRE) 103 [2] (6f, Newm, GF, Sep 25)
Luxembourg (IRE) 102 [1] (1m, Curr, Gd, Sep 25)
Chipotle 101 [1] (5f, Asco, GF, Jun 16)
Perfect Power (IRE) 101 [1] (6f, Newm, GF, Sep 25)
Flaming Rib (IRE) 100 [1] (6f 17y, Ches, Gd, Sep 25)
Native Trail 100 [1] (7f, Newm, Gd, Oct 9)
Castle Star (IRE) 99 [2] (6f, Newm, GF, Sep 25)
Wings Of War (IRE) 99 [1] (6f, Newb, Gd, Sep 18)
Berkshire Shadow 98 [1] (6f, Asco, GF, Jun 15)
Hierarchy (IRE) 98 [2] (6f, Newb, Gd, Sep 18)
Ebro River (IRE) 97 [1] (6f, Curr, Yld, Aug 8)
Go Bears Go (IRE) 97 [4] (6f, Newm, GF, Sep 25)
Royal Patronage (Fr) 97 [1] (1m, Newm, GF, Sep 25)
Zain Claudette (IRE) 97 [1] (6f, Asco, GF, Jul 24)
Caturra (IRE) 96 [5] (6f, Newm, GF, Sep 25)
Coroebus (IRE) 96 [2] (1m, Newm, GF, Sep 25)
Desert Dreamer 96 [2] (6f, Asco, GF, Jul 24)
Hello You (IRE) 96 [1] (7f, Newm, GF, Sep 24)
Lusail (IRE) 96 [1] (6f, York, GF, Aug 20)
Twilight Jet (IRE) 96 [5] (6f, Newm, GF, Sep 25)
Delmona (IRE) 95 [3] (6f, Asco, GF, Jul 24)
Sissoko (IRE) 95 [2] (1m, Donc, Sft, Oct 23)
Asymmetric (IRE) 94 [7] (6f, Newm, GF, Sep 25)
Bayside Boy (IRE) 94 [3] (1m, Donc, Sft, Oct 23)
Dr Zempf 94 [2] (6f, Curr, Yld, Aug 8)
Dubawi Legend (IRE) 94 [2] (7f, Newm, Gd, Oct 9)
Inspiral 94 [1] (1m, Newm, GS, Oct 8)
Coming Patch (IRE) 93 [2] (6f, Newb, Gd, Jul 16)
Eldrickjones (IRE) 93 [2] (6f, Asco, GF, Jun 15)
Gisburn (IRE) 93 [1] (6f, Newb, Sft, Oct 23)
Hannibal Barca (IRE) 93 [4] (1m, Donc, Sft, Oct 23)
Quick Suzy (IRE) 93 [1] (5f, Asco, GF, Jun 16)
Vertiginous (IRE) 93 [1] (5f, Ayr, GF, Sep 17)
Albahr 92 [1] (6f 212y, Hayd, GF, Jul 17)
Dig Two (IRE) 92 [2] (5f, Asco, GF, Jun 16)
Fearby (IRE) 92 [3] (6f, Newb, Gd, Sep 18)
Goldspur (IRE) 92 [1] (1m 2f, Newm, Gd, Oct 9)
Ladies Church 92 [1] (5f, Naas, Gd, Jul 21)
Sacred Bridge 92 [1] (6f, Curr, Gd, Aug 27)
Vintage Clarets 92 [3] (6f, Asco, GF, Jun 15)
Boonie (IRE) 91 [3] (5f, Asco, GF, Jun 16)
Cachet (IRE) 91 [2] (7f, Newm, GF, Sep 24)
Dhabab (IRE) 91 [4] (6f, Newb, Gd, Sep 18)
Dubai Poet 91 [1] (7f, Newb, Gd, Sep 18)
Imperial Fighter (IRE) 91 [5] (1m, Donc, Sft, Oct 23)
Masseto 91 [4] (6f, Asco, GF, Jun 15)
Mr Mccann (IRE) 91 [1] (1m 113y, Epso, Gd, Sep 26)
Sandrine 91 [3] (6f, Newm, GF, Sep 25)
Unconquerable (IRE) 91 [2] (1m 2f, Newm, Gd, Oct 9)

TOPSPEED: LAST SEASON'S TOP PERFORMERS 3YO+

KEY: Horse name, best Topspeed figure, finishing position when earning figure, (details of race where figure was earned)

Adayar (IRE) 118 [1] (1m 3f 211y, Asco, GF, Jul 24)
Mishriff (IRE) 118 [1] (1m 2f 56y, York, Gd, Aug 18)
Poetic Flare (IRE) 118 [1] (7f 213y, Asco, GF, Jun 15)
Creative Force (IRE) 117 [1] (6f, Asco, GS, Oct 16)
Snowfall (JPN) 116 [1] (1m 4f 6y, Epso, GS, Jun 4)
Hurricane Lane (IRE) 114 [1] (1m 6f 115y, Donc, GS, Sep 11)
Winter Power (IRE) 114 [1] (5f, York, GF, Aug 20)
Glen Shiel 113 [2] (6f, Asco, GS, Oct 16)
Lone Eagle (IRE) 113 [2] (1m 4f, Curr, Gd, Jun 26)
Master Of The Seas (IRE) 113 [2] (1m, Newm, GF, May 1)
Emaraaty Ana 112 [2] (5f, York, GF, Aug 20)
Lucky Vega (IRE) 112 [3] (1m, Newm, GF, May 1)
Rohaan (IRE) 112 [1] (6f, Asco, Sft, Jun 19)
Trueshan (Fr) 111 [1] (1m 7f 209y, Asco, GS, Oct 16)
Alenquer (Fr) 110 [1] (1m 2f, Linw, SD, Feb 26)
Dragon Symbol 110 [3] (5f, York, GF, Aug 20)
Starman 110 [1] (6f, Newj, GF, Jul 10)
Wonderful Tonight (Fr) 110 [1] (1m 6f, Good, Sft, Jul 31)
Love (IRE) 109 [3] (1m 3f 211y, Asco, GF, Jul 24)
Minzaal (IRE) 109 [3] (6f, Asco, GS, Oct 16)
Pyledriver 109 [1] (1m 4f 6y, Epso, GS, Jun 4)
Tashkhan (IRE) 109 [2] (1m 7f 209y, Asco, GS, Oct 16)
Al Aasy (IRE) 108 [2] (1m 4f 6y, Epso, GS, Jun 4)
Art Power (IRE) 108 [4] (6f, Asco, GS, Oct 16)
Helvic Dream (IRE) 108 [1] (1m 2f 110y, Curr, Hvy, May 23)
Mojo Star (IRE) 108 [2] (1m 6f 115y, Donc, GS, Sep 11)
Away He Goes (IRE) 107 [2] (2m, Good, Sft, Jul 27)
Broome (IRE) 107 [2] (1m 2f 110y, Curr, Hvy, May 23)
Danyah (IRE) 107 [1] (7f, Asco, GF, Jul 24)
Dream Of Dreams (IRE) 107 [1] (6f, Asco, Sft, Jun 19)
Siskany 107 [1] (1m 4f, Newm, GS, Oct 8)
Alcohol Free (IRE) 106 [1] (7f 213y, Asco, Hvy, Jun 18)
King's Lynn 106 [1] (6f 2y, Donc, Sft, Nov 6)
Lord Of The Lodge (IRE) 106 [1] (7f 1y, Linw, SD, Apr 2)
Space Blues (IRE) 106 [1] (7f, York, Gd, Aug 21)
Stradivarius (IRE) 106 [3] (1m 7f 209y, Asco, GS, Oct 16)
Tis Marvellous 106 [1] (5f, Asco, Sft, Oct 2)
Haqeeqy (IRE) 105 [1] (1m, Donc, Gd, Mar 27)
Sir Ron Priestley 105 [3] (2m, Good, Sft, Jul 27)
Sonnyboyliston (IRE) 105 [1] (1m 6f, Curr, Gd, Sep 12)
Subjectivist 105 [1] (2m 3f 210y, Asco, GF, Jun 17)
Albaflora 104 [2] (1m 3f 188y, York, Gd, Aug 19)
Battleground (USA) 104 [3] (7f 213y, Asco, GF, Jun 15)
Bolshoi Ballet (IRE) 104 [1] (1m 2f, Leop, Gd, May 9)
Lord North (IRE) 104 [2] (1m 2f, Linw, SD, Feb 26)
Naval Crown 104 [4] (1m, Newm, GF, May 1)
Oxted 104 [3] (6f, Newj, GF, Jul 10)
Sealiway (Fr) 104 [1] (1m 1f 212y, Asco, GS, Oct 16)
Solid Stone (IRE) 104 [1] (1m 31y, Wind, GS, May 10)
Suesa (IRE) 104 [4] (5f, York, GF, Aug 20)
The Mediterranean (IRE) 104 [3] (1m 6f 115y, Donc, GS, Sep 11)
Yibir 104 [1] (1m 3f 188y, York, Gd, Aug 18)
Amhran Na Bhfiann (IRE) 103 [1] (1m 6f, Curr, GF, Jun 27)
Atalis Bay 103 [3] (5f, Hayd, GF, Sep 4)
Bielsa (IRE) 103 [1] (6f, Ayr, Gd, Sep 18)
Chil Chil 103 [3] (6f, Hayd, GF, Sep 4)
Copper Knight (IRE) 103 [1] (5f 3y, Donc, Sft, Oct 23)
Falcon Eight (IRE) 103 [1] (2m 2f 140y, Ches, GS, May 7)
Fancy Man (IRE) 103 [3] (1m 2f, Linw, SD, Feb 26)
Hurricane Ivor (IRE) 103 [1] (5f 143y, Donc, GS, Sep 11)
Khuzaam (USA) 103 [1] (1m 1y, Linw, SD, Apr 2)
Lady Bowthorpe 103 [4] (1m, Newj, GF, Jul 9)
Lazuli (IRE) 103 [1] (5f, Newm, GF, May 1)
Maydanny (IRE) 103 [1] (1m, Good, GS, Jul 30)
Moss Gill (IRE) 103 [2] (5f, York, Gd, Jul 10)
Motakhayyel 103 [6] (7f, Asco, GF, Jul 24)
Qaader (IRE) 103 [1] (1m 1f 197y, Good, GS, Jul 29)
Snow Lantern 103 [1] (1m, Newj, GF, Jul 9)
Tribal Craft 103 [2] (1m 6f, Good, Sft, Jul 31)

TOPSPEED: LAST SEASON'S TOP PERFORMERS 3YO+

Twilight Payment (IRE) 103 [2] (1m 6f, Curr, Gd, Sep 12)
Al Suhail 102 [1] (6f 212y, Hayd, GF, Sep 2)
Bedouin's Story 102 [1] (1m 1f, Newm, GF, Sep 25)
Benbatl 102 [1] (1m, Newm, GF, Sep 24)
Create Belief (IRE) 102 [1] (1m, Asco, Hvy, Jun 18)
Dubai Honour (IRE) 102 [2] (1m 1f 212y, Asco, GS, Oct 16)
Forbearance (IRE) 102 [1] (1m 3f 188y, York, Gd, Aug 19)
Great Ambassador 102 [2] (6f, Ayr, Gd, Sep 18)
Gustavus Weston (IRE) 102 [1] (6f, Curr, Hvy, May 22)
Happy Romance (IRE) 102 [4] (6f, Hayd, GF, Sep 4)
Japan 102 [1] (1m 1f, Leop, Gd, Jul 15)
Johan 102 [1] (1m, Sali, GS, Jun 23)
Magical Spirit (IRE) 102 [2] (6f 2y, Donc, Sft, Nov 6)
Maximal 102 [4] (7f 213y, Asco, GF, Jun 15)
Mohaafeth (IRE) 102 [4] (1m 2f 56y, York, Gd, Aug 18)
Real World (IRE) 102 [1] (1m 2f, Newb, GF, Jul 17)
Spycatcher (IRE) 102 [1] (6f 1y, Linw, SD, Feb 5)
Top Ranked (IRE) 102 [1] (1m, Donc, Gd, Mar 27)
Toro Strike (USA) 102 [1] (7f, Thir, GF, Apr 17)
True Self (IRE) 102 [3] (1m 2f 110y, Curr, Hvy, May 23)
Urban Beat (IRE) 102 [3] (5f, York, Gd, Jul 10)
Vadream 102 [5] (6f, Asco, GS, Oct 16)
Zeyaadah (IRE) 102 [2] (1m 3f 75y, Ches, GS, May 5)
Aldaary 101 [1] (7f, Asco, Hvy, Oct 2)
Arecibo (Fr) 101 [1] (5f, Newm, Sft, May 22)
Domino Darling 101 [2] (1m 3f 188y, York, Gd, Aug 19)
Dubai Fountain (IRE) 101 [1] (1m 3f 75y, Ches, GS, May 5)
Hamish 101 [4] (1m 7f 209y, Asco, GS, Oct 16)
Happy Power (IRE) 101 [8] (6f, Asco, GS, Oct 16)
Highfield Princess (Fr) 101 [6] (6f, Asco, GS, Oct 16)
Liberty Beach 101 [6] (5f, York, GF, Aug 20)
Maker Of Kings (IRE) 101 [2] (1m 1f, Leop, Gd, Jul 15)
Mildenberger 101 [5] (2m 56y, Ncsw, SD, Jun 26)
Mooneista (IRE) 101 [1] (5f, Curr, Gd, Jul 17)
Mother Earth (IRE) 101 [2] (1m, Newj, GF, Jul 9)
Mutasaabeq 101 [1] (7f, Newm, Gd, Apr 13)
Perotto 101 [1] (1m, Asco, GF, Jun 17)
Victory Chime (IRE) 101 [2] (1m 1f 209y, Sand, Gd, Aug 21)
Accidental Agent 100 [2] (6f 212y, Hayd, GF, Sep 2)
Baron Samedi 100 [3] (1m 6f, Curr, Gd, Sep 12)
Brunch 100 [1] (1m 6y, Pont, GF, Jul 25)
Burning Victory (Fr) 100 [2] (2m 2f, Newm, Gd, Oct 9)
Buzz (Fr) 100 [1] (2m 2f, Newm, Gd, Oct 9)
Cape Byron 100 [1] (6f, Hayd, Hvy, May 8)
Chindit (IRE) 100 [5] (7f 213y, Asco, GF, Jun 15)
Dubious Affair (IRE) 100 [2] (1m 6f 34y, Asco, GF, Jun 15)
Escobar (IRE) 100 [3] (1m, Good, GS, Jul 30)
Glorious Journey 100 [3] (7f, York, Gd, Aug 21)
Kemari 100 [1] (1m 6f 34y, Asco, GF, Jun 16)
Logo Hunter (IRE) 100 [1] (5f, Naas, Sft, May 16)
Lord Glitters (Fr) 100 [2] (1m 177y, York, Gd, Aug 21)
Mac Swiney (IRE) 100 [5] (1m 2f 56y, York, Gd, Aug 18)
Pogo (IRE) 100 [2] (1m, Newm, GF, Sep 24)
Raaeb (IRE) 100 [1] (5f, Chmf, SS, Aug 3)
Santiago (IRE) 100 [4] (2m, Good, Sft, Jul 27)
Scope (IRE) 100 [1] (1m 6f 34y, Asco, GS, Oct 1)
Shelir (IRE) 100 [1] (7f 192y, York, Sft, Oct 8)
Storm Damage 100 [1] (1m, Newj, Gd, Aug 7)
The Grand Visir 100 [2] (2m 2f 140y, Ches, GS, May 7)
Twilight Spinner 100 [1] (6f, Hayd, Hvy, May 21)
Urban Artist 100 [2] (1m 6f, Good, Sft, Jul 31)
Ventura Diamond (IRE) 100 [7] (6f, Asco, GS, Oct 16)
Youth Spirit (IRE) 100 [3] (1m 3f 188y, York, Gd, Aug 18)
Acanella 99 [1] (1m 1f, Curr, Gd, Aug 27)
Ainsdale 99 [2] (5f, Hayd, Hvy, May 22)
Axana (GER) 99 [1] (7f, Ling, Sft, May 8)
Bangkok (IRE) 99 [1] (1m 2f, Linw, SD, Apr 2)
Brando 99 [7] (6f, Newj, GF, Jul 10)
Came From The Dark (IRE) 99 [2] (5f, Newm, GF, May 1)
Champers Elysees (IRE) 99 [2] (1m 1f, Curr, Gd, Aug 27)
Good Effort (IRE) 99 [3] (6f 1y, Linw, SD, Feb 5)
Interpretation (IRE) 99 [4] (1m 6f 115y, Donc, GS, Sep 11)
Laneqash 99 [2] (7f, Newb, Gd, Aug 14)
Make A Challenge (IRE) 99 [2] (6f, Curr, Hvy, May 22)
Nayef Road (IRE) 99 [5] (2m, Good, Sft, Jul 27)
Rhoscolyn 99 [2] (1m, Good, GS, Jul 30)
Sacred 99 [1] (7f, Newb, Gd, Aug 14)
Saint Lawrence (IRE) 99 [2] (7f, Newb, Gd, Apr 16)
Serpentine (IRE) 99 [6] (2m, Good, Sft, Jul 27)
Sir Lucan (IRE) 99 [4] (1m 3f 188y, York, Gd, Aug 18)
Spanish Mission (USA) 99 [3] (2m 3f 210y, Asco, GF, Jun 17)
Stone Of Destiny 99 [5] (5f, Hayd, GF, Sep 4)
Ville De Grace 99 [1] (1m 2f 23y, Yarm, GS, Sep 15)
Without A Fight (IRE) 99 [1] (1m 4f, Newm, GF, Sep 24)
Wordsworth (IRE) 99 [3] (1m 4f, Curr, Gd, Jun 26)
Almighwar 98 [2] (2m 110y, Newb, Gd, Apr 16)
Artistic Rifles (IRE) 98 [1] (1m 68y, Hami, GF, Jul 31)
Bay Bridge 98 [1] (1m 2f 56y, York, GS, Oct 9)
Beat Le Bon (Fr) 98 [4] (7f 14y, Ncsw, SS, Feb 23)
Boundless Power (IRE) 98 [1] (5f 3y, Donc, Sft, Oct 23)
Commanche Falls 98 [1] (6f 6y, Hami, Gd, Jul 16)
Derab 98 [2] (1m 2f, Newb, GF, Jul 17)
Emperor Of The Sun (IRE) 98 [7] (2m, Good, Sft, Jul 27)
Fame And Acclaim (IRE) 98 [2] (1m, Curr, Hvy, May 23)
Fresh 98 [2] (6f, Asco, Sft, Jun 19)
Jawwaal 98 [4] (5f, Hayd, GF, Sep 4)
Judicial (IRE) 98 [1] (6f 17y, Ches, GS, Aug 1)
Kinross 98 [9] (6f, Asco, GS, Oct 16)
Marie's Diamond (IRE) 98 [3] (1m, Ayr, Gd, Sep 18)
May Sonic 98 [1] (6f, Chmf, SD, Jul 20)
Megallan 98 [2] (1m 2f 56y, York, Gd, May 13)
Novemba (GER) 98 [4] (7f 213y, Asco, Hvy, Jun 18)
One Ruler (IRE) 98 [6] (1m, Newm, GF, May 1)
Palavecino (Fr) 98 [2] (1m 2f, Linw, SD, Apr 2)
Parent's Prayer (IRE) 98 [1] (1m 113y, Epso, GS, Jun 5)
Path Of Thunder (IRE) 98 [1] (1m, Newj, GF, Jul 8)
Real Appeal (GER) 98 [1] (1m, Leop, Gd, Sep 11)
Royal Crusade 98 [3] (5f, Hayd, GF, Sep 25)
Royal Fleet 98 [1] (1m, Donc, GS, Sep 11)
Saldier (Fr) 98 [5] (1m 6f 34y, Asco, GF, Jun 15)
Venturous (IRE) 98 [1] (5f, Ncsw, SS, Jan 2)
Waliyak (Fr) 98 [3] (7f 213y, Asco, GF, Jun 16)
A Case Of You (IRE) 97 [2] (5f, Curr, Gd, Sep 12)
Alounak (Fr) 97 [2] (1m 4f 63y, Ches, GS, Sep 11)
Azano 97 [3] (1m 6y, Pont, GF, Jul 25)
Baaeed 97 [1] (1m, Newj, GS, Jun 19)
Bounce The Blues (IRE) 97 [2] (7f, Ling, Sft, May 8)
Campanelle (IRE) 97 [2] (6f, Asco, Hvy, Jun 18)
Dhushan (IRE) 97 [4] (1m 5f 188y, York, Gd, Aug 21)
Foxes Tales (IRE) 97 [2] (1m 2f, Newj, GF, Jul 9)
Golden Pal (USA) 97 [7] (5f, York, GF, Aug 20)
Harry's Bar 97 [2] (5f, Naas, Gd, Apr 26)
Indigo Balance (IRE) 97 [1] (5f, Tipp, Yld, Apr 20)
Jumby (IRE) 97 [1] (6f, Newm, Gd, May 15)
Just Frank 97 [2] (7f 1y, Ches, Gd, Jun 26)
La Joconde (IRE) 97 [3] (1m 3f 188y, York, Gd, Aug 19)
Masen 97 [1] (7f, Leop, Gd, Oct 23)
Moshaawer 97 [2] (1m 5f 188y, York, Gd, Aug 21)
My Frankel 97 [1] (1m 3f 219y, Kemw, SS, Apr 9)
Nagano 97 [1] (1m 3f 218y, Good, Sft, Jul 28)
Nicholas T 97 [1] (2m 56y, Ncsw, SD, Dec 11)
Njord (IRE) 97 [3] (7f, Newb, Gd, Aug 14)
Passion And Glory (IRE) 97 [1] (1m 2f, Linw, SS, Jun 14)
Persuasion (IRE) 97 [1] (7f 37y, Hayd, GF, Apr 24)
Primo Bacio (IRE) 97 [5] (1m, Newj, GF, Jul 9)
Punchbowl Flyer (IRE) 97 [1] (6f 12y, Wind, Sft, Jun 28)

INDEX OF HORSES

INDEX OF HORSES

Horses in Training 2022
Edited by Graham Dench
PB £24.99

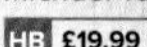

Steve Cauthen
English Odyssey
Michael Tanner
HB £19.99

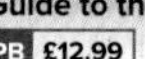

Guide to the Flat 2022
PB £12.99

100 Winners
Jumpers to Follow 2021-
Rodney Pettinga
PB £5.99

RACING POST SHOP

New for 2022

www.racingpost.com/shop
01933 304858

The History of Horse Racing in 100 Objects
Steve Dennis
HB £19.99

Puzzle Book
240 Puzzles
Alan Mortiboys
PB £9.99

A4 Notebook
£16.99

A5 Notebook
£14.99

Mug
£11.99

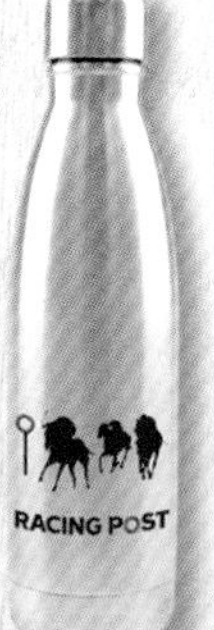

Drinks Bottle
£21.99

Travel Flas
£20.00

Parker Jotter Pen
£24.99

Stylus Pen
£7.99

Bottle Op
Key Fob
£7.99